TRC

~ *Forster's Narrative Vision*

Forster's Narrative Vision

BY BARBARA ROSECRANCE

CORNELL UNIVERSITY PRESS
ITHACA AND LONDON

First published 1982 by Cornell University Press.
Published in the United Kingdom by Cornell University Press Ltd., Ely House, 37 Dover Street, London W1X 4HQ.

CORNELL UNIVERSITY PRESS GRATEFULLY ACKNOWLEDGES
A GRANT FROM THE ANDREW W. MELLON FOUNDATION
THAT AIDED IN BRINGING THIS BOOK TO PUBLICATION.

Permission to quote from the novels of E. M. Forster is gratefully acknowledged. Excerpts from *Where Angels Fear to Tread*, *The Longest Journey*, *A Room with a View*, and *Howards End* appear with the permission of Alfred A. Knopf, Inc., and Edward Arnold Ltd. Excerpts from *A Passage to India*, copyright 1924 by Harcourt Brace Jovanovich, Inc., renewed 1952 by E. M. Forster, are reprinted by permission of Harcourt Brace Jovanovich, Inc., and Edward Arnold Ltd. Quotations from *Maurice*, copyright © 1971 by the Trustees of the Late E. M. Forster, are used with the permission of W. W. Norton and Company, Inc., New York, N.Y., and Edward Arnold Ltd. Quotations from *Arctic Summer* appear with the permission of Edward Arnold Ltd.

International Standard Book Number 0-8014-1502-0
Library of Congress Catalog Card Number 82-71598

Printed in the United States of America

Librarians: Library of Congress cataloging information appears on the last page of the book.

For Herman, Frances, and Dick

Contents

Acknowledgments

I am happy to thank those who have helped to bring this book to completion. These include the late A. N. L. Munby and Penelope Bullock of King's College Library, Cambridge, and the late Oliver Stallybrass, who helped facilitate my early researches in 1974; P. N. Furbank and Alan Wilde, who read and commented on parts of an earlier draft; Wilfred Stone, whose rigorous, thorough, and generous critique was of inestimable value; Bruce Johnson, for helpful suggestions and for his perception of the work's wider implications; and Katherine Gottschalk, Coraleen Rooney, and Mary Barrett, for typing the manuscript and its revisions. I am grateful also to Cornell University for a Faculty Humanities Research Grant; to Bernhard Kendler and Kay Scheuer of Cornell University Press for their professionalism and fine editing; to James McConkey, whose encouragement and respect for readings with which he sometimes disagreed were essential to the success of this project; and to my husband, Richard Rosecrance, for his help and patience, without which the idea of this book could not have become a reality.

BARBARA ROSECRANCE

Ithaca, New York

Preface

WRITING his novels in the first quarter of the twentieth century, E. M. Forster rendered his vision of a new world through techniques of narration widely employed by his Victorian predecessors. His use of an omniscient and intrusive narrator is a major part of his fictional method and appears in remarkable contrast to the practice of most of his contemporaries; as his biographer has noted, had he been a contemporary of George Eliot "this might have passed without notice, but in his own age it sets him apart as an English writer."[1] My interest in the narrator of Forster's novels originated in the belief that much of their effect is related to our sense of contact with a rich, didactic, elusive personality: that one reads Forster more for the pleasure and profit of acquaintance with the commenting author than because of engagement with sometimes limited characters and fantastic plots. This sense of the authorial presence in Forster's novels, a presence centrally embodied in the voice of his narrator, led me to a concern with the ways in

1. P. N. Furbank, "The Personality of E. M. Forster," *Encounter,* November 1970, p. 65.

which the narrator develops Forster's moral and philosophical
views and to an interest in voice both as it elucidates a unique
artistic presence and as it represents the survival of an author-
centered narrative mode in a world from which the author's
voice was fast disappearing.

This book undertakes to reinterpret Forster's novels through
an account of the interrelations between Forster's major themes
and his narrative voice. It deals with the six novels he published between 1905 and 1924, the most important posthumously published short stories, and the novel fragment, *Arctic
Summer*. It offers a reappraisal of the novels and a new interpretation of the shape of Forster's novelistic career.

Where Angels Fear to Tread, Forster's first novel, was published in October 1905. All the novels except for *A Passage to
India* were written between 1905 and 1914. Thus both the
First World War and a significant gap in time separate most of
Forster's fiction from his final novel and acknowledged masterpiece. That to a degree previously unseen *Howards End*
bridges this gap in metaphysical terms, revealing in preliminary
but substantial form the preoccupations of *A Passage to India*,
is part of my thesis in this book. Of Forster's homosexual
fiction, one should note that it remained unpublished until
after his death in 1970, and that it consists largely of *Maurice*,
written in 1913–14, and a group of stories written between
1903 and 1958.[2] I will discuss the relevance of this fiction and
of *Arctic Summer* to Forster's primary themes and to his other
fiction.

2. *Maurice* was published in 1971. The stories are collected in E. M.
Forster, *The Life to Come and Other Stories*, Abinger Edition, 8, ed. Oliver
Stallybrass (London: Edward Arnold, 1972); see p. vii for Stallybrass's chronology. A homosexual story fragment, "Little Imber," written in 1961, appears
in E. M. Forster, *Arctic Summer and Other Fiction*, Abinger Edition, 9, ed.
Elizabeth Heine and Oliver Stallybrass (London: Edward Arnold, 1972), pp.
226–235. *Arctic Summer* itself may be described as covertly homosexual because of its focus on a male friendship and its depiction of a romantic warrior-
hero as the object of attraction.

Forster's novels all present a search for absolute value, which is envisioned in the early works as the humanistic ideal of self-realization reached through personal relations and harmony with nature and in *Howards End* and *A Passage to India* as a cosmic unity no longer attainable through human efforts. Yet the germ of Forster's transcendent statement in *A Passage to India* is present in his first novel, *Where Angels Fear to Tread*. The journey to Italy that Philip Herriton undertakes is a voyage of the soul no less central in its more congenial context than the quest for metaphysical completeness that animates *A Passage to India*. Seen all together, the novels reveal a deepening pessimism about the possibility of human relations that culminates in the final novel in a vision of human limitation. But from the beginning, an inner tension appears in Forster's search for wholeness, a tension whose implications are fundamental to our reading of the novels. Perceptible in the first novel, this tension increases in *The Longest Journey*, reaches its apogee in *Howards End*, and achieves, finally, a form of resolution in *A Passage to India*. Manifest throughout as a conflict between the hopeful ideal of personal relations and a deep impulse to withdrawal from worldly concerns, it appears in the last two novels as a universal condition. In these novels the movement toward negation is dramatized as social disintegration and cosmic chaos; the possibility of solution exists only in metaphysical terms.

The tension between commitment and withdrawal engenders a paradox that begins in the first novel, where at the moment of his greatest insight Philip retreats from the embrace of life that Forster has advocated throughout. Furthermore, the detachment that was Philip's limitation appears at the end to be the necessary condition for his insight. The conclusion of *Where Angels Fear to Tread* creates a paradigm of conflict, which the ensuing novels dramatize, between Forster's continuing attempt to assert the possibility of harmony and the increasing pressure of a vision of disorder. For except for the triumph of Lucy

Honeychurch, the fates of Forster's protagonists reveal the opposite of what the novels claim to demonstrate. Only in *A Passage to India* does the relationship between withdrawal and the possibility of wholeness become fully and finally explicit: there Forster resolves the earlier contradiction of Philip's fate by enclosing it in a paradox that transcends the capacities or fates of individuals. Paradox is the mode, the acceptance of paradox the only hope.

The internal tension I have described is significant primarily because it permeates Forster's changing world view and influences his search for moral and metaphysical meaning. But we may also see the conflict in part as reflecting Forster's personal dilemma, the sense of himself as outsider. Forster's alienation is poignant, for his commitment to life, to the value of continuance that is so central in the novels, was at odds with his sexuality. The implications of his personal situation find expression not only in *Maurice* but in the careers of his young male protagonists in the early novels and in a discrepancy that all the novels present between the avowed connections and the real energies of the personal relationships they depict.

The schism between affirmation and negation in Forster's novels has important aesthetic consequences. Not the tension itself, but Forster's struggle to control and transcend it underlies the problems of coherence that mar *The Longest Journey* and *Howards End*. It is no accident that these novels present the greatest difficulties in both theme and voice. In *The Longest Journey*, Forster's ambivalence to his protagonist creates severe problems of authorial distance. In *Howards End*, the anticipations of apocalypse that in *A Passage to India* find expression in the controlling image of the Marabar caves undermine his assertions of synthesis and reconciliation.

Forster's search for belief is inseparable from his artistic voice, and analysis of their interrelations enables us to redefine both the meaning and the pattern of his artistic progress. Whereas *A Passage to India* has been viewed as disjunct from, if greater than, its predecessors, recognition of the prominence in *Howards End* of a prevision of chaos now causes us to locate the height of Forster's humanism not in that novel, but earlier, in *The Longest Journey,* to which the lighter *Room with a View* provides a valedictory coda. Concomitantly, we must now see *Howards End* as far closer in spirit to *A Passage to India.* The final novel marks the culmination of a movement, the end of a continuum that began with *Where Angels Fear to Tread,* and it follows a logic already present in the concluding pages of *Howards End.*

As primary agent of his creator's voice, the Forsterian narrator dramatizes himself through a distinctive diction. His categories and juxtapositions embody even as they seem to seek balance and order; they also convey an underlying sense of romantic mystery and religious absolutes. He uses both a spare, economical prose and a language of metaphor and personification that in the earlier novels approaches fantasy. This complex variety of language is unique to the narrator and is the greatest source of the novels' richness. The narrator seeks a relationship with the reader that both assumes and compels acceptance of his values, drawing the reader into the world not so much of the characters as of his own imaginative judgments. Pursuing the moral implications of character and action, he invites the reader to join him in the quest for meaning. Finally, the narrator's language and method are of great significance in creating our sense of structure and order within the work itself, a harmony of art that the novels seek in vain to discover in life. The artistic technique is thus ultimately both form and content of Forster's vision.

As Forster's themes become more complex, so alterations appear in his narrative voice. The narrator of the first novel inaugurates Forster's techniques of authorial intrusion, narrative control of structure, and the rudiments of rhythm that will reach full development in the final novel. In *The Longest Journey* and *Howards End,* Forster's attempts to explore the potentialities of human personality bring the personal narrator to the fore: in these novels his interventions increase and reach a climax in *Howards End*. In *A Passage to India*, Forster's voice is finally at one with the implications of his vision, and a contradiction no longer exists between ideology and presentation. From its remote perspective, Forster's voice depicts human limitation. The narrator no longer attempts to approach either characters or reader, and although this choice has other implications, its consequence in the novel is a coherence so complete that, whatever the contributing factors of his personal situation, Forster's artistic silence after *A Passage to India* seems the expression of a perfect logic.

We may see the final novel most clearly as the culmination of Forster's art if we follow the passage of Forster's own vision and voice.[3] And to do this, we must begin with his first voyager, Philip Herriton.

3. In forming my views of the novels, I have benefited from the rich array of contemporary criticism on Forster; but since reinterpretation of Forster's texts has been my purpose, I have allowed a very small number of critics to represent the parameters and progression of Forster interpretation and to bear the brunt of occasional reference. I do not mean to scant the many valuable articles and studies I have omitted from mention. Furthermore, with the service provided Forster readers and scholars by Frederick P. W. McDowell's comprehensive bibliography and its updates, to include a bibliography seemed superfluous. See Frederick P. W. McDowell, *E. M. Forster: An Annotated Bibliography of Writings about Him* (DeKalb: Northern Illinois University Press, 1976); Frederick P. W. McDowell, "Forster Scholarship and Criticism for the Desert Islander," in *E. M. Forster: A Human Exploration—Centenary Essays*, ed. G. K. Das and John Beer (London: Macmillan, 1979), pp. 269–282; Frederick P. W. McDowell, "'Fresh Woods, and Pastures New': Forster Criticism and Scholarship since 1975," in *E. M. Forster: Centenary Revaluations*, ed. Judith Scherer Herz and Robert K. Martin (London: Macmillan, and Toronto: University of Toronto Press, 1982), pp. 311–329.

Forster's Narrative Vision

1 ～

Where Angels Fear to Tread

EARLY in *Where Angels Fear to Tread* Philip Herriton spends an unforgettable evening.

> Dinner was a nightmare. They had the smelly dining-room to themselves. Lilia, very smart and vociferous, was at the head of the table; Miss Abbott, also in her best, sat by Philip, looking, to his irritated nerves, more like the tragedy confidante every moment. That scion of the Italian nobility, Signor Carella, sat opposite. Behind him loomed a bowl of goldfish, who swam round and round, gaping at the guests.[1]

The ensuing scene, which culminates in the revelation that Lilia and Gino Carella are already married, suggests Forster's concerns in this first novel and illustrates important aspects of his narrative method. The narrator's short declarative opening statement summarizes the entire episode.[2] His tone is assured

1. E. M. Forster, *Where Angels Fear to Tread*, Abinger Edition, 1, ed. Oliver Stallybrass (London: Edward Arnold, 1975), p. 22. All subsequent quotations are from this edition; hereafter page numbers will be indicated in the text.

2. For convenience, and where the context is unambiguous, I will sometimes use "narrator" and "Forster" interchangeably. Obviously there are many

yet ironic, sympathetic yet detached. His selection of details and his comic discriminations create the atmosphere and dominate the action. He separates Philip's view from his own, noting those elements in the scene which discomfit the fastidious Englishman—the "smelly" dining room and Miss Abbott's bearing. The narrator's ironic reference to Gino as "that scion of the Italian nobility" recalls Lilia's attempt to pacify her former in-laws by fabricating a pedigree for Gino. Such a judgment encompasses both Philip and Gino and prepares for the narra-

---

situations in which "narrator" cannot represent "Forster," but as Forster's direct representative, we may call the narrator by his name. "Forster" so designated is, of course, the "implied author" and not the historical man. I do not dismiss the distinctions between author, implied author, and narrator. On the contrary, I reiterate the obvious distinction between author (biographical man) and his fictional projection in the novels. The implied author, that projection, is more inclusive than the persona of a reliable narrator: as Wayne Booth says, "It includes, in short, the intuitive apprehension of a completed artistic whole; . . . we infer him as an ideal, literary, created version of the real man; he is the sum of his own choices" (see Wayne Booth, *The Rhetoric of Fiction* [Chicago: University of Chicago Press, 1967], pp. 73–75; see also Wolfgang Iser, *The Implied Reader* [Baltimore: Johns Hopkins University Press, 1974], pp. 30, 46–47). Thus the implied author permeates the work and appears both in his designated narrative persona and in the dialogue of characters. In distinction, a "reliable narrator" (as in Forster) is an explicit projection of the author's norms, dramatized to a greater or lesser degree: as Booth says, he is the author's "dramatic version of himself" (p. 217), and it should be noted that Booth interchanges the terms narrator and author when in distinguishing between this narrator and any character, he notes that "the author is always there on his platform to remind us, through his wisdom and benevolence, of what human life ought to be and might be" (217). This is a description of Fielding's narrator, but it could describe a Forsterian narrator. Although there are important differences between Forster and Fielding narrators, the point here is that a reliable, dramatized narrator represents the implied author, although he does not constitute the sum of that implied author's presence.

If one needs support for the distinction between biographical and implied author, Booth's definition of the latter as an "ideal, literary, created version of the real man" makes the important point. We need only to compare the often petty, waspish, tormented Forster whom P. N. Furbank reveals in his biography with the wise commentator of the novels: see P. N. Furbank, *E. M. Forster: A Life*, 2 vols. (London: Secker & Warburg, 1977, 1978).

tor's distancing of the entire group by his startling image of the bowl of goldfish that "loomed" behind Gino, gaping at the actors and comically dwarfing them all.

Gino has dirty hands, oily hair, a vulgar and ill-fitting suit, and he does not miss the handkerchief he appears to need. Philip's revulsion is comic though not unsupported. But suddenly the Italian reveals his true charm.

> For the youth was hungry, and his lady filled his plate with spaghetti, and when those delicious slippery worms were flying down his throat his face relaxed and became for a moment unconscious and calm. And Philip had seen that face before in Italy a hundred times—seen it and loved it, for it was not merely beautiful, but had the charm which is the rightful heritage of all who are born on that soil. But he did not want to see it opposite him at dinner. It was not the face of a gentleman. [P. 23]

The narrator's language evokes the thematic opposition of instinct and convention: Gino is beautiful because his behavior is spontaneous and unconscious. Philip shares the narrator's moral categories but lacks his fuller insight, as Forster distinguishes between Philip's capacity for appreciation and his slavery to convention.[3]

In a Forster novel, dialogue seldom speaks unaided. Conversations are set like gems in the framework of guiding descriptions and interpretations. The narrator defines issues, causes, and implications, creating the nuances of attitude and reaction that animate the scene.

> Signor Carella, heartened by the spaghetti and the throat-rasping wine, attempted to talk, and, looking politely towards Philip,

3. The association of beauty with an absence of self-consciousness is an early expression of the attitude that finds more complex statement in the Temple section of *A Passage to India*, where the villagers, chanting their celebration of Krishna's birth, are beautiful because they are unself-conscious and calm. By this time the repudiation of self-consciousness is more complete; its absence is the condition not only for beauty but for any possibility of affirmation.

said: "England is a great country. The Italians love England and
the English."
Philip, in no mood for international amenities, merely bowed.
[P. 23]

The narrator has motivated Gino's speech, recorded Philip's
unspoken response, and defined the situation by his summary
of Gino's dialogue as "international amenities." Comic irony
arises from the application of a term redolent of statecraft
and public decorum to this ludicrous encounter between a conventional and inhibited Englishman and a vulgar but relaxed
Italian.

Gino continues his conversation "a little resentfully," having
registered Philip's hauteur. The narrator's comment on Gino's
recitation of the first three lines of Dante's *Inferno* as "a quotation which was more apt than he supposed" (p. 24) emphasizes
his detachment from both characters. Philip, who no more
than Gino comprehends the peculiar aptness of the quotation,
would be the last to believe he might have anything in common
with the Italian. Yet for all their differences in culture and
temperament, the characters share an unawareness of their distance from the narrator's knowledge and an inability to approach his norms. His awareness reflects on their limitations.

Philip's evening culminates in his confrontation with Gino:
"Philip watched his face,—a face without refinement, perhaps,
but not without expression—watched it quiver and re-form
and dissolve from emotion into emotion. There was avarice at
one moment, and insolence, and politeness, and stupidity, and
cunning—and let us hope that sometimes there was love" (p.
29). Speaking in his own voice, Forster invites the reader directly to share his perceptions: "let us hope. . . ." "Us" in this
usage may include Philip, who has participated in the narrator's observation of the scene, but Gino is being revealed primarily to the reader. For the fundamental significance of the
"us" is to suggest a community of belief between narrator and
reader. It places the reader in the same position of moral judg-

ment and assumes that, far more than the characters, he or she is capable of making similar discriminations among the qualities of avarice, stupidity, cunning, politeness, and love.

After dinner, Philip lectures Lilia on the inappropriateness of her engagement. Moved by what he takes to be her painful acquiescence, he reprimands Gino and concludes, "he will be different when he sees he has a man to deal with" (p. 26). Forster might simply have rendered Lilia's reply. Instead, the narrator's mock-epic simile foretells the effect of future action before allowing it to proceed.

> What follows should be prefaced with some simile—the simile of a powder-mine, a thunderbolt, an earthquake—for it blew Philip up in the air and flattened him on the ground and swallowed him up in the depths. Lilia turned on her gallant defender and said:
> "For once in my life I'll thank you to leave me alone. I'll thank your mother too. For twelve years you've trained me and tortured me, and I'll stand it no more. . . . 'Bully?' 'Insolent boy?' Who's that, pray, but you? But, thank goodness, I can stand up against the world now, for I've found Gino, and this time I marry for love!" [Pp. 26–27]

The narrator's interruption, by emphasizing the unexpected quality of Lilia's response, provides a context for the dialogue that demonstrates to Philip and the reader how far Philip has misinterpreted Lilia's attitude, and it shows the reader how deeply Lilia has resented the years of Herriton patronization and mistreatment. The narrator's tone mocks Philip's pretensions: he is ineffective, he has been genuinely moved only by his assumption that Lilia agrees with him, and he has deceived himself.

Such a passage shows the narrator in the act of arranging his story, creating emphases where he chooses. Its effect is to draw attention to the teller of the tale, to strengthen his position and authority, and to increase the importance of the substance and manner of his telling over that of the action itself. The narrator, then, may be seen as the key to the novel's meaning: in his insights and his special relationship to the reader lies the primary basis for interpretation.

The scene just discussed reveals Forster's narrator exploiting the comic possibilities implied in the limited awareness of his characters and in the conflict of values they enact. Let us look at a passage late in the novel that embodies a quite different intention.

> Philip looked away, as he sometimes looked away from the great pictures where visible forms suddenly become inadequate for the things they have shown to us. He was happy; he was assured that there was greatness in the world. There came to him an earnest desire to be good through the example of this good woman. He would try henceforward to be worthy of the things she had revealed. Quietly, without hysterical prayers or banging of drums, he underwent conversion. He was saved. [P. 139]

In this crucial passage, the narrator implies a world beyond phenomenological reality in his notation that visible forms may "suddenly become inadequate for the things they have shown to us." That he concurs in this idea is shown by his generalization of Philip's perception to include Philip, himself, and the reader in common response. Philip's vision brings him certainty—"he was assured." Where the narrator has so often before tumbled down his character's false interpretations of the world, he here supports Philip's experience and his belief. "Quietly" is set against "hysterical": Philip operates within the decorum of rational intellectuals. Yet his experience is religious and nonrational. It transcends the limits of his often-seen aestheticism, for although Philip has seen eyes like Caroline's, "full of infinite pity and . . . majesty" "in great pictures but never in a mortal" (p. 139), he moves beyond aestheticism in requiring commitment and activity ("to be good . . . to be worthy") of himself. The narrator's terse final sentence declares the outcome of Philip's vision: "he was saved."

The moment that this passage renders distills the novel's essence. Everything that precedes it moves toward its peculiar contention; everything that comes after follows from its implications. The concept of salvation declares Forster's fundamental concern with moral states and with a journey of the soul. More a mystery play than a comedy of manners,[4] *Where Angels Fear to Tread* traces the process by which Philip moves from his early complacency to salvation and beyond.

Philip's spiritual journey begins at Sawston, a town suburban both in geography and morality. Instrumental to his enlightenment is the major confrontation with Italy and Gino Carella, who presents the values of instinct and spontaneity against which the conventions of Sawston and the inhibitions of the "undeveloped heart" are measured, and to which they are inadequate. Philip's development is also crucially abetted by Caroline Abbott, a young Englishwoman who, in remorse for her complicity in the mismating of Lilia and Gino, at first seeks to aid the Herritons in procuring Gino's baby, but who later changes sides. Caroline herself undergoes a kind of conversion in her acceptance of the claims of instinct and her eventual self-knowledge. She alone of the characters perceives that Philip must renounce his passivity, commit himself to a moral position, and act. Philip is granted two visions, both embodied in the image of Caroline Abbott. In the first, his apprehension of Caroline's majesty and compassion impels him to conversion and salvation. In the second, Philip receives "something indestructible" from Caroline's assertion that she is not "refined," that she accepts her nature. But the receipt of this second vision impels Philip's withdrawal, a retreat whose implications underlie the conflicts in Forster's subsequent novels.

From the outset Forster as narrator presides over the moral progress of his characters, defining the limits of their relative

4. As I. A. Richards noted in "A Passage to Forster: Reflections on a Novelist," *The Forum*, 78 (December 1927), 914–920, reprinted in *Forster*, ed. Malcolm Bradbury (Englewood Cliffs, N.J.: Prentice-Hall, 1966), p. 16.

awareness. Contemplating Lilia's trip to Italy, Philip "found the situation full of whimsical romance: there was something half attractive, half repellent in the thought of this vulgar woman journeying to places he loved and revered. Why should she not be transfigured? The same had happened to the Goths" (p. 5). Philip's mother, on the other hand, "did not believe in romance, nor in transfiguration, nor in parallels from history, nor in anything else that may disturb domestic life" (p. 5). Philip is naive and comically fastidious in seeing Lilia as a "Goth" and in fantasying her transformation. But although the categories in which he views the world may need refining by the narrator's superior vision, the categories themselves are associated with both Philip and the narrator. Although the former may misuse them, he perceives their validity.

That Mrs. Herriton has no such perception becomes evident when the narrator applies these categories to her. His voice and style appear in the juxtaposition and apparent equivalence of the series of abstractions—romance, history, transfiguration—with anything "that may disturb domestic life." To suggest such an equivalence is to expose Mrs. Herriton's fallacious point of view, an incapacity for insight that Forster describes in terms of faith: she did not "believe in" such things.

For Mrs. Herriton, "domestic life" consists simply in the maintenance of her rule and the preservation of appearances. When the narrator notes a period of "quiet profitable existence" (p. 5) for the Sawston characters, his language exposes Herriton limitations, for with its moral vacuity, such a life could be "profitable" only to a Herriton. The "quiet" contrasts with the conceptions soon to be developed of life in Italy, which is always associated with noise. "Profitable" evokes Mrs. Herriton's opportunism; moreover, with its mercantile implications, "profitable" suggests the Herriton view that values can be measured in terms of monetary gain and that money can buy things of the soul.[5]

5. Such Benthamite concepts will be turned to more serious uses in *The Longest Journey*, where a monetary metaphor is specifically associated with

Against the background of Lilia's Italian marriage, Philip moves to center stage:

> He was a tall, weakly-built young man, whose clothes had to be judiciously padded on the shoulders in order to make him pass muster. His face was plain rather than not, and there was a curious mixture in it of good and bad. He had a fine forehead and a good large nose, and both observation and sympathy were in his eyes. But below the nose and eyes all was confusion, and those people who believe that destiny resides in the mouth and chin shook their heads when they looked at him. [P. 54]

The narrator's attitude toward Philip mixes detachment and sympathy. Even as he notes that "Philip himself, as a boy, had been keenly conscious of these defects" (p. 54), he keeps the reader aware of the gap between Philip's perceptions and his own. His summary of Philip's uncertain attempts to find a place for himself suggests Philip's promise: "At all events he had got a sense of beauty and a sense of humour, two most desirable gifts" (p. 54). But Philip's aesthetic sense includes not only the awareness of beauty but a lack of human understanding: "At twenty-two he went to Italy with some cousins, and there he absorbed into one aesthetic whole olive-trees, blue sky, frescoes, country inns, saints, peasants, mosaics, statues, beggars" (p. 54). The narrator has done this with a single word—the incongruous inclusion of "beggars" in the catalogue.

When Philip finds himself unable to change Sawston, the narrator posits values more powerful than those Philip knows, carefully distinguishing Philip's mistaken conclusions from his own certainty: "He concluded that nothing could happen, not knowing that human love and love of truth sometimes conquer where love of beauty fails" (p. 55). When Philip tries to solace himself through humor, the narrator implies that the solution

---

spiritual values, and in *Howards End*, where the relationship of money to the inner life is explored. For a recent discussion of economic imagery in Forster's moral universe, see Wilfred Stone, "Forster on Profit and Loss," in *E. M. Forster: A Human Exploration*, ed. G. K. Das and John Beer (London: Macmillan, 1979), pp. 69–78.

is inadequate by casually recording its ephemeral character. "If he could not reform the world, he could at all events laugh at it, thus attaining at least an intellectual superiority. Laughter, he read and believed, was a sign of good moral health, and he laughed on contentedly, till Lilia's marriage toppled contentment down for ever" (p. 55).

Disillusioned by his sister-in-law's death at the hands of a "cad," Philip abandons his vision of Italy. Mrs. Herriton adroitly plays on his state of mind.

> "Here beginneth the New Life, then. Do you remember, mother, that was what we said when we saw Lilia off?"
> "Yes, dear; but now it is really a New Life, because we are all at accord. Then you were still infatuated with Italy. It may be full of beautiful pictures and churches, but we cannot judge a country by anything but its men."
> "That is quite true," he said sadly. And as the tactics were now settled he went out and took an aimless and solitary walk. [P. 57]

To Mrs. Herriton, the "new life" means simply that her children are at last happily subservient to her policies. But Philip must find a genuine "vita nuova." Moreover, a "new life," Lilia's child, has literally and disturbingly been introduced into the consciousness of the Herritons and the plot of the novel.

As the dialogue indicates, Mrs. Herriton has lost no opportunity to impress on Philip his mistakes about Italy. But why does Forster have the narrator record Philip's next action as an "aimless and solitary walk?" Is not a relationship being implied between this and the settling of tactics? Each of the narrator's words carries a weight of implication. Philip, "aimless," seems to have no further function; his instinct for honesty has no avenue for expression in Mrs. Herriton's Sawston. Morally isolated, he is thrown back on solitude.

Philip is jolted from ennui by an awareness that his mother is using her weapons against him. It is characteristic of Forster that even in the act of redeeming basically sympathetic characters, he is likely to use their human frailty in the process: "Philip started and shuddered. He saw that his mother was not sincere. Her insincerity to others had amused him, but it was disheartening when used against himself" (p. 68). Philip and his mother part moral company: "In one moment an impenetrable barrier had been erected between them" (p. 68), and Philip moves toward insight:

> And though she was frightening him, she did not inspire him with reverence. Her life, he saw, was without meaning. To what purpose was her diplomacy, her insincerity, her continued repression of vigour? Did they make any one better or happier? Did they even bring happiness to herself? Harriet with her gloomy peevish creed, Lilia with her clutches after pleasure, were after all more divine than this well-ordered, active, useless machine. [Pp. 68–69]

Philip's perception of his mother's insincerity is the first step in his spiritual education. He has arrived at an awareness that the narrator has had all along: the phrases "he saw" and "were, after all, more divine," assume that the truth exists to be found. Philip shows a concern with the meaning of life that approaches Forster's own preoccupation, and the problem is couched in religious terms. "She did not inspire him with reverence." Lilia and Harriet are "more divine" than Mrs. Herriton, whose calculated diplomacy renders her a "machine." Foolish or mistaken, Lilia and Harriet approach "divinity" insofar as they are sincere. To make others happy, secondarily, to make oneself happy, can inspire "reverence." Defined thus, right living partakes of ultimate sanction.

Supernatural implication also accompanies nonrational modes of apprehension. Philip, about to embark for Italy, characterizes the country as "dangerous" and Gino as "mysterious and terrible." Forster comments that "he seemed to be inspired," a statement whose connotations evoke religious prophecy. From the "inspiration" that visits Philip when he talks of Italy, Forster moves to its comic vernacular: the fellow passengers on

Philip's train have "the usual Italian gift of divination" (p. 15)
and help him off at the correct stop. But whether issuing in
intimations of the divine or in the magic of divination, such
spontaneous modes of apprehension are perceived by Forster's
narrator and Philip alike as virtues.

Italy emerges through the narrator's view:

> They travelled for thirteen hours downhill, whilst the streams
> broadened and the mountains shrank, and the vegetation
> changed, and the people ceased being ugly and drinking beer,
> and began instead to drink wine and to be beautiful. And the
> train which had picked them at sunrise out of a waste of gla-
> ciers and hotels was waltzing at sunset round the walls of Ve-
> rona. [P. 75]

The juxtapositions and contrasts—aesthetic, emotional, ideo-
logical—between Switzerland and Italy, the balanced clauses,
the whimsical personifications of the landscape, all characterize
the narrator's language and define his unique personality. Only
he can articulate such associations, although Philip, sharing
his love for Italy, can perceive them. But even when Philip
initiates an observation, the narrator moves the perception
from Philip's mind to his, and turns the occasion to his own
preoccupations: "Italy was beastly, and Florence station is the
centre of beastly Italy. But he had a strange feeling that he was
to blame for it all; that a little influx into him of virtue would
make the whole land not beastly but amusing" (p. 76). The
narrator's generalization about Florence has the effect of ob-
jectifying Philip's complaint. Florence station epitomizes the
heat, bustle, discomfort, and irritation that beset all travelers.
Yet simultaneously Philip realizes that his mood affects his
perceptions, that "a little influx of virtue" would change everything. Even playfully, the narrator speaks in moral categories.
He approves both Philip's irritation—Florence station *is* beastly—and Philip's self-awareness. In corroboration, the narrator
addresses the landscape, which exists not only as Philip's perception, but as a reality:

For there was enchantment, he was sure of that; solid enchantment, which lay behind the porters and the screaming and the
dust. He could see it in the terrific blue sky beneath which they
travelled, in the whitened plain which gripped life tighter than a
frost, in the exhausted reaches of the Arno, in the ruins of
brown castles which stood quivering upon the hills. [Pp. 76–77]

It becomes evident that the narrator has been leading Philip in
order to follow his own concern with the symbolic power of
Italy, and he will bring Philip increasingly within the orbit of
that power. Already under the influence of Italy, Philip is moved
to observe of Gino, against whose turpitude Harriet has been
railing, that " 'because he was unfaithful to his wife, it doesn't
follow that in every way he's absolutely vile.' He looked at the
city. It seemed to approve his remark" (p. 78). Expressing for
the first time a sense of the complexity of good and evil, Philip
is beginning his moral education.

What a journey to Italy represents is implied in an earlier
description of the way to Monteriano: "When the bewildered
tourist alights at the station of Monteriano, he finds himself in
the middle of the country. . . . He must take what is suitably
termed a *legno*—a piece of wood—and drive up eight miles of
excellent road into the Middle Ages. For it is impossible, as
well as sacrilegious, to be as quick as Baedecker" (p. 15). The
notion that Monteriano is medieval had been introduced in a
letter from Lilia, who wrote that "looking out of a Gothic
window every morning, it seems impossible that the Middle
Ages have passed away" (p. 7). Although Lilia is not normally
acute, the narrator has reinforced her perception by noting her
"not unsuccessful description of the wonderful little town" (p.
7). The superlative denotes the narrator's own valuation of
Monteriano. Lilia's achievement, the "not unsuccessful description," indicates her approach to the prevailing standard of
value. Her statement, with its imaginative visualization of the
past in the present, its instinctive bow to the importance of
history, its explicit awareness of the categories of art, seems to
place Monteriano in the value-framework of the novel.

The narrator's reiteration that Monteriano is a medieval town confirms its position. But in his language there is no suggestion of subjective perception. Monteriano does not "seem" to be medieval; rather, the tourist will move toward a verity: he will "drive up eight miles of excellent road into the Middle Ages." Even more significant, however, are the conditions of his journey. The "legno" is a wooden carriage that moves slowly along the road and implies religious value as well as physical necessity. For Forster's narrator emphasizes that it is "sacrilegious" to go faster. The journey is thus purposefully structured and beset with conditions: the narrator's attitude and language suggest a ritual pilgrimage or quest.

The details of Philip's journey are consistent with such an idea. He passes "endless rows of olive-trees, regular yet mysterious." These express opposition to the values in which he has previously acquiesced, and the olive trees accompany him throughout the trip. As the carriage traverses a little wood whose significance will emerge, the narrator notes that Philip's eyes have "registered the beauty" and enjoins him not to forget "that the road to Monteriano must traverse numerous flowers." Philip is accompanied by a guide, the indigenous driver who knows more than he. Finally, appearing high on a hill, Monteriano partakes of visionary qualities: "The hazy green of the olives rose up to its walls, and it seemed to float in isolation between trees and sky, like some fantastic ship city of a dream" (p. 20).

Arrived in Monteriano, Philip discovers that Caroline Abbott has got there before him. When she reports that Gino has inquired apologetically for him, Philip's rejoinder, "What a memory the fellow has for little things" (p. 88), only partially expresses his response. The narrator, using his unique ability to see Philip's face and read his thoughts, interprets the information that dialogue conveys. "He turned away as he spoke, for he did not want her to see his face. It was suffused with pleasure. For an apology, which would have been intolerable eighteen months ago, was gracious and agreeable now" (p. 88). Gino's compliment has restored Philip's humor after a day of trivial frustration in which the Englishman has failed even to locate Gino and has been defeated as would-be diplomatist by the Italian's illiterate housekeeper. Philip's entire mood changes.

> What did the baby matter when the world was suddenly right way up? . . . For romance had come back to Italy. . . . And Miss Abbott—she, too, was beautiful in her way, for all her gaucheness and conventionality. She really cared about life, and tried to live it properly. And Harriet—even Harriet tried.
> This admirable change in Philip proceeds from nothing admirable, and may therefore provoke the gibes of the cynical. But angels and other practical people will accept it reverently, and write it down as good. [Pp. 88–89]

The narrator has used Philip's reaction to express a more fundamental preoccupation. Like the narrator, Philip is concerned with the question of how life should be lived. His judgment here echoes his earlier realization that his mother is insincere and that he cannot accord her "reverence."

Forster now enlarges on his primary subject, the moral life. Although Philip's new idealism originates in personal vanity, the narrator insists that reverence should be accorded those who view the world with benevolence and charity rather than with cynicism. The unexpected juxtaposition of "angels and other practical people," and the narrator's description of Philip's attitude as "this admirable change" align narrator and angels; the reader can scarcely go with the cynics. The religious motif appears again in the narrator's terminology: "angels" approve Philip's benevolence; "reverence" is the appropriate response to such an attitude.

Forster's tone in this passage, apparently casual, is curiously elaborate. Philip's vanity is not admirable, but his new-found benevolence is. At the same time, there is more than a suggestion that in regaining his paradise, Philip is merely recapturing his old romantic infatuation: "Romance had come back to

Italy; there were no cads in her: she was beautiful, courteous, lovable, as of old" (p. 88). The angels, theoretical beings and therefore scarcely pragmatic, are practical because they care about the result rather than the cause of Philip's change of heart. The narrator seems unequivocal in his assertion that the result is good. Nevertheless, a quality of evasion is discernible in this passage: here a kind of archness, it will reappear in more primary contexts as Forster seeks to cover or elude inner inconsistencies in concept and characterization.

Another sign of change in Philip is his movement closer to Caroline Abbott, recorded in the narrator's language. When Caroline, responsive to the charms of Italy, declares that she wishes she were Harriet, the narrator describes her as "throwing an extraordinary meaning into the words" (p. 89). Pondering her reaction, Philip "believed she had paid homage to the complexity of life. For her, at all events, the expedition was neither easy nor jolly. Beauty, evil, charm, vulgarity, mystery—she also acknowledged this tangle, in spite of herself" (p. 89). "Neither easy nor jolly" recapitulates an earlier comment by Philip, in the context of a frustrating encounter with the simplistic Harriet. There he had summed up his dilemma: " 'Things aren't so jolly easy,' said Philip, more to himself than to her" (p. 78). Detached from both characters, the narrator uses Philip's phrase to render his own judgment on Harriet. "But for Harriet things were easy, though not jolly" (p. 78).

Reintroducing the phrase in relation to Caroline's comment, the narrator associates Caroline with his values and emphasizes her antithesis to Harriet. Her "extraordinary desire" to be like Harriet expresses the discomfort that accompanies her new awareness of moral complexities. Philip is right then, and his insight is validated by his use of the narrator's categories—"beauty, evil, charm, vulgarity, mystery." The phrases embodying "jolly" and "easy" initially registered Philip's sense of the difficulty of enlarging Harriet's understanding and then defined Harriet's limitations. Now they contrast her simplistic awareness with Caroline's and Philip's greater capacities. Although such words and the concepts they imply appear both in dialogue and in the narrator's voice, it is the latter who controls their reiteration, defines their contexts, and directs their incremental meanings.

Philip and Caroline move yet closer in common front as Philip refrains from "betraying" Caroline's desire to go to the opera. He manages Harriet here in a manner almost worthy of his mother, convincing her by an appeal to her notion of duty, "classical, you know." The narrator demonstrates the correctness of Philip's tactic by describing its effect. "Harriet's face grew restrained." The dialogue here among Philip, Caroline, and Harriet is punctuated by the narrator's observation of the subtleties of nuance and alteration in the relationships among characters.

The opera scene continues the growing accord between Caroline and Philip. As always, the standard comes from the narrator, who tells us that Philip "had grasped the principle of opera in Italy—it aims not at illusion but at entertainment" (p. 94). Caroline understands, too: "[She] fell into the spirit of the thing. . . . and rejoiced in the existence of beauty" (p. 95). Philip and Caroline communicate, and the narrator interprets their common awareness: "'Don't you like it at all?' he asked her. 'Most awfully.' And by this bald interchange they convinced each other that Romance was here" (p. 94).

Since Philip's moral growth is the novel's subject, we may ask why Caroline Abbott's concerns are given so much development. The reason is that Caroline becomes a kind of touchstone for Philip's salvation. Like the narrator, she is aware of Philip's limitations. Whereas Philip shares the narrator's aesthetic sensibility, she begins with his sense of moral responsibility. Caroline is not so much deluded as inhibited, bound though reluctantly to the imperatives of Sawston, which have heretofore passed for morality with her. Her own potentialities may ultimately be unrealized, but her moral authority is important

for its effect upon Philip. Her struggle and conversion must
therefore be accorded weight.

After the night at the opera, Caroline fights the enchantment
of Italy: "she began to beat down her happiness, knowing it to
be sinful" (p. 98). Although "knowing" usually signifies the
narrator's authority, in those instances where characters "know"
things that have been shown to be incorrect, it is invariably a
preparation for reversal. The narrator has paid tribute to the
mystery, the evil, the vulgarity, and the complexity of Italy. But
he has also endorsed, in his own analyses and in the rendered
experiences of Caroline, Philip, and even such a limited character as Lilia, Italy's beauty and its capacity for joy. Caroline's
denial is followed by a dream in which she sees Monteriano's
historical antagonist, Poggibonsi: "Poggibonsi was revealed to
her as they sang—a joyless, straggling place, full of people who
pretended. When she woke up she knew that it had been Sawston" (p. 99). "Knew" in this case does embody the narrator's
authority. His own previous judgments and the exposures of
characters who represent Sawston values accord with Caroline's vision. The diction is religious: Poggibonsi-Sawston
"was revealed"—an unsought but compelling vision that Caroline is not yet ready to accept.

When Caroline seeks Gino with the intention of persuading
him to relinquish his child, the narrator intervenes to evoke by
his mock-epic manner the disparity between her unenlightened
view and his superior understanding: "she prepared to do battle with the powers of evil" (p. 101). As she waits uneasily in
the desolate parlor, Gino enters the house and passes the open
door of the room in which she sits without seeing her. Increasingly uncomfortable, Caroline is mesmerized by Gino's smoke
ring, which has floated out across the landing. "The ring had
extended its pale blue coils towards her. She lost self-control. It
enveloped her. As if it was a breath from the pit, she screamed"
(p. 103). Gino too reacts: "he, too, was frightened, and perspi-
ration came starting through the tan. For it is a serious thing to

have been watched. We all radiate something curiously intimate when we believe ourselves to be alone" (p. 103).

The scene, with its depiction of human anxiety, its penetration beneath the witty surface of comedy of manners, reveals attitudes and an early anticipation of material that become of major importance in *A Passage to India*. Forster shows here his concern with a common vulnerability and notes the helplessness of human beings under stress. His description of Philip and Harriet descending from the Alps into Italy expresses a similar perception and foreshadows his use of the weather and its effect on man in *A Passage to India*. "And on the second day the heat struck them, like a hand laid over the mouth. . . . From that moment everything went wrong" (p. 75). The coils of smoke which threatened to envelop Caroline and which cause her to lose control of herself anticipate the coiling serpents and the echo of the Marabar caves, which so crucially affect both Mrs. Moore and Adela Quested. A suggestion of the ultimate futility of human attempts to communicate is already present, as the narrator discourses on the unequal love of parents and children, an observation inspired by the image of Gino and his baby: "For a wonderful physical tie binds the parents to the children; and—by some sad, strange irony—it does not bind us children to our parents. For if it did, if we could answer their love not with gratitude but with equal love, life would lose much of its pathos and much of its squalor, and we might be wonderfully happy" (p. 111). The sense of human futility appears again as Caroline tries to inspire Philip with conviction: "she could not prove it. No argument existed. Their discourse, splendid as it had been, resulted in nothing, and their respective opinions and policies were exactly the same when they left the church as when they had entered it" (p. 121). Finally, a sense of the irony of human arrangements awaits Philip at the novel's close, where it is used to support his withdrawal: "here was the cruel antique malice of the gods, such as they once sent forth against Pasiphaë. Centuries of aspiration and culture—and the world could not escape it" (p. 146).

But although this first novel takes note of man's helplessness in the face of nature and his own physiology, it also celebrates the life force. Watching Gino and his son, Caroline Abbott perceives that "she was in the presence of something greater than right or wrong" (p. 109); "this was something too remote from the prettiness of the nursery. The man was majestic; he was a part of Nature; in no ordinary love scene could he ever be so great" (p. 111). Miss Abbott's response to this scene is "reverently" to avert her eyes and "humbly" ask if she can help wash the baby. She performs this ritual, "strangely exalted by the service" (p. 112). The supremacy of instinct and nature are thus associated through the narrator's language with religious truth.

The baby himself reinforces Miss Abbott's vision. As Gino and Caroline approach, he ceases crying, "and his arms and legs were agitated by some overpowering joy" (p. 111). The baby obviously cannot speak for himself. The narrator's grasp of the baby's response augments the reader's view of Caroline's capacities. But not content to render the infant's reaction alone, the narrator intervenes. "She understood little babies . . . and Gino soon ceased to give her directions, and only gave her thanks" (p. 111).

The narrator has described Caroline's reaction to the power of Gino's passion for his child in terms of religious ritual: he now arranges a tableau, in explicit association with Renaissance iconography. Forster's narrator here shares with Philip the tendency to view the materials of life in aesthetic terms, a collapse of distance whose implications become more overt at the novel's conclusion:

> He put a chair for her on the loggia. . . . There she sat, with twenty miles of view behind her, and he placed the dripping baby on her knee. It shone now with health and beauty; it seemed to reflect light, like a copper vessel. Just such a baby

Bellini sets languid on his mother's lap, or Signorelli flings wriggling on pavements of marble, or Lorenzo di Credi, more reverent but less divine, lays carefully among flowers, with his head upon a wisp of golden straw. . . . he knelt by the side of the chair, with his hands clasped before him.

So they were when Philip entered, and saw, to all intents and purposes, the Virgin and Child, with Donor. [P. 112]

As the tableau dissolves, Miss Abbott flees. Although he is curious to discover the cause of her peculiar behavior, Philip remains detached: "he was quite indifferent to the outcome. . . . He was only extremely interested" (p. 116). Philip still considers himself "an emissary of civilization and as a student of character" (p. 117). His condescension contrasts with Caroline Abbott's ease. She is now more in tune with Italy than he, implicitly the result of her acceptance of the claims of nature. "Instinctively she led the way to the famous chapel" (p. 118). But under the influence of Caroline's sincerity, Philip is slowly beginning to feel rather than to abstract. "He thought less of psychology and feminine reaction" (p. 118). He is, however, still content to observe.

In the service of Philip's movement toward commitment, the narrator reintroduces Santa Deodata, whose sanctity has consisted in such detachment that she allowed the devil to fling her mother downstairs before her eyes: "But so holy was the saint that she never picked her mother up, but lay on her back through all, and thus assured her throne in Paradise. She was only fifteen when she died, which shows how much is within the reach of any schoolgirl" (p. 79). A fresco shows Santa Deodata avoiding life, her evasion rendered by symbols explicitly linked with Philip's recent view of Gino and his baby. The narrator sharpens the implied analogy between Santa Deodata and Philip, to whom passivity is still "agreeable."

His eyes rested agreeably on Santa Deodata, who was dying in full sanctity, upon her back. There was a window open behind her, revealing just such a view as he had seen that morning, and

on her widowed mother's dresser there stood just such another
copper pot. The saint looked neither at the view nor at the pot,
and at her widowed mother still less. . . . In her death, as in
her life, Santa Deodata did not accomplish much. [P. 119]

Caroline Abbott poses the central issue to Philip, put, as she
says, "dispassionately enough even for you" (p. 120). Criticizing his passivity, she asks him to commit himself to a position
and act upon it. Philip's response constitutes a major judgment
on him, prepared by the narrator's careful chronicling of his
detachment: "you are quite right: life to me is just a spectacle,
which—thank God, and thank Italy, and thank you—is now
more beautiful and heartening than it has ever been before" (p.
121). Caroline articulates a need that the impetus of action and
the narrator's own judgments have made the reader feel. She
sees that deep moral consequences are involved in the question
of commitment, and she experiences Philip's refusal to accept
responsibility as "blasphemy." "There's never any knowing,"
Caroline warns him, "which of our idlenesses won't have things
hanging on it for ever" (p. 123). The narrator's language again
frames the crucial antitheses between art and life, detachment
and involvement, ratiocination and feeling, as he interprets Philip's response. "He assented, but her remark had only an aesthetic value. He was not prepared to take it to his heart" (p.
123). Supported by the narrator, Caroline's intuition has car-
ried the moral authority; Philip's detachment bars him from
salvation.

Forster has early begun to prepare the denouement through
the introduction of images and details that will reach full meaning in the novel's climactic scene.

At that moment the carriage entered a little wood, which lay
brown and sombre across the cultivated hill. The trees of the
wood were small and leafless, but noticeable for this—that their
stems stood in violets as rocks stand in the summer sea. There
are such violets in England, but not so many. Nor are there so
many in art, for no painter has the courage. The cart-ruts were

channels, the hollows lagoons; even the dry white margin of the road was splashed, like a causeway soon to be submerged under the advancing tide of spring. [P. 18]

The narrator's language defines this brief episode. Although he notes that the wood is "brown and sombre" as later he will emphasize its darkness, in its initial appearance the wood is associated with spring. The trees are leafless, but the wood is carpeted in a profusion of violets. The narrator discriminates for the reader those aspects that are important. Developing his theme, he moves from the violets themselves to a comparison with the presence of life in England and in Art. The tone is declarative: the trees "were small and leafless, but noticeable for this," "there are no such violets . . . nor are there . . . the cart-ruts were channels . . ." "for no painter has the courage." No imagination but that of Forster as narrator can conceive the profusion of flowers as an exercise in boldness and use the comparison to emphasize the power of natural creation.

When Philip first reached Monteriano, he found Gino complacently reciting the opening lines of Dante's *Inferno*:

> Nel mezzo del cammin di nostra vita
> Mi ritrovai per una selva oscura
> Che la diritta via era smarrita. [P. 24]

The "selva oscura" intensifies the comedy of Philip's condescension and ignorance, displayed at length in the dinner scene already discussed. But Dante's term implies also the deeper darkness of Philip's unenlightened moral state. Philip's way will not be clear until he has reentered the little wood, when it will have become the dark wood and will figure in a drama of death and rebirth.

As catastrophe impends, apparently casual details reemerge as significant. Gino has predicted rain, and rain comes with the "extraordinary darkness" through which Philip and his party will travel inexorably into the dark wood. The narrator evokes a symbolism which reflects Philip's growing sense that some-

thing is amiss. The Monteriano tower that Philip has earlier
fantasied as representing a heaven at its apex, hell at its base, is
now seen in its base only, "fresh papered with the advertise-
ments of quacks" (p. 126). The connotations are of sordid
deceit. An idiot enters. Like the passively malignant Santa Deodata, he has visions of the saints. The narrator uses him to
frame yet another illustration of ways in which Italy represents
Nature, here noting its acceptance of all creatures. "Philip then
saw that the messenger was a ghastly creature, quite bald, with
trickling eyes and grey twitching nose. In any other country he
would have been shut up; here he was accepted as a public
institution, and part of Nature's scheme" (p. 126). The idiot
runs after Philip's carriage, seeking to return small change,
because "it was part of the idiot's malady only to receive what
was just for his services" (p. 127). The narrator's comment
implies that honesty is an illness of idiots and pariahs. Yet the
idiot's services have contributed to evil, as has Philip's inaction.[6]

The narrator describes Philip's panic in terms that prefigure
the cosmic chaos of *Howards End* and *A Passage to India*. "He
was frightened . . . the whole of life had become unreal" (p.
127). When Harriet enters the carriage with the baby, Philip
can only conjecture that Gino has crumpled beneath her "intense conviction" and has sold his child. The narrator does not
enlighten either Philip or the reader. Instead he records Philip's
increasing apprehension, as the scene moves toward a pitch of
intensity from which only the accident in the wood will bring
relief.

The narrator provides the images and controls the elements
of this scene, contrasting Harriet and Caroline throughout. After
speculating on Harriet's victory, Philip remembers the intensity

6. This episode anticipates Forster's developed expression of the nature of
good and evil, and the inclusiveness of human participation by many means,
in *A Passage to India,* where Professor Godbole comments, after the catastrophe in the Marabar caves, that all participate in an evil action.

of Caroline's opposing conviction. Only he has remained un-
committed. The suggestions of darkness accumulate. Philip does
not yet know the true cause of the baby's presence. He nevertheless experiences the situation as "sombre," an adjective last
used to characterize the little wood. Every detail suggests associated meanings. Philip compares Harriet, who "dandled the
bundle laboriously," to his most recent memory of the baby,
"sprawling on the knees of Miss Abbott, shining and naked,
with twenty miles of view behind him, and his father kneeling
by his feet" (p. 128). The narrator had described the earlier
scene in nearly identical language.

The idea of a view is associated with the moral truths that
Philip and Caroline seek. The view entered as Baedeker's assurance that "the view from the Rocca (small gratuity) is finest
at sunset" (p. 89). Philip likes views; Harriet cannot tolerate
them. When Philip insists that she look out the train window
to see Virgil's birthplace, she gets a smut in her eye. Caroline begins to appreciate views as she moves toward consonance with her instincts, leading Philip to the window of their
hotel to look out at Monteriano. Shut in the viewless reception
room that houses forgotten memories of Lilia, Caroline becomes hysterical.

Once she has accepted the forces of nature, Caroline herself
becomes associated with the view. Her antagonist, Harriet,
cloaked and umbrellaed, is shut in the carriage that moves
through darkness toward death. The narrator has compared
the baby to the glowing infants of Bellini, Signorelli, and Di
Credi, and Caroline to the Virgin. In Harriet's hands the baby
becomes a "bundle." Harriet herself, in contrast to the sen-
suous religio-aesthetic celebrations of Renaissance art, has
stepped from the vindictive Old Testament: she is "like some
bony prophetess—Judith, or Deborah, or Jael" (p. 128). The
"dripping baby" was wet from the bath in which he had been
joyously splashing; here he is with Harriet and the darkness

and the silent rain, the last an image mirrored in the baby's
silent weeping, of which Gino had said, "then you may be
frightened" (p. 110).

Moved by his recollections of the baby and the contrast
between the past and present scene, Philip is "filled with sorrow and with the expectation of sorrow to come" (p. 128). As
the narrator reiterates the converging associations, the intensity
of his language moves the scene toward catastrophe: "It was as
if they were travelling with the whole world's sorrow, as if all
the mystery, all the persistency of woe were gathered to a
single fount" (p. 129). The carriage overturns "in the wood,
where it was even darker than in the open" (p. 130). In a prose
almost devoid of adjectives, the narrator records Philip's actions. "He shook the bundle; he breathed into it; he opened his
coat and pressed it against him. Then he listened, and heard
nothing but the rain and the panting horses, and Harriet, who
was somewhere chuckling to herself in the dark" (pp. 131–
132). Swiftly and economically the narrator has moved Philip
and the reader to the moment of tragic knowledge. As Philip
wipes from the baby's face the silent rain and silent tears, the
narrator approaches his climactic verdict. "The face was already chilly, but thanks to Philip it was no longer wet. Nor
would it again be wetted by any tear" (p. 132).

The death in the wood brings new awareness to Philip. From
the "selva oscura," evidences of a genuine "vita nuova" emerge:
"as yet he could scarcely survey the thing. It was too great.
Round the Italian baby who had died in the mud there centred
deep passions and high hopes. People had been wicked or
wrong in the matter; no one save himself had been trivial" (p.
133). Philip acknowledges responsibility in a confrontation
with Gino that the narrator counterpoints to Caroline's earlier
visit: "The woman took him to the reception-room, just as she
had taken Miss Abbott in the morning. . . . But it was dark
now, so she left the guest a little lamp" (p. 134). The details
are stark and functional. The lamp that Perfetta leaves for

Philip will be thrown out the window by the grief-maddened
Gino. Caroline will use the baby's milk to reestablish peaceable
behavior between Gino and Philip. On receiving the news, Gino
twists Philip's broken arm and chokes him in a masochistic
scene that expresses Forster's ambivalence to his prototypes, an
attitude dramatized in subsequent novels as pleasure in sexual
brutality directed to his weak and refined protagonists by lower-
class partners. Caroline Abbott's entrance ends this curious
display: she comforts Gino, and Philip achieves "salvation."
The fruition of his moral sense is the climax of Philip's education: from aestheticism and self-delusion, he has moved to
awareness of nature's supremacy, to comprehension of the complex nature of good and evil, and thence to the realization—a
penultimate one, as will be seen—of the necessity for personal
commitment.

Where Angels Fear to Tread expresses what becomes an
archetypal concern with the problem of living life properly; the
narrator largely articulates the modes of doing so. These modes
coalesce finally in the desire for an inclusive vision that demonstrates Forster's occupation from the first with an ideal of completeness, a unity of mind, body, and soul. As Philip walks
through Monteriano to Santa Deodata's, the narrator notes the
city's points of interest: "The Piazza with its three great attrac-
tions—the Palazzo Publico, the Collegiate Church, and the Cafe
Garibaldi: the intellect, the soul, and the body—had never
looked more charming" (pp. 116–117). Completion is also implied in Forster's insistence on the mixed nature of life, dramatized in character, action, and setting. Thus, the natural environment—"vast slopes of olives and vineyards, with more
olives and more farms, and more little towns outlined against
the cloudless sky"—is "terrible and mysterious all the same"
(p. 43). The freedom and spontaneity of Italian life belong to
its men but not its women. The opera combines beauty and
vulgarity—glorious music with a fat diva who sweats pro-
fusely, an opera hall majestic in its bad taste, which "observes

beauty, and chooses to pass it by. But it attains to beauty's confidence" (p. 93). After a *festa,* the church of Santa Deodata smells of incense and garlic. The sacristan's little daughter wears a tinsel crown made for Saint Augustine, while the sacristan removes scarlet calico from the columns in the nave. The sacristan's little son sweeps the nave, "more for amusement than for cleanliness, sending great clouds of dust over the frescoes and the scattered worshippers" (p. 117). The inclusion in religious observance of incense and garlic, theatrical regalia, saints, children, and dust foreshadows the coalescence of gaiety, vulgarity, and metaphysical truth in the Temple section of *A Passage to India.*

Yet despite its implicit ideal of completion and its explicit plea for commitment, the novel concludes amid ironies and limitations. Revealing that Philip is now in love with Caroline, the narrator shapes the tone and creates the depressed mode of this final scene. His verbs authorize Philip's perception: "all the excitement was over. . . . He was convalescent, both in body and spirit, but convalescence brought no joy. . . . He had seen the need for strenuous work and for righteousness. And now he saw what a very little way those things would go" (p. 142). Twice in a single sentence Philip looks "mournfully" out the train window. Caroline, insisting that " 'all the wonderful things are over,' . . . looked at him so mournfully that he dared not contradict her" (p. 144).

The stage is set for a denouement, as Philip begins to hope. Caroline appears interested: she will write; she hopes they will meet often; she is tempted to reveal her feelings. The narrator allows the reader to be misled: "Their faces were crimson, as if the same thought were surging through them both" (p. 145). It would appear that Philip has attained his ideal. But the moment of revelation presents unexpected ironies: "She said painfully, 'That I love him.' Then she broke down. Her body was shaken with sobs, and lest there should be any doubt she cried between the sobs for Gino! Gino! Gino!" (p. 145). The emphatic "and lest there should be any doubt" is directed to the effect of Caroline's revelation upon Philip and the reader. Caroline does not call Gino's name for Philip's benefit: unaware that he loves her, she speaks only from her own distraction. The narrator's language, not Caroline's, emphasizes the disparity between her awareness and Philip's.

Compounding the ironies, Philip rises to the occasion. He has to endure the consequences of Caroline's trust. "I dare tell you this," she confides, "because you're without passion; you look on life as a spectacle" (p. 145). Caroline's confidence is thus contingent on the passivity from which she had sought to free Philip. And passive Philip remains. With authorial self-contradiction, Forster describes Philip's behavior as an act of heroic unselfishness: "In that terrible discovery Philip managed to think not of himself but of her. He did not lament. He did not even speak to her kindly, for he saw that she could not stand it" (p. 146).

In compensation, Philip is granted a vision. Caroline insists that he cease to think of her as refined, that her love is earthly and carnal. "As she spoke she seemed to be transfigured, and to have indeed no part with refinement or unrefinement any longer. Out of this wreck there was revealed to him something indestructible—something which she, who had given it, could never take away" (p. 147). Again the vision is expressed in religious terms. Caroline is "transfigured," meaning is "revealed": finally, Caroline becomes a "goddess," albeit from the myth of Endymion: "This woman was a goddess to the end. . . . To such a height was he lifted that without regret he could now have told her that he was her worshipper too" (pp. 147–148).

This conclusion is curiously foreshadowed in an early encounter with Caroline Abbott. The issue is whether the conventions are invincible; Philip's answer is prophetic: "But your real life is your own, and nothing can touch it. There is no power on earth that can prevent your criticizing and despising mediocrity—nothing that can stop you retreating into splendour and beauty—into the thoughts and beliefs that make the real life—the real you" (p. 62). The novel's action seeks to dislodge Philip from the position he asserted here, from the safety of retreat. He is "saved," and a symbology of death and resurrection, responsibility and suffering, worship and admission to the mystic vision accompany the process of his salvation. Yet the conclusion suggests salvage rather than salvation.

It is true that Philip, at the novel's end, is some considerable distance from his initial moral and emotional situation. He has become aware of the values that activate the novel; he has earnestly tried to shoulder responsibility and to participate in life. And his life does not return entirely to the old pattern. He is trying to free himself from what Forster sees as the source of his self-deceptions, by leaving Sawston. With Caroline he must settle for friendship. As the novel ends, they return to the performance of small services, to what Caroline had earlier repudiated as "petty unselfishness," to the custodianship of the unaware. At the least, Philip and Caroline are united and endure their lots in a moral universe far different from that of the Sawston characters. They have moved through experience to revelation and have made for themselves a place in which to endure the "outer" world.

Clearly Forster endorses the concept of Philip's salvation. But that he persuades the reader of Philip's transfiguration is questionable. In the light of the narrator's careful development of Philip's situation, the shock of the accident in the wood seems adequate motivation for the character's new awareness of responsibility. Philip's acceptance of responsibility and consequent suffering are likewise consistent with the evidence of character and action and with the narrator's voiced attitudes. That under the stress of recent physical suffering and strong emotion Philip should be moved by Caroline's compassion is understandable. That an impressionable young man whom we know to have been uncritically romantic should see the girl as a goddess is not in itself unbelievable. But the narrator suddenly collapses the distance between himself and Philip when he asserts that Philip's salvation is the result of this vision.

The narrator's involvement here is problematic. Our sympathy for Philip has grown through Forster's depiction of his gradual abandonment of pretension, and the narrator's superior insight details Philip's essential innocence as well as his limitations. But when the narrator himself abandons his detachment, a moment mirrored in multiple levels of engagement as Philip "sees" Caroline seeing Gino, Forster's pronouncement that "Philip was saved" fills us with unease. For in this observation Forster implicates himself in all the ambiguities of Philip's position: what apparently "converts" Philip is the tableau he sees, clearly a Pietà which moves him in much the same way as art. "Such eyes he had seen in great pictures but never in a mortal" (p. 139). And averting his eyes, "as he sometimes looked away from the great pictures where visible forms suddenly become inadequate for the things they have shown us," Philip "underwent conversion" (p. 139). Forster thus seems both to assume the character's naivete and to share the aesthetic attitude toward life that he has represented throughout as Philip's limitation. In moving from the sympathetic recording of Philip's vision to a view of its effect on Philip as "salvation," Forster appears to have fallen prey to his character's self-beguiling romanticism.

This collapse of distance exemplifies a significant failure of technique, as Forster's narrator assumes the character's aestheticizing flaw. Behind the abandonment of authorial detachment here, as behind Philip's deflection from union with Caroline, lies Forster's homosexuality and his concomitant need to disguise this personal vantage point. Philip's education should have led him to self-realization. Yet, in the novel's terms of earnest heterosexuality, such self-realization is impossible. What we witness in Forster's identification with Philip is the transformation into aesthetic and symbolic terms of an emotion that can find embodiment only in theory. For in *Where Angels Fear to Tread,* as in all the subsequent novels except *A Room with a View,* the really important relationships occur between persons of the same sex. The crux of this first novel is not Philip's affection for Caroline, nor is Caroline the focal point of the triangle that the ending sketches. Rather, the novel's energy resides in Philip's friendship with Gino; the telling confession is not Caroline's, but Philip's "I love him too." Philip's homosexual temperament and Forster's need for concealment make the repudiation of love a comprehensible if not satisfactory outcome. But in the ending of this first novel we confront the artistic consequences of a fundamental tension between aspiration and reality in Forster's own system of values that far transcends its partial bases in his sexuality.[7] For not only does *Where Angels Fear to Tread* begin what will be seen in the subsequent novels as a pattern of schism between explicit ideals and real energies, but Philip's inaction presents a paradigm that the ensuing novels will formulate in increasingly complex terms as Forster's search for wholeness moves toward the articulation of a metaphysic.

Where Angels Fear to Tread lauds the life natural and preaches acceptance of passion and the necessity of engagement. But Forster's two sympathetic characters retreat to a singularly arid position. Furthermore, Forster not only has Philip withdraw, he makes this a condition for insight. Philip was "saved" when he vowed "to be good through the example of this good woman." But the generous act required of him is merely withdrawal. Despite the pains Forster has taken to purge Philip of his pretensions and intellectualizations, the final meaning of Philip's "salvation" seems to lie in the exercise of his observing intelligence, which relies on words, not actions, and which can suggest the meaning of experience only by viewing

7. For a more detailed discussion of the consequences of Forster's sexuality in the novels, see my essay "Forster's Comrades," *Partisan Review,* 4 (1980), pp. 591–603.

it at a remove. Thus, the impulse to wholeness, articulated throughout the novel as Philip's necessary movement toward responsibility and personal commitment, culminates in his removal from the possibility of action. Philip's situation is doubly paradoxical, for not only does the novel's conclusion present the opposite of what it appears to demonstrate, but the idea of withdrawal as the necessary condition for insight directly counters the substance of Forster's humanistic ideal. Not until the transforming insights of *A Passage to India* will the tension adumbrated in this first novel approach resolution. Yet *Where Angels Fear to Tread* harbors the germ of Forster's mature achievement, not only in its formulations and problems, but in its genuine harmony of form and content, a coherence and tonal consistency seen in no other novel before *A Passage to India*. And despite its strangely foreboding sterility, *Where Angels Fear to Tread* projects the exuberance of its embrace of Italy and leads directly to Forster's more complex but still hopeful exploration of youth and possibility in *The Longest Journey*.

2 ～

The Longest Journey

SHOULD Rickie Elliot acknowledge his illegitimate half-brother? As the brash young Stephen Wonham stands beneath his window, Rickie ponders his course:

> It seems to me that here and there in life we meet with a person or incident that is symbolical. It's nothing in itself, yet for the moment it stands for some eternal principle. We accept it, at whatever costs, and we have accepted life. But if we are frightened and reject it, the moment, so to speak, passes; the symbol is never offered again.[1]

The unheroic hero of *The Longest Journey* fails his own greatest test. But the insight he is unable to follow stands behind Forster's preoccupations and problems in this turbulent second novel, which dramatizes a search for meaning that encompasses but far transcends the tragedy of Rickie's life.

Like *Where Angels Fear to Tread, The Longest Journey* is concerned with the problem of living rightly. As sincerity was

---

1. E. M. Forster, *The Longest Journey* (New York: Alfred A. Knopf, 1953), p. 158. All subsequent quotations are from this edition; hereafter page numbers will be indicated in the text.

for Philip, so truth for Rickie becomes the crucial value. But where Philip's limited attempt to participate in life resulted in his "salvation," Rickie's more complex and fuller effort ends in disaster. Thus more tragic than its predecessor, *The Longest Journey* is yet more affirmative, as the search for truth finds application in an ideal of romantic heroism that allows the novel to conclude on a note of prophetic hope. This solution engenders strange contortions of direction and mode. What began as a *Bildungsroman,* the account of Rickie's growth and salvation, becomes a drama of displacement and idealization in which the condition of Stephen's survival becomes Rickie's death. The sentimental victory of the pastoral hero presents a reduction of the complex inquiries into epistemology and ethics, art and society, love and friendship, civilization and nature, that give the novel its impetus and breadth. Yet in its vindication of the romantic hero, *The Longest Journey* reveals an essential optimism that reappears only in its close but limited successor, *A Room with a View.* Thus, we must locate the most developed expression of Forster's belief in possibility early in his novelistic career and read *The Longest Journey* as the distillation and climax of his youthful hope.

In this second novel Forster's subjects are more complex, his method more intricate, the development of character, setting, and the structure of metaphysical inquiry more profound. His interventions accelerate, as the narrator steps more often between reader and action: the authorial personality imposes itself, and Forster flings aside restraint and any pretense of realism to intrude into his narrative. But even as it dominates, the authorial voice creates and compounds problems of thematic confusion and aesthetic distance. For Rickie exists in ambiguous relation to the novel's emotional and moral structure, and Forster's ambivalence toward his ego-surrogate undermines the very coherence of this passionate and flawed book, which was Forster's own favorite of his novels.[2]

2. See P. N. Furbank, *E. M. Forster: A Life,* Vol. 1, *The Growth of the Novelist (1879–1914)* (London: Secker & Warburg, 1977), p. 149.

The Longest Journey's first sentence announces the search for meaning, as Ansell, the undergraduate philosopher, contends that "the cow is there" (p. 11).[3] Later, when Rickie has made a catastrophic marriage and been drawn into the deadening conventions of Sawston School, the cloud of unreality that encompasses him reverberates: "He explained that it was nothing of any practical importance, nothing that interfered with his work or his appetite, nothing more than a feeling that the cow was not really there" (p. 203). Rickie's failure to seize the symbolic moment plunges him into ever deepening unreality. "The heart of all things was hidden. . . . had he not known the password once—known it and forgotten it already?" (p. 167).

As Rickie begins the longest journey, contending elements war for his soul. Forster's tripartite division of the novel allies Rickie with his moral categories, an inclusion that seems to place Rickie on the road to salvation traveled by his predecessor, Philip. "He was equally sensitive to places. He would compare Cambridge with Sawston, and either with a third type of existence, to which, for want of a better name, he gave the name of 'Wiltshire'" (p. 170). Symbolizing intellectual and imaginative truth, Cambridge imparts education as an embodiment of the Edwardian good life: "The air was heavy with good tobacco-smoke and the pleasant warmth of tea. . . . In the morning he had read Theocritus, whom he believed to be the greatest of Greek poets; he had lunched with a merry don and had three Zwieback biscuits; then he had walked with people he had liked, and . . . he would go and have supper with Ansell, whom he liked as well as any one" (pp. 13–14). Steeped

3. For discussions of the philosophic background of *The Longest Journey*, particularly of the importance of G. E. Moore, see S. P. Rosenbaum, "The Longest Journey: E. M. Forster's Refutation of Idealism," in *E. M. Forster: A Human Exploration*, ed. G. K. Das and John Beer (London: Macmillan, 1979), pp. 32–54, and P. N. Furbank, "The Philosophy of E. M. Forster," in *E. M. Forster: Centenary Revaluations*, ed. Judith Scherer Herz and Robert K. Martin (London: Macmillan, and Toronto: University of Toronto Press, 1982), pp. 37–49.

in these influences Rickie stands at the brink of life, eager and apprehensive. Like Philip, he has a sense of beauty. But Rickie is far more complex than Philip: truthful, intuitive, and egalitarian, he would seem better equipped to live rightly.

Yet Rickie's virtues cannot withstand contact with the great world, a place the Cantabridgian Ansell claims does not exist, but which for Rickie materializes as "Sawston." Unworldly truth and worldly falsity struggle for Rickie in a dialectic whose outcome is not, as some have suggested, a synthesis, but rather the rejection of Sawston and absorption of Cambridge in the novel's third moral and structural category, pastoral Wiltshire.[4]

Sawston's major representative, Agnes Pembroke, initially seems an ordinary young woman who has done nothing more reprehensible than to interrupt the cogitations of Ansell and his philosophers. Her first action is to turn on the electric light, revealing the philosophers "with unpleasing suddenness" (p. 14). Her perceptions are limited: the implications of Rickie's apology for the rudeness of Ansell, who as an inconsistent philosophical realist has denied her existence, do not strike her. She contrasts Gerald, "her own splendid lover," with the "unhealthy undergraduates" (p. 16), a judgment not entirely inappropriate.

Agnes's successful attempt to block Rickie's path to the window beneath which Stephen stands moves Rickie helplessly into the Sawston world. The marriage reveals Agnes in her pettiness and conventionality. She approves bullying and takes pleasure in the suffering of its victims. She is spitefully jealous of Rickie's feeble attempts to pursue old friendships and minimally sustain the life of imagination. She patronizes and pities

4. Contrary to Frederick Crews's contention that the three categories are "rival outlooks that contend for [Rickie's] loyalty," Cambridge and Wiltshire complement each other. Although Wiltshire emerges as England's hope, Cambridge is necessary to its definition and sustenance. See Frederick Crews, *E. M. Forster: The Perils of Humanism* (Princeton: Princeton University Press, 1962), p. 53.

Ansell, insults his sister when they meet by chance in a London department store, and is gratified at Ansell's failure to get a fellowship. Finally, she uses Rickie's account to her of an incident in which Stephen drunkenly sang scurrilous songs about his patroness to turn Aunt Emily against Stephen and evict him from her house. Stephen rebounds upon Rickie, and in a melodramatic scene, Ansell declaims the truth of their relationship to a horrified chorus of assembled Sawstonites. Rickie collapses, but Sawston's ascendancy is over.

As in the first novel, "Sawston" represents convention, appearance, power, and insincerity. But where the earlier Sawston was largely a projection of Mrs. Herriton's domestic manipulations, Sawston School is something more important, an aggregation of modern, urban, institutional claims. The town in which it is set is nondescript, its fog a sketch for the more potent image of urban disintegration in *Howards End*. The school has lost its rural environment and historical purpose: "Sawston School . . . was then a tiny grammar-school in a tiny town, and the City Company who governed it had to drive half a day through the woods and heath on the occasion of their annual visit . . . the intentions of the founder had been altered, or at all events amplified, instead of educating the 'poore of my home,' he now educated the upper classes of England" (p. 54). Modernity has engendered homogeneity: the school "aimed at producing the average Englishman, and, to a very great extent, it succeeded" (p. 55) and the destruction of spontaneity describes even its living arrangements: "Nothing in the house was accidental, or there merely for its own sake. [Rickie] contrasted it with his room at Cambridge, which had been a jumble of things. . . . And then he contrasted it with the Ansells' house, to which their resolute ill-taste had given unity" (p. 179). As in *Where Angels Fear to Tread*, the idea of inclusion—Rickie's "jumble" avoids exclusion or gradations—and the unity of the Ansells' house imply the impulse to wholeness that becomes the cosmic preoccupation of *A Passage to India*. The organized exclusions of Sawston depict a social fragmentation that finds ultimate expression in the caves of the final novel. Thus, to the schoolmaster Herbert Pembroke, life is a "ladder"; Wilbraham, the Sawston-like manager of Mr. Failing's farm, lives by his "map" of society, keeping everyone in his place: "The line between the county and the local, the line between the labourer and the artisan—he knew them all, and strengthened them with no uncertain touch. Everything with him was graduated—carefully graduated civility towards his superior, towards his inferiors carefully graduated incivility" (pp. 115–116). The regulated and hierarchical world of Sawston School is, Mr. Pembroke avers, "the world in miniature" (p. 182). And school spirit produces a patriotism of imperial fantasy and self-congratulation: "Taking a wider range, he spoke of England, or rather of Great Britain, and of her continental foes. Portraits of empire-builders hung on the wall, and he pointed to them. He quoted imperial poets. . . . And it seemed that only a short ladder lay between the preparation room and the Anglo-Saxon hegemony of the globe" (p. 182).

Just as Rickie perceives Sawston's rigidities, he also sees through Herbert's worldliness. But the narrator's portrayal of Rickie's acuity contrasts oddly with the novel's dramatization of Rickie's acquiescence in Herbert's manipulations. In Rickie's strange mixture of misapprehension and truth, we glimpse the authorial inconsistency that flaws the novel.

While Rickie languishes at Sawston, Ansell awaits the moral opportunity: "Do you suppose that I didn't want to rescue him from that ghastly woman? Action! Nothing's easier than action; as fools testify. But I want to act rightly" (p. 208). This requires "the Spirit of Life."

> You can't fight Medusa with anything else. If you ask me what the Spirit of Life is, or to what it is attached, I can't tell you. I can only tell you, watch for it. Myself I've found it in books.

> Some people find it out of doors or in each other. Never mind.
> It's the same spirit, and I trust myself to know it anywhere, and
> to use it rightly. [P. 209]

Noting that in this insight Ansell has "trespassed into poetry"
(p. 209), Forster goes to the crux of Rickie's quest for meaning.
"Poetry" and the coalescent "spirit of life" represent the novel's
convergent values of truth, reality, and meaning. Rickie has
already distinguished between life and death-in-life in his insistence that "poetry, not prose, lies at the core" (p. 201). "Prose"
animates Sawston—the values of a pragmatic, expedient, and
conventional world. It finds embodiment also as the death-in-
life that awaits those who stray from the inner truth of their
natures, a fate Forster defines as "beating time." Thus even
Agnes has her tragedy: having lost the man she genuinely loved,
"she continued her life, cheerfully beating time" (p. 229).

There are hints in this novel that Forster is moving toward
acknowledgment that "prose" may represent a necessary if secondary reality. The narrator struggles to give Herbert his due,
observing over Rickie's shoulder that it "is so easy to be refined and high-minded when we have nothing to do" (p. 178).
Although Rickie uses this insight to rationalize his moral compromise, Forster's uneasiness at the idea of the aesthete is evident. It is for *Howards End* to define the Sawston values as
"necessary grit," and to seek a reconciliation between "poetry"
and "prose."

With Stephen's dramatic reintroduction, the theme of England's inheritance emerges as central. Stephen is Ansell's "spirit
of life," the answer to Rickie's search for truth, and Forster
invests Stephen's rural environment with spiritual authority,
comparing a Wiltshire rainstorm with the Creation: "It seemed
the beginning of life. Again God said, 'Shall we divide the
waters from the land or not? Was not the firmament labour
and glory sufficient?'" (p. 101). Notable here is the comfortable importation of the God of Genesis into the narrator's
commentary. Forster will retain throughout the novels the habit

of biblical diction, but as his vision of earthly possibility becomes more bleak, the allusions express the growing separation of man from God. By *Howards End,* God is distinct from anthropomorphic Christianity; the prevailing question of *A Passage to India* is the existence of deity itself.

The Wiltshire countryside presents the first of Forster's embodiments of the national essence: "The fibres of England unite in Wiltshire, and did we condescend to worship her, here we would erect our national shrine" (p. 147). The landscape embodies a mythic, pagan past. Soldiers and gold lie buried beneath the Cadbury range; the mounds and regressing circles of turnips with a lone tree at the center identify the scene with epistemological and moral truth, for the ancient track that leads from the outer circle through the two inner circles to the central tree makes the same figure as Ansell's ever-regressing circles and squares, which locate reality and truth at the innermost point. So at the center of the Cadbury rings stands Stephen, leaning against the tree.

Removal from Wiltshire is a descent into Hades. Stephen, expelled from Cadover, leaves behind him the crystalline waters of the country rivers and approaches "a solemn river majestic as a stream in hell," which gathers together the waters of central England and makes them "intolerable ere they reached the sea" (p. 279). "But the waters he had known escaped. Their course lay southward into the Avon by forests and beautiful fields, even swift, even pure. . . . Of these he thought for a moment as he crossed the black river and entered the heart of the modern world" (p. 279).

The city's inhabitants are no less corrupted than their environment. Stephen's urban fellow-workers are "hurried and querulous" (p. 280). His companions in Wiltshire had been men like Fleance Thompson, who exemplifies the rural noblesse: he beats Stephen fairly "by trying often"; he provides the disinherited Stephen with his own Sunday clothes, and his rustic companions subscribe their meager wages toward the youth's survival. To these men Forster contrasts the working-class Londoner:

> [Stephen] loathed the foreman, a pious humbug who allowed no swearing, but indulged in something far more degraded—the Cockney repartee. The London intellect, so pert and shallow, like a stream that never reaches the ocean, disgusted him almost as much as the London physique, which for all its dexterity is not permanent, and seldom continues into the third generation. [P. 280]

All who abandon the rural verities present variations in sterility, and Forster details the evil urbanity of Mr. Elliot, the spiritual bankruptcy of his brilliant but insensitive sister, Mrs. Failing, and the ultimate tragedy in store for Fleance Thompson's family, forced after generations to leave Wiltshire for London.

The inventions of modern technology are part of the urban phenomenon and fall under the same condemnation. The electric light with which Agnes disrupts the young philosophers becomes a metaphor for her: Widdrington: "Well I am inclined to compare her to an electric light. Click! She's on. Click! She's off. No waste. No flicker." Ansell: "I wish she'd fuse" (p. 206). Technology, urbanism, and convention are linked in opposition to the natural world. Mrs. Failing, the most subtle and intelligent champion of the conventions, is never without her electric bell. Her windows are closed to keep out the elements of nature. When Rickie makes his momentous decision to offer himself to the "beneficent machine" of Sawston School, he is surrounded by the greyness of urban fog, and he has had to sit for an extra half hour on the train, "listening to the unreal noises that came from the line, and watching the shadowy figures that worked there" (p. 175). The train is an instrument of death and disruption. When Rickie first rides it to Cadover, he is an unwitting participant in the death of a child, killed as he pursued his spurious ideal (at the moment of tragedy he is embracing Agnes). Although modern inventions do not account for all tragedy—Rickie's mother and her lover die naturally induced if arbitrary deaths—the train does Rickie in, and it was only an accident that everyone was not killed when the Cambridge tram lost its wheels. The train last appears carrying Herbert Pembroke away from the productive and tranquil world over which Stephen Wonham presides at the novel's end. "The silence of the night was broken. The whistle of Mr. Pembroke's train came faintly, and a lurid spot passed over the land— passed, and the silence returned" (p. 327). The disturbance is momentary but it will recur.

The deaths of his parents and of his protector, Mr. Failing, leave Stephen to grow up as a kind of noble savage. Himself inarticulate, Stephen does not doubt his mission: "Though he could not phrase it, he believed that he guided the future of our race, and that, century after century, his thoughts and his passions would triumph in England. The dead who had evoked him, the unborn whom he would evoke—he governed the paths between them" (p. 326). Serious and truthful, Stephen illustrates Ansell's formula for salvation, and the critical philosopher admires Stephen without reservation as the touchstone of "reality," whose symbol is appropriately the clod of earth that initiated their friendship in a Forsterian scene of male combat. Rickie seems to attain Ansell's view of Stephen: "Against all this wicked nonsense, against the Wilbrahams and Pembrokes who tried to rule our world Stephen would fight till he died. Stephen was a hero" (p. 316). When Stephen breaks his word and drinks, Rickie views his behavior as "the end of everything for a hero" (p. 318), but the weight of consensus is clearly on Ansell's side. Whether fighting injustice, farming, rescuing Rickie, or merely brawling, Stephen suffers no inhibitions to action. Intrinsic to Forster's ideal of romantic heroism, the ability to act disappears or becomes irrelevant in the later novels as the possibilities for action diminish. But in *The Longest Journey* action is still a desideratum, right action, as Ansell has perceived, the ideal. When Ansell dramatically champions Stephen's cause, he momentarily approaches this ideal state,

striking out "like any ploughboy" (p. 208). But Ansell knows
his limitations: "There [in the British Museum] he knew that
his life was not ignoble. It was worth while to grow old and
dusty seeking for truth though truth is unattainable, restating
questions that have been stated at the beginning of the world.
. . . He was not a hero, and he knew it" (p. 204).

Thus, as in *Where Angels Fear to Tread,* a divorce persists
between thought and action. The sensitive intellectuals are necessary to express the problem and to create art. But they cannot save the Republic:[5] only the spontaneous and inarticulate
hero can act. It is interesting in this connection to note the
worldly failure of all the self-consciously intelligent and sensitive characters. Stephen's patron Tony Failing's life-work was
an unsuccessful attempt to put his utopian theories into practice. Ansell, Rickie's "clever friend," philosopher, rationalist,
seeker after truth, eventually loses his place at Cambridge because his dissertations successively fail. Ansell has repudiated
Rickie's notion of the existence of the "great world," but even
in the narrow society of Cambridge he has no place. Nor can
Rickie contend, either in the "great world" or in Ansell's "small
societies, good or bad" (p. 77). His course illustrates the condition that prevails for all the novel's artists and intellectuals. But
Rickie's failure is special. When ultimately, he is permitted
the opportunity for salvation through right action, Rickie approaches his moment of heroism "wearily" dying in an agony
of spiritual self-negation. The articulate Mrs. Failing renders

5. Tony Failing discourses on "the beloved Republic . . . of which Swinburne speaks" (*The Longest Journey,* p. 271). Swinburne's line, "Even Love
the Beloved Republic, that feeds upon freedom and lives," is from *Hertha.* As
Wilfred Stone notes, Forster used the phrase several times, most conspicuously
in "What I Believe," where he describes democracy, for which he gives two
cheers, as an approach to the Beloved Republic, which alone deserves three.
See E. M. Forster, "What I Believe," *Two Cheers for Democracy,* Abinger
Edition, 11, ed. Oliver Stallybrass (London, Edward Arnold, 1972), pp. 66–
67. See also Wilfred Stone, *The Cave and the Mountain: A Study of E. M.
Forster* (Stanford: Stanford University Press, 1966), pp. 61–62.

the world's judgment of him as "one who has failed in all he undertook; one of the thousands whose dust returns to the dust, accomplishing nothing in the interval. Agnes and I buried him to the sound of our cracked bell, and pretended that he had once been alive" (p. 319). A terrible conclusion for a character who has sought with such ardent simplicity to penetrate the meaning of life. The destruction of Rickie seems gratuitously complete. Wilfred Stone aptly subtitled his chapter on *The Longest Journey*, "The Slaughter of the Innocent."[6] His epithet suggests the importance of a closer look at Forster's treatment of Rickie.

Rickie Elliot begins the world of *The Longest Journey* with many impressive credentials. He starts with a breadth of insight and sympathy that his predecessor Philip never attains. Free of Philip's pretension and the aestheticism which separates that character from salvation, Rickie is appealingly without a false—or true—sense of his worth. Rickie's imaginative spontaneity contrasts gracefully with the rationalism of the more confident Ansell, and he embodies a plea for the merits of intuition and art over logic and criticism. The narrator's creation of the Apostolic scene advances Rickie's claims.[7]

It is all very interesting, but at the same time it is difficult. Hence the cow. She seemed to make things easier. She was so familiar, so solid, that surely the truths that she illustrated would in time become familiar and solid also. Is the cow there or not? This was better than deciding between objectivity and subjectivity. So at Oxford, just at the same time, one was asking, "What do our rooms look like in the vac.?" [P. 11]

Patronizingly affectionate to the undergraduates playing at philosophy, the narrator creates universality within a very small

6. Stone, *The Cave and the Mountain*, p. 184.

7. This scene recapitulates a typical session of the prestigious and secret Society of Apostles, the Cambridge Conversazione Society, founded in 1820 and still extant, to which Forster was elected in 1901. See Furbank, *E. M. Forster: A Life*, 1:75–78.

world. His explanation of undergraduate motives and attitudes emphasizes his distance from them. His adverbs are restrained but pointed: a quibbler speaks "brightly," the undergraduates "honestly" try to think the matter out. Rickie is at once differentiated from the others. If Forster patronizes Rickie here, it is only in asserting his own superior insight. For Forster is far closer to Rickie's imaginative whimsy than to the earnest rationalism of the other undergraduates.

Confronted with the problem of Ansell's cow, Rickie stays out of the discussion. "It was too difficult for him. He could not even quibble. . . . He preferred to listen, and to watch the tobacco-smoke stealing out past the window-seat into the tranquil October air" (p. 12). Rickie dreamily observes the passing scene, intermittently recalling himself to attention:

> Was she there or not? The cow. There or not. He strained his eyes into the night.
> Either way it was attractive. If she was there, other cows were there too. The darkness of Europe was dotted with them, and in the far East their flanks were shining in the rising sun. Great herds of them stood browsing in pastures where no man came nor need ever come, or plashed knee-deep by the brink of impassable rivers. . . .
> Suddenly he realized that this, again, would never do. As usual, he had missed the whole point and was overlaying philosophy with gross and senseless details. . . . And what would Ansell care about sunlit flanks or impassable streams? [P. 13]

For skill in logic, Rickie substitutes an energetic imagination, an awareness of beauty, and an appreciation of his luck that Forster endorses with sympathy. Rickie's alert observation of the collegiate scene and his imaginative extrapolations from the cow reveal his brightness and belie his self-accusation.

Thus imaginative, Rickie is also honest. He admits to Agnes that he has forgotten her impending visit, and Forster intrudes to note that Rickie would have been equally and not more contrite had he behaved thus to a servant. Rickie's lack of pretension opposes Agnes's sense of class distinctions. Rickie's bedmaker, to whom he shows the same respect as he does to Agnes, is a character witness. "His one thought is to save trouble. I never seed such a thoughtful gentleman. The world, I say, will be the better for him" (p. 18). The world does not appreciate Mrs. Aberdeen but, like Rickie, Forster does, underlining her comments by his authority: "Bedmakers have to be comic and dishonest. . . . In a picture of university life it is their only function. So when we meet one who has the face of a lady, and feelings of which a lady might be proud, we pass her by" (p. 19).

As the catalogue of Rickie's virtues develops, Forster equates Rickie's attitude to his dell with that of the ancient Greeks, who could include holiness with laughter. And in contrast to the "delighted aesthete" who would bar common humanity from the dell, Rickie shares with his uncle Tony Failing the insight that he must not exclude: "*'Procul este, profani!'* . . . was never to be the attitude of Rickie. He did not love the vulgar herd, but he knew that his own vulgarity would be greater if he forbade it ingress, and that it was not by preciosity that he would attain to the intimate spirit of the dell" (p. 28). Forster applauds Rickie's sensitivity and his ideals. "Rickie was open to the complexities of autumn: he felt extemely tiny— extremely tiny and extremely important; and perhaps the combination is as fair as any that exists. He hoped that all his life he would never be peevish or unkind" (p. 29). The narrator's explanations create sympathy for Rickie as he contends with the formidable Ansell: "'I maintain,' said Rickie—it was a verb he clung to, in the hope that it would lend stability to what followed" (p. 30). Setting the story of Rickie's childhood in the frame of his own perceptions, Forster shamelessly intrudes to introduce the flashback: "With this invitation Rickie began to relate his history. The reader who has no book will be obliged to listen to it." But contrary to his own assertion, he does not actually let Rickie tell the story: "Some people spend their lives in a suburb, and not for any urgent reason. This had been the fate of Rickie" (p. 32). In the ensuing account of Rickie's childhood, the narrator's structure dominates, shaping the reader's response.

> These were the outlines. Rickie filled them in with the slowness and accuracy of a child. He was never told anything, but he discovered for himself that his father and mother did not love each other, and that his mother was lovable. . . . Mr. Elliot had not one scrap of genius. . . . In reality he never did or said or thought one single thing that had the slightest beauty or value. And in time Rickie discovered this as well. [P. 34]

Forster thus emphasizes the pathos of Rickie's boyhood, noting the boy's loneliness, illustrating his solitary games, and adding a dialogue passage that reveals Mr. Elliot's brutality and indifference to wife and son. Forster's account of the suffering of these two innocents at the hands of the evil Mr. Elliot expands into the momentary hope provided by the father's death. Rickie is to be redeemed from the brutalities of the public school, his mother, once more vigorous and young, is to live with him (and his unbeknownst brother) in Wiltshire. Her unexpected death is one of Forster's jarring demonstrations of the insecurity of life. Rickie, orphaned, is at the mercy of the world. The acuteness and scope of the narrator's perceptions intensify the reader's sympathy for Rickie's plight. When Forster claims that "such, in substance, was the story which Rickie told his friends" (p. 38), he misleads; for Rickie has scarcely told the story at all. It is the narrator who has defined Rickie's experience.

Young though he is, Rickie seems already to have achieved a grace and vision not given to any other character. When Herbert Pembroke attempts to reinforce Rickie's religious orthodoxy with "a few well-worn formulae," Forster's comment transcends the issue of Rickie's formal religion.

> The props were unnecessary. Rickie had his own equilibrium. Neither the Revivalism that assails a boy at about the age of

fifteen, nor the scepticism that meets him five years later, could sway him from his allegiance to the church into which he had been born. But his equilibrium was personal, and the secret of it useless to others. He desired that each man should find his own. [Pp. 58–59]

Rickie's effort to avoid taking sides in Sawston factional disputes is an attempt to maintain this equilibrium, and Forster approves his awareness of complexity: "For Rickie suffered from the Primal Curse, which is not—as the Authorized Version suggests—the knowledge of good and evil, but the knowledge of good-and-evil" (p. 197).

Just as Forster has opposed Rickie's intuition and creative imagination to Ansell's logic, similarly he elevates Rickie's understanding above the theoretical quality of Ansell's comprehension and that of Cambridge:

> Ansell could discuss love and death admirably, but somehow he would not understand lovers or a dying man. . . . Would Cambridge understand them either? He watched some dons who were peeping into an excavation, and throwing up their hands with humorous gestures of despair. These men would lecture next week on Catiline's conspiracy, on Luther, on Evolution, on Catullus. They had dealt with so much and they had experienced so little. Was it possible he would ever come to think Cambridge narrow? [P. 70]

Forster's comment does not so much corroborate Rickie's suspicion that he may someday find Cambridge limited as suggest the extent of its limitation. By comparison with Ansell, Rickie is wise. His experience has enabled him to perceive truths about the chaos and brutality of life shared only by Forster: "In his short life Rickie had known two sudden deaths, and that is enough to disarrange any placid outlook on the world. He knew once for all that we are all of us bubbles on an extremely rough sea." In validating Rickie's reflections on earthly insecurity— a motif dramatized in this novel by its many sudden deaths— Forster amplifies his own preoccupation with human limitation:

> Ah, the frailty of joy! Ah, the myriads of longings that pass
> without fruition, and the turf grows over them! . . . These are
> morbid thoughts, but who dare contradict them? There is much
> good luck in the world, but it is luck. We are none of us safe.
> We are children, playing or quarrelling on the line, and some of
> us have Rickie's temperament, or his experiences, and admit
> it. [P. 129]

Rickie's virtues thus appear fundamental; the source of crucial insights, he seems a sympathetic and reliable character. But
Rickie is also fallible and weak. The problem is not that falli-
bility and sympathy are incompatible: it is rather that Forster's
attitude toward Rickie is so ambivalent. The mixture of ap-
probation and hostility that pursues Rickie throughout the novel
makes him ambiguous; the narrator's conflicting pronouncements call his own authority into question. As the central
assumption of the novel is the narrator's wisdom, this failure
of authority impugns the narrative voice and strikes at the core
of the novel's power.

Whereas some of Rickie's limitations bespeak a not unap-
pealing diffidence, Forster treats other characteristics with equivocation or even hatred. Biographical information supports a
reading of Rickie's lameness as an emblem for homosexuality.[8]
Ansell early warns Rickie that he is unsuited for heterosexual
love, and when he marries, he is cruelly punished for his pre-
sumption not simply by the failure of the marriage but by the
birth of a child even more handicapped than he. To contemplate the importance of the limp and its magnified appearance
in Rickie's child is to see in Forster's punishment of Rickie
his own revulsion from the alienation Rickie represents.

The first mention of Rickie's difficulty occurs when we see

8. In September 1904 Forster encountered a lame shepherd boy at the
Figsbury Rings near Salisbury (the Cadbury Rings of the novel). This incident,
notes Furbank, combined "in one symbol so many elements with meaning for
him: the ideal English landscape, heroic human quality in a working-class
guise, and an inherited handicap (as it might be, homosexuality) courageously
overcome" (Furbank, *E. M. Forster: A Life*, 1:119).

him "nervously limping" (p. 14) toward the doorway where Agnes stands, contrasted in height and assurance: a "tall young woman stood framed in the light." Left to wait in Rickie's room, Agnes sees his shoes: but it is Forster who furnishes the telling explanation that "Rickie was slightly deformed" (p. 17). Rickie's shoe presages other shoes, "a whole row of them, all deformed" (p. 18). For Agnes, this represents "her first great contact with the abnormal, and unknown fibres of her being rose in revolt against it" (p. 21). Forster's term "abnormality" is significant: although Agnes's heterosexual "normality" includes a dose of sadism, it is Forster who has defined Rickie's difference as "deformity," and his treatment of the other references to abnormality in Rickie suggests agreement with the judgments of the "normal" world. For example, when Rickie becomes engaged to Agnes, she kisses him. His response is to start, and passionately to interpose the greater claims of her dead lover, Gerald. In the circumstance, Agnes's reaction seems justified: "She was frightened. Again she had the sense of something abnormal" (p. 89).

Rickie perceives himself as a deformity of nature. His love for beauty enjoins self-rejection. As he tells Agnes,

> I like people who are well-made and beautiful. They are of some use in the world. I understand why they are there. I cannot understand why the ugly and crippled are there, however healthy they may feel inside. Don't you know how Turner spoils his pictures by introducing a man like a bolster in the foreground? Well, in actual life every landscape is spoilt by men of worse shapes still. [P. 84]

Agnes's rejoinder that Rickie sounds like a bolster with the stuffing out seems a sensible refusal to indulge his masochism. Rickie perceives her common sense as "a puff of humorous mountain air" (p. 85), and fancies Agnes as a Meredithian heroine who blows his "cobwebs" away. The cobwebs reappear when, after the marriage, Agnes tries "with a vengeance" to undermine Rickie's belief that "poetry, not prose, lies at the core" (p. 201). But although Forster links the scenes by using the same metaphor—the image of blowing or sweeping cobwebs away—Agnes's two actions are very different. Whereas in the later incident she is clearly villainous, her rejection of Rickie's self-evaluation suggests her correctness here and Forster's ambivalence to his central character.

Other characters note Rickie's weakness or pass judgment on his incapacity. In the book's single genuine love-scene, Ansell and Rickie plait flower garlands in a Cambridge meadow. When Rickie tries to leave, Ansell prevents him:

> "Lemme go, Stewart."
> "It's amusing that you're so feeble. You—simply—can't—get—away. I wish I wanted to bully you."
> Rickie laughed, and suddenly overbalanced into the grass. Ansell, with unusual playfulness, held him prisoner. [P. 79]

That the confluence of eroticism and cruelty which this passage displays is integral to Forster's conception of love, *Maurice* and the posthumously published homosexual stories verify. We may note also the affinity of Ansell's "unusual playfulness" with the despised Agnes's "thrill of joy when she thought of the weak boy in the clutches of the strong one" (p. 63). But whatever its other implications, the passage emphasizes Rickie's helplessness. Agnes's observation that Rickie is "cracked on beauty" (p. 85) becomes Mrs. Failing's association of Rickie with "the cracked church bell" (p. 149) to whose "pang" he is eventually buried.

Forster's description of Rickie's father is the most naked expression of hatred in all the novels: it also provides the only reference to Rickie's physical appearance. "Mr. Elliot was a barrister. In appearance he resembled his son, being weakly and lame, with hollow little cheeks, a broad white band of forehead, and stiff impoverished hair" (p. 32). Mrs. Failing maliciously pursues the association, likening Rickie and Agnes to Rickie's parents. But the most reliable observer, Forster himself, reiterates the comparison, associating Rickie with the hereditary weakness and malice of the Elliots.

> Weakly people, if they are not careful, hate one another, and when the weakness is hereditary the temptation increases. Elliots had never got on among themselves. . . . they always turned outwards to the health and beauty that lie so promiscuously about the world. Rickie's father had turned, for a time at all events, to his mother. Rickie himself was turning to Agnes. [P. 141]

Bad heredity, epitomized in the Elliot infirmities and symbolized by Rickie's limp, yields to good heredity, exemplified by Stephen's health and vigor. Rickie's disability results in double death, for his crippled daughter and eventually for himself. Thus with a wealth of hatred, the burden of being an Elliot falls on Rickie.

Although Forster repeatedly associates Rickie with his own values, what he gives with one hand, he frequently withdraws with the other. Having approved Rickie's perception that Wiltshire, Sawston, and Cambridge are moral categories, the narrator undercuts him: "It must not be thought that he is going to waste his time. These contrasts and comparisons never took him long, and he never indulged in them until the serious business of the day was over. And, as time passed, he never indulged in them at all" (p. 180).

Forster regards Rickie's predicament with a mixture of sympathy and pleasure, as when Rickie discovers that his wife has connived to have Stephen turned out of Cadover. "Then Herbert overbore him, and he collapsed. He was asked what he meant. Why was he so excited? Of what did he accuse his wife? Each time he spoke more feebly, and before long the brother and sister were laughing at him. He felt bewildered, like a boy who knows that he is right but cannot put his case correctly" (p. 233). The narrator's simile reveals his sympathy, but "collapsed" and "feebly" emphasize Rickie's weakness and present the reader with the spectacle of his humiliation. Yet

when Rickie is tormented by visions of his own annihilation
and Stephen's survival, Forster interposes his sympathy between Rickie and the reader. "Henceforward he deteriorates.
Let those who censure him suggest what he should do. He has
lost the work that he loved, his friends, and his child. He
remained conscientious and decent, but the spiritual part of
him proceeded towards ruin" (p. 223).

When Rickie leaves Agnes, Forster seems to arrest this dete-
rioration, commenting about Rickie's rehabilitation, "he was
not vindictive. In the dell near Madingley he had cried, 'I hate
no one,' in his ignorance. Now, with full knowledge, he hated
no one again" (p. 297). Rickie and Forster seem at one as
Rickie contemplates "the Ansells' memorable façade."

> The spirit of a genial comedy dealt there. It was so absurd, so
> kindly. The house was divided against itself and yet stood. Meta-
> physics, commerce, social aspirations—all lived together in
> harmony. Mr. Ansell had done much, but one was tempted to
> believe in a more capricious power—the power that abstains
> from "nipping." [P. 298]

The accumulated evidence of plot and character accords with
these comments. Rickie and Forster have earlier been associated in appreciation of the harmony and virtue of the Ansells.
Likewise, they have shared the common perception of the ca-
priciousness of life. The reference to "nipping" is Stephen's
formulation, of which Forster but not Rickie had been aware.
Allied now with Stephen, Rickie quotes him and opens his
Shelley. The longest journey seems to have come full circle,
with Forster's approval of Rickie's acquired wisdom.

Reversal comes with the failure of Rickie's insight. Regarding Stephen's broken promise as betrayal, Rickie seems to have
lost everything. Once again he has made a standard of the
dead. Once again he has, as he himself phrases it, echoing the
narrator's terminology, "gone bankrupt" (p. 318). But the
bankruptcy lies not, as he believes, in his having "trusted the

earth" (p. 318) but rather in his unreal idealization of another human being. Robbed of belief, Rickie cannot find meaning even in his own annihilation. In the context of such negation, is Rickie's earlier accession of insight meaningless, and are the negative feelings directed toward him at the end—Leighton the butler's "chill of disgust," Mrs. Failing's triumphant epitaph— conclusive statements? The epiloguelike final chapter seems to rescue Rickie from his own and the world's judgments. But his life appears meaningful only by virtue of his sacrifice. Stephen will continue the values that Rickie sought to live, he has preserved the ambiguous best of Rickie in achieving publication of Rickie's stories, and their common heritage continues in the child who has been given their mother's name.

Forster's treatment of Rickie's art further reveals Rickie's problematic status. Initially, Forster encourages his protagonist. When the undergraduate Rickie is cowed by Herbert Pembroke's businessman approach to the idea of creative effort, Forster takes up the cudgels. His defense acknowledges that Rickie is, however embryonically, an artist.

> He never thought of replying that art is not a ladder—with a curate, as it were, on the first rung, a rector on the second, and a bishop, still nearer heaven, at the top. He never retorted that the artist is not a bricklayer at all, but a horseman, whose business it is to catch Pegasus at once, not to practice for him by mounting tamer colts. This is hard, hot, and generally ungraceful work, but it is not drudgery. For drudgery is not art, and cannot lead to it. [P. 25]

The seriousness of Rickie's artistic intention shines the brighter for Agnes's incomprehension, literature being to her "something that just lasts the hour" (p. 87). Imagination is to Agnes a quality unknown; her enthusiasm introduces ambiguity into the idea of Rickie's art, when she advises the young man to "plunge," a course Rickie himself observes not even his closest friend Ansell has suggested. The ambiguity increases, as Mrs. Failing, whose intellectual capacities are not in doubt, pronounces the writing bad. Is her qualifying "But. But. But." intended only to leave "a pleasurable impression" (p. 124), or does it suggest a potentiality beyond honest but misguided effort? The editor who rejects Rickie's story is "slow of soul"[9] and conceives of imagination in art as "ghost stories." But Rickie's work appears wanting. His literary fantasizing about Nature is cant to the authentically natural Stephen, and Agnes's bald outline of Rickie's intended allegory—"Man = modern civilization (in bad sense). Girl = getting into touch with Nature"—seems simultaneously to do it injustice and reveal its inadequacy.[10]

When Rickie has repudiated Agnes and the Sawston world, he returns to his lapsed vocation. But here again its status is unclear, for Forster emphasizes the sincerity of Rickie's self-expression rather than the possibilities of his art: "Two men I know—one intellectual, the other very much the reverse—burst into the room. They said, 'What happened to your short stories? They weren't good, but where are they? Why have you stopped writing? Why haven't you been to Italy? You *must* write. You *must* go. Because to write, to go, is you'" (pp. 312–313).

Only when Rickie himself has been destroyed does his art receive any confirmation. And although earlier Stephen and Ansell have encouraged Rickie for reasons other than the likelihood of his worldly success (he had hesitated because the story was not likely to "pay"), the world's standards seem a significant part of the final estimate. The novel's final chapter begins with Stephen's hard-headed query about Rickie's posthumously published writings: "You guarantee they'll sell?" (p. 320). And Rickie has benefited by a change in fashions: the editor who

9. Forster added this limiting characterization to the final version: in the manuscript the editor is merely kind (manuscript of *The Longest Journey*, Cambridge, England, King's College Library, Folio Volume 6, F249, p. 294). The editor is evidently based on Holbrook Jackson.

10. This is, of course, Forster's story "Other Kingdom."

rejected Rickie's story because it "does not convince" (p. 166) is paid at last. Stephen: "I'd got the idea that the long story had its points, but that these shorter things didn't—What's the word?" Pembroke: " 'Convince' is probably the word you want. But that type of criticism is quite a thing of the past. Have you seen the illustrated American edition?" (p. 320) Finally, even Rickie's worldly success is open to question, for Stephen asserts that it was "the introduction with all those wrong details that sold the other book" (p. 321).

So Rickie: equivocally an artist, ambiguously and posthumously a worldly success, while alive, unable to contend in any world, not Ansell's, Pembroke's, Stephen's, or his own inner world of imagination.

Forster's role in this has been not only elusive but downright misleading. For the best of Rickie has been seen in some of the very qualities whose insufficiency to contend in the world Forster has demonstrated. Rickie has shown sanity, warmth, compassion, balanced judgment, and a unique capacity for insight. Imagination has been the source of both his percipience and his corruption—he arrived at his ill-conceived love for Agnes through the same quality that has armed him with a vision whose power even Agnes acknowledges. "Through all her misery she knew that this boy was greater than they supposed. . . . his meagre face showed as a seraph's who spoke the truth and forbade her to juggle with her soul" (pp. 66–67). Rickie's mistake originates in idealism and inexperience.

> He is, of course, absurdly young. . . . He has no knowledge of the world; . . . He believes in Humanity because he knows a dozen decent people. He believes in women because he has loved his mother. And his friends are as young and as ignorant as himself. They are full of the wine of life. But they have not tasted the cup—let us call it the teacup—of experience, which has made men of Mr. Pembroke's type what they are. Oh, that teacup! To be taken at prayers, at friendship, at love, till we are quite sane, efficient, quite experienced, and quite useless to God or man. [P. 75]

The bitterness of Forster's tone here indicts the conventional world; his eloquence defends Rickie's innocence and idealism. However wrongly Rickie's imagination may transfigure reality, his values are generous. He is open, unpossessive, undogmatic. Beside his intuition and engaging whimsy, Ansell's obsessive rationalism often seems pretentious. Rickie's ideas of beauty and value are Forster's own.

Yet Rickie's lack of equilibrium belies Forster's early description of his moral balance. In this, he reflects the greater failure of Forster's aesthetic distance and a concomitant confusion of theme. It is Forster's lack of clarity and control of his attitude to Rickie and the meaning of Rickie's values that causes the novel, as Trilling put it, to "not so much fall apart as fly apart."[11]

Forster's unsteadiness toward Rickie has repercussions in the portrayal of other characters, particularly Ansell. Rickie's friend is the most prominent of those in the novel who approach the narrator's standards: Ansell's penetrating and uncompromising judgments lead straight from diagnosis of Rickie to recognition of Stephen. But Rickie and Ansell seem at times held in a wavering balance, in which the weaknesses of one are the strengths of the other. We have seen that Rickie's intuition successfully opposes Ansell's rationalism and that his awareness of tragedy transcends Ansell's donnish theorizing. Although Ansell is an "extremist," despising physical beauty and strength, Rickie knows better: "he had escaped the sin of despising the physically strong—a sin against which the physically weak must guard" (p. 49). Whereas Rickie's desire to reconcile wife and friend expresses both emotion and the ideal of inclusion, Ansell's antagonism to Agnes is, despite his claim to principle, clearly the resentment of a jealous lover.[12]

11. Lionel Trilling, *E. M. Forster* (Norfolk, Conn.: New Directions, 1964), p. 76.

12. Rickie's response to Ansell's caveat locates the crux of love in the novel: "this letter of yours is the most wonderful thing that has ever happened to me

The balance shifts gradually but definitively from Rickie to Ansell. But his elevation requires small but distinct reversals in authorial attitude, as Ansell, with his creator's approval, moves abruptly to worship of Stephen. The reader finds it hard to eradicate the sense that Rickie cannot so easily be divested of capacities for insight that earlier countered Ansell's. Yet the narrator's approval is unequivocal:

> In many ways he was pedantic; but his pedantry lay close to the vineyards of life—far closer than that fetich Experience of the innumerable teacups. He had a great many facts to learn, and before he died he learnt a suitable quantity. But he never forgot that the holiness of the heart's imagination can alone classify those facts—can alone decide which is an exception, which an example. [P. 240]

Having deputized him, Forster seems concerned that Ansell not eclipse his creator. Ansell views the events he is witnessing as "the Greek Drama, where the actors know so little and the spectators so much" (p. 250), expressing a privileged awareness that Forster is curiously compelled to correct. "Ansell prepared himself to witness the second act of the drama; forgetting that all this world, and not part of it, is a stage" (p. 250). The narrator thus reminds us that only he has complete vision: however adept an observer, Ansell is part of the show. The disembodied creator is not caught, his comment asserts, in the web of plot and personality. Yet in this he is mistaken, for the narrator is the most prominent actor, and in this novel his attachments and revulsions belie the attempt at an impartial godliness.

Wilfred Stone's contention that the works of Forster "are sapped by a moral anxiety to sacrifice dramatic representation for some swifter, purer, more direct statement of truth" as-

---

yet—more wonderful (I don't exaggerate) than the moment when Agnes promised to marry me" (p. 98). See also manuscript of *The Longest Journey*, Folio Volume 6, F104, p. 116. *Maurice* makes this sexuality explicit.

sumes that direct statements in the author's own voice lack the
status of art.[13] Without sharing that assumption, we may attrib-
ute Forster's insistence on purveying his primary moral insights
in his own voice to the didactic and missionary quality of his
impulse. But that Forster considered his narrator's efforts as art
is unquestionable and is seen in his very unwillingness to give
his own richness completely to any character. He places confidence, rather, in direct explication, in an author-centered universe, where the narrator as author-surrogate possesses the
greatest moral and linguistic resources. He demonstrates also an
aesthetic confidence in words, in the artistic scope and arrangement of language of which only he, as narrator, is capable.

The consequence of Forster's decision to vest his artistic
power so much in his narrator is that the success of his novels
becomes heavily dependent on the commentator's control, especially as the subjects of his observation become increasingly
complex. The centrality of the author's voice intensifies the
need for his consistent authority. Where problems arise, they
do so not because the narrator's presence vitiates the novel's
potentiality as art, but because the narrator himself embodies
the novel's crucial confusions of distance and theme.

The Longest Journey's famous "coinage" chapter illustrates
the dominance of moral preoccupations that Forster contin-
ually refers for expression to his own voice. It is the only
chapter in all of Forster's novels devoted entirely to the narrator's philosophic commentary and devoid of direct reference to
character or action. The chapter's three short paragraphs present Forster's exploration of the proper relationship between
man and man, man and God. While Rickie's collapse at hearing the truth about his brother's origin is the "bankruptcy"
that impels Forster to his reflections, nowhere in this chapter
does the narrator imply the relevance of his speculations to
Rickie or any other character. That this separation of general-

13. Stone, *The Cave and the Mountain*, p. 184.

ization from action is intentional is illustrated by the presence in the manuscript of *The Longest Journey* of an earlier ending to this chapter, in which Forster applied his reflections directly: "Here is the problem for Rickie. In this poverty, which coinage is he to choose?"[14] Forster's omission of this reference in the published novel emphasizes his overriding concern with moral implication and metaphysical possibility. In the context of this emphasis, the "coinage" chapter is in substance and function something quite different from what one critic regards as the "blurting out" of "an exact confession of what he [Forster] himself wants the story to mean."[15]

Forster moves in this chapter from definition of his initial metaphor of spiritual currency to discussion of its consequences: the soul's "bankruptcies" may actually enrich. Error and suffering can be a "discipline" by which the soul learns to "reckon clearly" and thus to attain the best possibilities of human relationships and earthly fulfillment. Contrasted to man's "coinage" is God's, incorruptible and incapable of error. But its expression is an ascetic mysticism in which the soul renounces alike the values and bankruptcies of human life. As the chapter

---

14. Manuscript of *The Longest Journey,* Folio Volume 6, F391, p. 464.

15. Crews, *E. N. Forster,* pp. 59–62. Crews misreads badly in his interpretation of this important chapter. For Rickie's "bankruptcy" is not attributable to a discovery that twin temptations of sexual love and a position of authority have ruined his life. The kind of sexuality his union with Agnes represents is, to put it blandly, ambiguous, and Rickie never seeks authority but rather suppresses his own instincts in the hope that "doing good" will renew his vanished insight. Rickie's first bankruptcy occurs as a result of his idealization of his mother. He moves to the second and final bankruptcy through a similar mistake, in which he compounds the initial excess by regarding Stephen as their mother's incarnation. Nor does "the most important connection" between the character's adventures and Forster's own passages of commentary lie in the coinage chapter's definition of the "central difficulty" as "that of properly evaluating human life" (Crews, p. 60). For the "coinage" chapter affirms the value of human life. Nor is Forster concerned in this chapter with the question of upholding "our private standards of value in a world that is indifferent to our existence" (Crews, p. 60). Rather he seeks a path to truth in which distortion and error are ultimately means to a fuller life.

concludes, Forster reiterates the superior value of human relationships and pleasures, and the moral utility of error. Human
life with its joys and imperfections is better than ascetic withdrawal and freedom from error.

The "coinage" chapter, then, is a plea for engagement with
life. In all his imperfection, Rickie pursues the moral choice by
his agonized attempts to live fully. Although tempted to the
safer contemplation of the divine, Rickie is saved from such a
withdrawal by Ansell: "If he had not been there, Rickie would
have renounced his mother and his brother and all the outer
world, troubling no one. The mystic, inherent in him, would
have prevailed" (p. 295). But the import of Forster's speculations in the "coinage" chapter really run counter to their implications for Rickie, for whom the correct choice brings no
fulfillment in life. The utility of his suffering is vitiated, the
discipline of his bankruptcy denied in Rickie's inability to
"reckon clearly." The chronicle of Rickie's doomed existence is
relieved only by a temporary clarity which Forster reveals as
illusory.

Nevertheless, proper reading of this chapter not only implies
the substance of Rickie's bankruptcy but reveals the extent of
Forster's optimism. The commentary attacks asceticism, detachment, and withdrawal. It affirms the belief in personal
relations and the search for humanistic values. The triumph
of the inarticulate but active Stephen, with his philosophy of
"Here am I, and there are you" (p. 303), is the ultimate illustration of the possibility for affirmation. The "coinage"
chapter is ineffective as applied to Rickie's life, and the discrepancy between Forster's hopeful metaphysic and the travails
of his major character shows that the ambiguities of *The Longest Journey* appear in theme as well as technique. The treatment of Rickie shows also that, at this stage, Forster cannot
transcend his inner conflict to give a coherent rendering of the
human condition.

We have seen that Rickie's symbolizing imagination has been

an ambiguous virtue, that it underlies both his insight and his fatal error. The equivocal portrait of Rickie raises fundamental questions about his creator's intention. Is Forster castigating the symbolizing activity or is he concerned only to repudiate Rickie's spurious vision? I think we must say the latter, but Stone is certainly correct in noting "cross-purposes," and his observation that *The Longest Journey* is "a negation of art that foreshadows Forster's own retirement" suggests something of the consequences of Forster's opacity.[16]

Rickie's problem is not that he symbolizes, but that he sometimes symbolizes wrongly. His imagination transfigures people as well as moments, and his excesses in this cause his two "bankruptcies." Here, as I have noted, Forster's treatment of Rickie runs counter to his theorizing. For Forster claims that bankruptcy is not destruction but opportunity, that the moral discipline of suffering leads to temporal and spiritual reward. The aftermath of Rickie's first bankruptcy seems correlative, but his second obliterates all the gains. Yet Forster insists that misperception is better than withdrawal, and that its consequences are enlargement, not repudiation of man's moral and imaginative vision. But in Rickie's destruction and Stephen's victory, he further evades the implications of his theory, for Stephen's virtues are irrelevant to those of the imagination. The Wiltshire farmer will never face the difficulties truth must meet: truth is his by instinct.

Stephen's position in the novel reveals yet another difficulty in the embodiment of theme. For Forster himself does what he punishes Rickie for. Stephen's importance is clearly symbolic. The "Wiltshire" theme develops his credentials as guardian of the English rural tradition. Ansell has saved Rickie from the mystic withdrawal decried in the "coinage" chapter by convincing him that "only one thing matters—that the Beloved should rise from the dead" (p. 283). Forster himself explains

16. Stone, *The Cave and the Mountain*, pp. 184–185.

that Rickie follows Stephen—an action clearly intended as re-juvenating—because in Stephen's voice, so like their mother's, "he had found a surer guarantee": "Habits and sex may change with the new generation, features may alter with the play of a private passion, but a voice is apart from these. It lies nearer to the racial essence and perhaps to the divine; it can, at all events, overleap one grave" (p. 292). The telling association of "racial essence" and "divine" finds implicit validation in the novel's concluding portrait of Stephen as guardian.

It would seem that Rickie's error is not excessive idealization but too little faith. Either way, his vision is repudiated. The misperceptions of the artistic imagination are clearly at vari-ance with the possibilities for affirmation. Art opposes the simple exercise of right instincts. At the same time, Forster himself has noted Stephen's limitations and exemplified the uses of the symbolizing imagination. The severe thematic and aesthetic difficulties of the novel mirror these ambiguities.

Yet *The Longest Journey* is of all Forster's books the most alive. Its extremes of love and hate, fulfillment and destruction, express a passionate concern for the possibilities of life, and the language projects extraordinary eloquence and a poignant awareness of both human potentiality and human waste. One can understand Forster's own preference for this novel. At the same time, we must say of Forster here, as Ansell says of Rickie, that he stands too near to settle.

3 ∿

A Room with a View

WE move with some relief from the torments of Rickie to the more hopeful dilemma of Forster's first heroine, Lucy Honeychurch, and one can speculate that Forster finished his second Italian novel as a respite from the intensities of *The Longest Journey*. Less complex than its predecessors, *A Room with a View* is, like them, a novel of initiation and discovery. But whereas the first two novels explore the nature of salvation and the meaning of truth, the moral absolute of *A Room with a View* is sexual self-realization, and questions of ultimate meaning cheerfully trim themselves into the confines of Lucy's progress to enlightenment. The novel's conclusion represents Forster's only real victory for personal relations and marks his single harmonious association of personal fulfillment with heterosexual love.

The acceptance of sexuality is the issue, dramatized both as rebellion against a parental generation whose authority manifests itself in the conventions of spinsters and clerics, and as a conflict within the heroine's psyche, a war between conscious motive and unconscious desire. Lucy's internal schism is the dominant motif, and Forster confronts sexual love with sur-

83

prising directness, given his evasions in the other novels and the
limitations of his background and orientation. Besides elaborat-
ing Lucy's psychic war, the novel hints at other concerns, with
sexuality, social change, and art. Lucy's self-delusion ultimately
threatens the comic mode, for although Forster rescues his heroine from herself, he skates thinly over tragedy, and an under-
tone of anxiety accompanies the dilemmas of Lucy and the
valedictory celebration of her environment. To the informing
motif of self-realization, *A Room with a View* adds Forster's
only portrayal of a harmonious society in its sketch of Lucy's
Surrey microcosm; altogether the novel is more diverse in its
concerns and nuances than its creator acknowledged or critics
have perceived.

Forster himself was ambivalent about *A Room with a View*:
he regarded it as "thin" and was troubled about the morality
of a happy ending in modern fiction. "A hundred years ago, or
fifty years ago, this would have seemed a very good answer,"
he commented in a 1906 paper, "Pessimism in Literature."
"But [the modern novelist] wants to end his book on a note of
permanence, and where shall he find it? . . . Where shall such a
man find rest with honour? Scarcely in a happy ending."[1] Yet
he recognized something of his accomplishment, noting that
"the characters seem more alive to me than any others that I
have put together" (xiii), and he defended the novel against the
strictures of Edward J. Dent, the model for Philip Herriton and
probably for Cecil, by his observation that "the character of
Lucy, on which everything depends, is all right: she and Mr.
Beebe have interested me a great deal" (xiv). In 1958, Forster
qualified the happy ending in a retrospective essay, "A View
without a Room," in which he speculated with depressed charm
on the subsequent fates of Lucy and George, living into the
post–World War II era.[2]

---

1. E. M. Forster, *A Room with a View*, Abinger Edition, 3, ed. Oliver
Stallybrass (London: Edward Arnold, 1977), pp. xvi–xvii. Subsequent references are to this edition; hereafter page numbers will be indicated in the text.
2. Ibid., Appendix, pp. 210–212.

A Room with a View is, as Forster noted, his "nicest" book (xiv). But it is more than nice, and its history goes far to explain the novel's mixture of naivete and polish, restriction of purpose and resource in execution. Among its endearing qualities are the heroine's warmth and lack of pretension, the affectionate treatment of family life, the tolerance for what in other Forster novels would be excoriated as philistinism, the wit and observation of its comic exposures, and its straightforward plea for sexuality and self-knowledge.

The novel's genesis also helps explain its peculiar location in the Forster canon, as a third novel whose outlook and preoccupations appear to designate it an earlier work. For *A Room with a View* occupies a dual position in the chronology of Forster's fiction. It was almost the first novel conceived—the abortive projection of an early Rickie in an unfinished sketch called "Nottingham Lace" occupies that position—[3] but it was the first novel begun and sustained, over two drafts and several years, before Forster put it aside for his first two published novels, thus giving the more complex *Where Angels Fear to Tread* precedence in appearance as his first Italian novel. Begun in the winter of 1901–1902 during Forster's first trip to Italy, *A Room with a View* started as a fragment that Forster called "Old Lucy" to distinguish it from the "New Lucy" which followed in 1903. Both these attempts at an Italian novel predate the writing of *Where Angels Fear to Tread*. Only fragments of the two *Lucy* novels have survived, but we may infer from chapter headings and the substance of the drafts that the existing sections accurately reflect their projected scope.[4] To compare the two *Lucy*s with *A Room with a View*, which was completed in 1907 and published in 1908, is to see the ways in which the novel represents the reworking of an earlier concep-

3. In E. M. Forster, *Arctic Summer and Other Fiction*, Abinger Edition, 9, ed Elizabeth Heine and Oliver Stallybrass (London: Edward Arnold, 1980), pp. 1–66.

4. See E. M. Forster, *The Lucy Novels: Early Sketches for A Room with a View*, Abinger Edition, 3a, ed. Oliver Stallybrass (London: Edward Arnold, 1977).

tion, revised and refined after the writing of two full-length novels. It is possible to identify elements in the earlier drafts that emerge in the novel and to see in the finished version the development of a fuller vision that nevertheless retains the germ of its inception in the *Lucy* drafts. We can thus understand why *A Room with a View* appears at once so simple and so deft, how it combines the preoccupations of a young man and the aura of an earlier time with a continuity of development and sophistication in technique that mark it as the creation of an experienced writer.

The first *Lucy* focuses on the comic exposure of English tourists in Italy. It contains Lucy, Charlotte, and a hero variously surnamed. The plot centers on a fund-raising concert to be given by the resident English, but Forster was unable to decide what should happen. The dissimilarities between *Old Lucy* and the published novel are more instructive than the likenesses. As in the novel, there is tension between Lucy and Charlotte, but Lucy eventually flees to Rome not with Charlotte as in the novel, but to avoid her. In *Old Lucy*, furthermore, Lucy is not the major character: Forster has a greater interest in the young man, Arthur, a would-be artist who undergoes a crisis of vocation. The friendship of Lucy and this character is platonic. The most significant incident, "a catastrophe," is the death of a young Italian man in the Piazza Signoria, an incident similar to the murder that brings Lucy and George Emerson together in *A Room with a View*. But in the early draft, Lucy is not present. Narrated from Arthur's point of view, the episode consists largely of a lurid and erotic description of the dying "naked youth." The sight of "the young Italian's perfect form lying on the fountain brim"[5] causes Arthur to renounce art in favor of life, as he tells Lucy, "to promote human intercourse and bring about the brotherhood of Man."[6]

5. Ibid., p. 37.
6. Ibid., p. 47.

Forster did not include this piece of adolescent homosexuality in the finished novel; by 1903 in *New Lucy* his story had become a heterosexual romance. But *New Lucy* presents some comparable elements. The homosexual countercurrent seen in *Old Lucy* as concentration on the male hero and his fantasies appears in *New Lucy* in the greater attention given Mr. Beebe's proclivities. The parson shares a romantic interlude in the woods at night with George, during which he tries unsuccessfully to persuade George to renounce Lucy. His failure provokes in Mr. Beebe what is clearly jealous anger. Although Mr. Beebe's homosexuality is not explicit, the scene and Mr. Beebe's puzzled speculations about the intensity of his feelings for George provide a motivation for what in *A Room with a View* is more mysterious, Mr. Beebe's hostile withdrawal from the lovers.

The other major difference in plot between *New Lucy* and the published novel is that in the draft Forster kills off George, with typical suddenness, in a bicycle accident that follows his unsuccessful attempt to persuade Lucy to elope.[7] It is Forster's irony that if Lucy had agreed they would have taken another route and avoided the disaster. George's reprieve became necessary to Forster's conception of the logic of his plot: "Oh mercy to myself I cried if Lucy don't get wed" he announced in September 1907, in a postcard to R. C. Trevelyan (xii). But the marriage reinforced or defined for Forster the novel's thinness, a "moral matter" because the happy ending is an easy way out; for as Forster said in his 1906 paper, a "conscientious and artistic" writer "knows that healthiness and simplicity are not, in all cases, identical with truth" (xvii). The unease of the modern world requires separation, not celebration, and in his awareness of what he considered an outmoded solution Forster demonstrates both the distance he has traveled from the Victorian novel and his realization that, in his mature acceptance of an earlier logic, he has written a novel whose atmosphere and

7. Ibid., p. 130.

solutions are closer to the nineteenth century than to the twentieth. Yet he moves toward a modern view in that the potential tragedy in *A Room with a View* is not, as in *New Lucy,* an external disaster that would nullify Lucy's brave choice but a condition of inner alienation, a disaster of the individual psyche.

A Room with a View retains the shape and the comparative restriction of the drafts. Like *New Lucy* it is only half an Italian novel, its second part set in an England through which the reminiscent breath of Italy blows but which embodies its own verities. As in *Old Lucy,* the treatment of Italy is superficial, restricted to the tourist mentality and the tourist enterprise. In this respect the published novel reflects its genesis in Forster's first Italian journey, in which, traveling with his mother, he had little opportunity for the contact with "real" Italians that Philip is able to accomplish in *Where Angels Fear to Tread. New Lucy* presents Miss Bartlett, Mr. Beebe, and the Cecil-Lucy-George triangle. But in the published novel Forster directed the story to Lucy's growth. Her sexual awakening, fear, self-delusion, and enlightenment now constitute a carefully structured thematic development that unifies both halves of the novel. Gone are the excesses of the earlier Lucys—old Lucy mannered and pert, new Lucy at times verbose and melodramatic: she has become a sympathetic and consistent character whose adventure in self-discovery is the paradigm of entrance into adulthood. The tourists of *Old Lucy* among whom she was an incidental member become the chorus of chaperones who impede the emerging Lucy of *A Room with a View.* The finished novel thus clarifies a theme that reflects the preoccupations of a writer himself at the verge of adulthood. At the same time, its consolidation of theme, its intricate plotting, the virtuosity of its comic dialogues and its hints of greater complexity bear witness to the experience Forster gained from the novels he wrote before returning to transform the two *Lucys* into the bright tour-de-force that is *A Room with a View.*

The motif of rebellion against parental authority appears in

Where Angels Fear to Tread and *The Longest Journey*, but its
greater energy and more direct influence in *A Room with a
View* testify also to the novel's early genesis. The early sections of *Where Angels Fear to Tread* develop Philip's rebellion
against his mother. The novel's conclusion makes us question
the degree of his emancipation, just as Forster himself remained
psychically with the Philips and Cecils. But if Philip's internal
burden never really lifts, as least he gropes toward insight without the supervisory presence of the parental generation. Free in
Italy from chaperones, Philip comes to the responsibility of
adulthood. In *The Longest Journey* the parents are dead, the
children struggle on their own. As antagonists and members of
an older generation, Herbert Pembroke and Mrs. Failing med-
dle and impinge. But repressive though they are, they function
rather as symbols of evil than as parental authority. *A Room
with a View*, on the other hand, opposes older and younger
generations. The parental generation is a force throughout the
novel, appearing in the first half as the English tourists who
"protect" Lucy, in the second as the benevolent regime of her
mother, from which Lucy nevertheless must separate herself to
reach adulthood.

Chaperones surround Lucy. Chief among these is her cousin,
Miss Bartlett. Their tense relationship presents a conflict between Miss Bartlett's fearful conventions and Lucy's rebellious
instincts; it also reveals a syndrome of anxiety, resentment, and
guilt, in which Lucy struggles against the manipulations of a
quasi-parent who seeks to repress her growth. Subsidiary chaperones echo the theme. The unreliable Miss Lavish conducts
Lucy to Santa Croce, the early Victorian Miss Alans articulate
a decorum against which Lucy rebels. Even the perceptive Mr.
Beebe expresses his pastoral concern for Lucy as an admonition not to go out alone. The other chaplain, Mr. Eager, aligns
himself against youth and love by separating two young Italian
lovers: appealing to Lucy, the couple asserts instinctual kinship
with her.

In the wings is Lucy's real parent, Mrs. Honeychurch, and
the restrictions of pension elders yield to the ease and intimacy
of Lucy's family life at Windy Corner. Her imprisonment is by
now self-imposed, the condition of liberation victory in an inner
struggle. Yet to be free Lucy must eventually separate herself
even from her loved mother, and at the crisis the entire adult
world unites against Lucy. Her mother's opposition creates the
definitive break between generations. The struggle, no longer
inner, devolves on Lucy, and Lucy rather than George, who
"was a boy, after all" (p. 206), emerges at the conclusion as
adult. That the price, her expulsion from Windy Corner, is
paradise lost, suggests the degree to which, despite the happy
ending, Forster implies a modern condition.

The novel's opening scene forms a prelude to its catalytic
episode, Lucy's sexual awakening in the Piazza Signoria. Confronted with old Mr. Emerson's offer to exchange rooms, Lucy
perceives that the issue is more than rooms and views: "she
had an odd feeling that whenever these ill-bred tourists spoke
the contest widened and deepened" (p. 4). Miss Bartlett's reception of the offer as masculine "brutality" and her "repression" of Lucy's attempts to respond introduce the sexual issue.
When the clergyman's mediation enables Miss Bartlett to accept, she insists on "protecting" Lucy by taking the young
man's room herself. Lucy "again had the sense of larger and
unsuspected issues" (p. 12). These become explicit with Lucy's
sexual attraction to George, whom she imagines as a Michel-
angelo nude: "She saw him once again at Rome, on the ceiling
of the Sistine Chapel, carrying a burden of acorns" (p. 24).
Lucy is soon moved to flout her pension elders and walk alone
in Florence at dusk, newly aware of her discontent though not
of its cause.

The scene that follows is extraordinary in the directness of
its symbolism. Lucy witnesses the murder of a young Italian:
fainting, she awakens in the arms of George Emerson, who
happened to be there. The incident marks the birth of passion

for Lucy and George, and its sexual nature is clear throughout. The tension of Lucy's rebellion from authority begins the scene. "She would really like to do something of which her well-wishers disapproved" (p. 40), so she buys forbidden reproductions, most significantly Botticelli's *Birth of Venus*. As she enters the Piazza Signoria in which "the Loggia showed as the triple entrance of a cave," Forster opposes the passivity of age to what he will dramatize symbolically as the sexuality of youth: "An older person at such an hour and in such a place might think sufficient was happening to him, and rest content. Lucy desired more. . . . She fixed her eyes wistfully on the tower of the palace, which rose out of the lower darkness like a pillar of roughened gold. It seemed no longer a tower, no longer supported by earth, but some unattainable treasure throbbing in the tranquil sky. Its brightness mesmerized her" (p. 41).[8]

The dying man now looks at Lucy "as if he had an important message for her" and blood comes from his mouth. As Lucy faints, "the palace itself grew dim, swayed above her, fell onto her softly, slowly, noiselessly, and the sky fell with it" (p. 41). "Oh what have I done?" repeats Lucy three times during the postlude. And "The palace tower had lost the reflection of the declining day, and joined itself to earth" (pp. 42–43). Lucy realizes "that she, as well as the dying man, had crossed some spiritual boundary." She next discovers that George has thrown her pictures into the river because they are covered with blood— one in particular has been stained: of course it is the Botticelli Venus. George echoes Lucy's awareness that "something tremendous has happened" (p. 43), as the river Arno roars out the "unexpected melody" of Beethoven's Opus 111, whose triumphant performance by Lucy had revealed her "greatness." Under the circumstances, Forster's chastely sententious summa-

8. Cf. "A tang of sweat spread as he stripped and a muscle thickened up out of gold": "The Other Boat," in E. M. Forster, *The Life to Come and Other Stories*, Abinger Edition, 8, ed. Oliver Stallybrass (London: Edward Arnold, 1972), p. 173.

tion is anticlimactic: "they had come to a situation where character tells, and where Childhood enters upon the branching
paths of Youth" (p. 45).

Lucy's symbolic loss of virginity brings reaction as, frightened at the discovery of her passionate self, Lucy avoids George.
The moment and her retreat from it inaugurate a pattern that
structures the action and binds together the contrasted settings
of the novel's two sections. From the moment of recognition in
the piazza and its immediate denial, Lucy's every advance toward conscious awareness brings a counteraction in which,
however abetted by outside repression, Lucy places herself in
the enemy's hands. Her experience in the piazza is initially
liberating, as she recognizes the voyeurism of her respectable
compatriots Mr. Eager and Miss Lavish who, seeking details of
the murder, "nibble after blood" (p. 51), and defends old Mr.
Emerson from the innuendoes of Mr. Eager: "For the first time
Lucy's rebellious thoughts swept out in words" (p. 54). Yet she
moves with a mixture of abjection and repulsion into the orbit
of Miss Bartlett, clinging almost literally to the chaperone's
skirts on an excursion of all the English to Fiesole, although
she envies the sexual happiness of the Italian lovers who drive
her carriage. Miss Bartlett's surveillance does not prevent George
from kissing Lucy at the picnic amid violets and associated
images of fecundity and fruition.[9] But the repressed conscious
looms as Miss Bartlett, "brown against the view" (p. 68). Torn
between fear of sexuality and anger at the chaperone's manipulations, Lucy "could not modulate out of the key of self-
abasement" (p. 75) and allows Miss Bartlett to take her off to
Rome. However simple the character of Lucy may appear—a
naive young woman of generous impulse and limited self-aware-

9. ". . . violets ran down in rivulets and streams and cataracts, irrigating
the hillside with blue, eddying round the tree stems, collecting into pools in
the hollows, covering the grass with spots of azure foam. . . . this terrace was
the well-head, the primal source whence beauty gushed out to water the
earth" (pp. 67–68).

ness—the nuances of her inner struggle, Miss Bartlett's exploitation, and the tonalities of awareness and conflict are intricate and subtle. Cross-examined about the kiss, Lucy "could not think" and cannot accept what she feels. Of all this the chaperone is aware, and knowing "perfectly well that Lucy did not love her, but needed her to love" (p. 77), she extracts from Lucy a promise of secrecy. Lucy on her side realizes that Miss Bartlett "had really been neither pliable nor humble nor inconsistent. She had worked like a great artist; for a time—indeed, for years—she had been meaningless, but at the end there was presented to the girl the complete picture of a cheerless, loveless world in which the young rush to destruction until they learn better—a shamefaced world of precautions and barriers which may avert evil, but which do not seem to bring good" (pp. 78–79).

In the novel's second half Lucy moves toward this world: her struggle for self-subversion intensifies as the impetus to truth grows stronger. The point to be made here is that despite the change of setting from Italy to England and the introduction of new characters—Cecil Vyse, the Honeychurches, citizens of the Surrey community Summer Street—the novel's second half is a continuity and does not create, as Stone has suggested and Trilling implied, a schism between the comic mode and a presentation of greater symbolic complexity.[10] Whereas the first half defines the sexual issue and locates the inner nature of Lucy's struggle, the second half follows the course of her accelerating self-deception to crisis and resolution.

The arrival of Cecil Vyse in Rome had been the news that interested Lucy least: her first act in the second half is to engage herself to Cecil, an exchange, as she soon discovers, of one chaperone for another. As Lucy's discomforts grow with the realization that her fiancé is a snob and that through his

10. See Wilfred Stone, *The Cave and the Mountain: A Study of E. M. Forster* (Stanford: Stanford University Press, 1966), p. 218; Lionel Trilling, *E. M. Forster* (Norfolk, Conn.: New Directions, 1964), pp. 99–100.

intervention George and his father will move into Summer Street, her warring subconscious emerges. Telling a story about the Emersons, she seeks to avoid reality by disguising them as "Harris." Shortly after this, Cecil kisses her, in a parody of Forster's less ironic love scenes. Her response to the comic failure of this attempt, in which Cecil's pince-nez becomes flattened between him and the object of his desire, is "Emerson the name was, not Harris" (p. 108). Cecil has made her instinctively recall the passionate George. "Safe" in London, Lucy plays not the triumphant Beethoven but Schumann, whose significance is "the sadness of the incomplete" (p. 121), symbolizing the sterility of her connection with Cecil; in London also she wakes in nightmare that recollects the kiss and the contrast between men. When she attempts to put George in a casual context and purge herself by telling Cecil about George's kiss, "her body behaved so ridiculously that she stopped" (p. 121).

Lucy's conscious mind had rehearsed the inevitable meeting with George, but their reunion occurs unexpectedly in the woods as George emerges from the "Sacred Lake" in the Edwardian discretion of Lucy's brother's trousers but otherwise free of the encumbrances of convention. Reborn himself from the ritual bathe, he greets Lucy "with the shout of the morning star." Lucy's instincts respond: "She had bowed across the rubbish that cumbers the world" (p. 134). But this affirmation belies her dutiful tolerance of Cecil's shortcomings, a course identified with the falsity of her former chaperone: "No one is perfect, and surely it is wiser to discover the imperfections before wedlock. Miss Bartlett, in deed, though not in word, had taught the girl that this our life contains nothing satisfactory. Lucy, though she disliked the teacher, regarded the teaching as profound, and applied it to her lover" (pp. 134–135). Additionally beset with her mother's accurate perception of Cecil, Lucy must defend him, but the subconscious surges forward as "the ghosts began to gather in the darkness" (p. 139). In Florence, Lucy had entered the Piazza Signoria at "the hour of unreality—the hour, that is, when unfamiliar things are real" (p. 41). Next day, as the chaperone conducted her through the same square, "for a moment she understood the nature of ghosts" (p. 47). Now, as Lucy tries to confirm herself in error, her subconscious threatens her rationalizing actions. With a visit from Miss Bartlett impending, "the ghosts were returning; they filled Italy, they were even usurping the places she had known as a child. . . . How would she fight against ghosts? For a moment the visible world faded away, and memories and emotions alone seemed real" (p. 141).

Forster chronicles Lucy's mounting crisis in chapter headings that indicate the internal nature of her conflict, as "How Lucy Faced the External Situation Bravely" gives way to "The Disaster Within," which leads to four chapters in which Lucy lies—to George, Cecil, Mr. Beebe et al, and Mr. Emerson, at the same time moving precariously toward revelation and acceptance. In this phase, Lucy dismisses her subconscious as "nerves": explaining George's kiss as the result of his subconscious, she makes a nice slip: "What I mean by subconscious is that Mr. Emerson lost his head. I fell into all those violets, and he was silly and surprised. I don't think we ought to blame him very much. It makes such a difference when you see a person with beautiful things behind him unexpectedly" (p. 147). George's second kiss, his plea to Lucy and Cecil's dismissal as "the scales fell from Lucy's eyes" (p. 168) follow, but because she has lied to George, Cecil, and herself about her sexual love for George, retribution threatens to overwhelm the novel's comic mode as Lucy enters a condition of death-in-life:

> She gave up trying to understand herself, and joined the vast armies of the benighted, who follow neither the heart nor the brain, and march to their destiny by catchwords. The armies are full of pleasant and pious folk. But they have yielded to the only enemy that matters—the enemy within. They have sinned against passion and truth, and vain will be their strife after virtue. [P. 174]

Lying to George, Lucy suddenly became aware of autumn, of decay and darkness. The manifestations of her inner darkness begin in apathy, as Mr. Beebe quietly approves, the vivacious Freddy opposes Lucy's new choice of music:

> Stop thine ear against the singer—
> From the red gold keep thy finger;
> Vacant heart, and hand and eye,
> Easy live and quiet die. [P. 189][11]

The Lucy who had once rebelled against the conventions of elderly tourists now cast her lot with the earliest Victorians of them all, the Miss Alans, for a trip to Greece by which she hopes to avoid George and self-knowledge. Lucy's entrance into the night that "received her, as it had received Miss Bartlett thirty years before" (p. 174), has its logical and ironic consequence—her metamorphosis into that figure. Her always perceptive mother recognizes it: "'Oh, goodness,' her mother flashed. 'How you do remind me of Charlotte Bartlett!'" (p. 193).

Against Lucy's determination to escape self-knowledge, her subconscious can now provide only muted resistance, in the rhythmic melody of the horses' hooves that sings to her of George's fidelity, "He has not told—he has not told" (p. 194). Denouement and reversal arrive in the nick of time, as Lucy's encounter with Mr. Emerson brings her finally to acceptance and psychic integration: "He gave her a sense of deities reconciled, a feeling that, in gaining the man she loved, she would gain something for the whole world. . . . He had robbed the body of its taint, the world's taunts of their sting; he had shown her the holiness of direct desire" (p. 204). Thus alone

---

11. As Oliver Stallybrass notes, this song was sung by Lucy Ashton in Scott's *The Bride of Lammermoor*. It is highly appropriate to its context in *A Room with a View*; beyond this it may reflect a wry comic association with the *Lucia* scene in *Where Angels Fear to Tread*. See *A Room with a View*, Note to p. 188, p. 235; *Where Angels Fear to Tread*, pp. 94–96.

among the novels, *A Room with a View* fulfills its ideology of personal relations and self-realization. Moreover, in its depiction of a successful heterosexual love it harmonizes these values with the imperative of continuance and suggests the worldly achievement of completion. Lucy, crediting Mr. Emerson, articulates the vision: "It was as if he had made her see the whole of everything at once" (p. 204).

A Room with a View succeeds as a novel of rebellion and initiation, in its affirmation of sexual love that includes Lucy's desire for comradeship with the man she loves. But another ideal of comradeship creates a strong undercurrent to the mainstream on which Forster's craft floats. The interest Forster expressed in Mr. Beebe indicates the direction of this second current. Despite Forster's omission of the more explicit material that appeared in both *Lucys*, the homosexual energy persists in two aspects of the novel that balance and qualify the unmitigated triumph of the heterosexual ideal. One is the celebration of male comradeship in the Sacred Lake; the other appears in the characterization of Mr. Beebe, whose turnabout at the novel's denouement has provoked much critical perplexity.[12]

Forster's decision not to include the homosexual material from the *Lucy* drafts strengthened his presentation of the romance between Lucy and George. Lucy's story remains central, and Forster either did not wish to or dared not undercut it directly. The former explanation seems more likely because with one exception, imagery and structure all advance the central motif. The exception is the placement of the male bathing scene, by which Forster suggests its importance. The two chapters in the novel that deal with sexual episodes are "Fourth Chapter," the piazza scene early in Part I, and "Twelfth Chap-

12. See, for example, Trilling, *E. M. Forster*, pp. 108–109; Stone, *The Cave and the Mountain*, pp. 231–232; Stallybrass, *A Room with a View*, xvii–xviii; Jeffrey Meyers, "Vacant Heart and Hand and Eye: The Homosexual Theme in *A Room with a View*, *English Literature in Transition*, 13 (1970), 181–192, and *passim*.

ter," in which Mr. Beebe, George Emerson, and Freddy Honeychurch bathe nude in a woodland pool. (The three kisses of
the novel punctuate rather than describe.) In contrast to all the
other chapters, these two have numerical rather than summa-
rizing titles. In "Fourth Chapter" Lucy undergoes transformation; in "Twelfth Chapter," George, who had retreated into
apathy after Lucy's flight to Rome, emerges from the pond
naked and filled with the desire to live. The exigencies of theme
bring George at this point to Lucy, but the experience that the
chapter describes excludes her—the arrival of women ends the
male idyll, whose significance is in its celebration of the male
body, male play, and the ritual, sanctifying quality of immersion. "The holiness of direct desire" echoes in Forster's summation of the scene: "It had been a call to the blood and to the
relaxed will, a passing benediction whose influence did not
pass, a holiness, a spell, a momentary chalice for youth" (p.
133). The scene has no further consequences: rather it distills a
male ideal of comradeship, a moment of truth in the communion of the pool whose implications could not be allowed
to emerge directly or to overbalance the focal theme.

The *Lucy* materials, the appearance of *Maurice,* and Furbank's biography make plain the "profound reasons" for Mr.
Beebe's chilliness toward the opposite sex: a homosexuality
that Forster disguises in the novel as celibacy and aestheticism.
Here matters become less plain, for Forster's attitude to Mr.
Beebe is ambiguous. There is some evidence that Forster can
treat him with irony: the parson writes in his "philosophic
diary" about the behavior of maiden ladies; Forster's observation that "his chief pleasure was to provide people with happy
memories" implies Mr. Beebe's fear of intimacy; the parson's
aestheticism is sometimes inappropriate, as when he disap-
proves Lucy's new dress, which he noticed while preaching.
But for most of the novel Forster permits Mr. Beebe to remain
above the battle and endows him with tolerance, good temper,
and sympathy—the qualities of an early Fielding. On all sub-

jects except the psychology of young women, Mr. Beebe is acute, and the narrative voice supports his attempts to further social harmony and approves the naturalness of his demeanor. When, faced with Lucy's maundering explanation of her broken engagement and with Charlotte's urgings to support Lucy's escape to Greece, Mr. Beebe is obtuse, his bachelor naivete may be invoked. But when, confronted with the revelation of Lucy's love for George, Mr. Beebe withdraws in hostility, the rejection is clearly directed to George, who "no longer interests" him. Forster has explained Mr. Beebe's sudden reversal by his early hint about the parson's chilliness and by the later assertion that Mr. Beebe's "belief in celibacy, so reticent, so carefully concealed beneath his tolerance and culture" (p. 186) "alone explains his action subsequently, and his influence on the action of others" (p. 187). Yet readers experience the turnabout as a mystery, and here the authorial attitude to Mr. Beebe comes into question.

Forster defines Mr. Beebe as ascetic and aesthetic, as the possessor of qualities he condemns in Cecil Vyse, to whom the parson admits kinship when he observes that they are both "better off detached." Yet the aestheticism that Forster repudiates in Cecil he seems, albeit with comic ironies at the parson's expense, to tolerate in Mr. Beebe. More than this, Forster seems here—as in *Where Angels Fear to Tread,* when at the crucial moment of vision he sees as Philip—unable to cure himself of the disease of his protagonist, but instead to share Mr. Beebe's aesthetic view. Like Philip, Mr. Beebe sees in images and tableaux. As Lucy sits amid her family,

> Her mother bent over her. Freddy, to whom she had been singing, reclined on the floor with his head against her, and an unlit pipe between his lips. Oddly enough, the group was beautiful. Mr. Beebe, who loved the art of the past, was reminded of a favourite theme, the *Santa Conversazione,* in which people who care for one another are painted chatting together about noble things—a theme neither sensual nor sensational, and therefore ignored by the art of today. [P. 188]

The narrator endorses both the mode and content of this observation, approving the subject matter—the Santa Conversazione—and the perception by which living people acquire moral significance through transformation into art. This is the very sin that forced Cecil from the field—his conception of Lucy as a work of art. Yet the narrative voice is one with Mr. Beebe here.

After the denouement, the chill of Mr. Beebe's transformation into "a long black column" and the force of his permanent disapproval, in which he carries Mrs. Honeychurch with him, cast a shadow on the harmonious conclusion. Perhaps this is Forster's way of withholding full approval from the romantic couple. Their validation lies in their power of continuance, and Forster must side with fruition against sterility. But the unacknowledged degree of his identification with Mr. Beebe makes that character remain partly a mystery. Mr. Beebe's influence is ultimately dual—like the swim in the Sacred Lake, a bow to the "unregistered" life, on the other hand, a repudiation that allows the triumph of the forces that the lovers represent.

On the subject of other sexualities, we may note Forster's command of the psychology of spinsters. Miss Bartlett is a portrait of sexual hysteria, from her fascinations with keys, locks, and secret passages to her voyeuristic obsession with Lucy's sexual life, the details of which she recounts to her friend, the lady novelist. As George notices, Miss Lavish's descriptions reflect Miss Bartlett's intensity, and it is the chaperone who returns without cease to George's kiss, forcing the issue on Lucy. At the crisis, Charlotte apparently aids the lovers she has tried to sunder: even if her reversal seems unconvincing, it has Forster's support, for in "A View without a Room" he announced that Miss Barlett had left the lovers "her little all. (Who would have thought it of Cousin Charlotte? I should never have thought anything else.)" (p. 210). The cousin's effusive affection for Lucy appears essentially a deflection of her repressed sexuality. Forster's keen observation bespeaks his history of intimacy with female relatives; on the same theme he presents with comic pathos the sexual anxiety of Miss Alan who, seeing Mr. Beebe and Lucy in conversation, "sidled towards them and sat down, self-conscious as she always was on entering a room which contained one man, or a man and one woman" (p. 33).

Mr. Beebe and Miss Bartlett provide the most direct suggestions of complexity in a novel notable for its large cast of characters and for the comic interplay of character and theme. Yet only in his scorn for the sinister chaplain, Mr. Eager, and Miss Lavish, the caricature of a feminist novelist, is Forster univocal. He delineates pathos as well as rigidity in elderly spinsters, nobility along with pretension in Lucy's fiancé.

Cecil Vyse is the unacknowledged major character of *A Room with a View*, an unreconstructed Philip, simplified and cast as villain. Cecil is an aesthete, more beautiful than Philip and similarly a lover of beauty, who sees Lucy as a "Leonardo" and collects such odd acquaintances as the Emersons for his amusement. To insure the centrality of the heterosexual theme Foster has reduced the scope of a character who represents, as Wilfred Stone has noted, the author's rejected self, the successor to Philip and Rickie.[13] Cecil's defeat represents an affirmation of the humanistic ideal and an evasion of its contradictions. Furthermore, it is significant in the light of Forster's more characteristic formulation that Cecil emerges most forcefully at the moment of his withdrawal: "On the landing he paused, strong in his renunciation, and gave her a look of memorable beauty" (p. 173). The extent of Forster's identification became clear in "A View without a Room." Here finally, Cecil comes into his own, slyly vanquishing the forces of British jingoism to affirm the claims of intelligence and culture.[14]

13. Stone, *The Cave and the Mountain*, p. 229.

14. "With [Cecil's] integrity and intelligence he was destined for confidential work, and in 1914 he was seconded to Information. . . . I had an example of his propaganda, and a very welcome one, at Alexandria. A quiet little party

The remaining characters align themselves more or less cheerfully with the thematic oppositions, although the vigorous
Mrs. Honeychurch transcends her maternal role to preside over
Forster's celebration of the Surrey microcosm. George Emerson
is intended to represent a fit consort for Lucy because he can
feel passion, as opposed to Cecil Vyse, who cannot. He represents also, as I have suggested, an idealized love object for both
male and female characters. He is a version of the lower-class
hero, an intellectualized Stephen Wonham. But he alternates
between a silence that is unconvincingly implied to be preg-
nant and pompous speeches that are especially silly from a
young man. Occasionally George has flashes of spontaneity—
in a vulnerability to which Lucy responds, in dramatized kindness to his father. But Forster doesn't enlarge the characterization of George by views inside the hero's mind. His Carlylean
gestures are merely adolescent, and he seems almost as much a
contrivance as his father. Of the "childish but not senile" Mr.
Emerson, who enters the crisis quoting Butlerean aphorisms,
others have said enough (most lucidly Stone and Stallybrass, who
take opposing views).[15] That Mr. Emerson expresses Forster's
religious impulse in this novel and articulates the redemptive
ethos is unarguable: Forster summarizes his position as Lucy,
about to confront her mother with the estranging truth, "turned
to Mr. Emerson in despair. But his face revived her. It was the
face of a saint who understood" (p. 204). Mr. Emerson presents two related problems. First, the didacticism that is his
chief characteristic is more acceptable from the narrator be-

---

was held on the outskirts of that city, and someone wanted a little Beethoven.
The hostess demurred. Hun music might compromise us. But a young officer
spoke up. 'No, it's all right,' he said, 'a chap who knows about those things
from the inside told me Beethoven's definitely Belgian.'
    "The chap in question must have been Cecil. That mixture of mischief and
culture is unmistakable. Our hostess was reassured, the ban was lifted, and
the Moonlight Sonata shimmered into the desert" (p. 212).
    15. See Stone, *The Cave and the Mountain*, p. 222; Stallybrass, *A Room
with a View*, p. xviii.

cause there it is part of a more complex personality. Second, although Mr. Emerson is sententious, the narrator does not treat him with irony. Rather, Forster seems to have used Mr. Emerson as a transparent vessel for his views. Neither informed by self-perception nor clarified by authorial distance, Mr. Emerson does not convince.

The novel's pursuit of the values Mr. Emerson proclaims and its classification as an "Italian novel" do not reflect the degree to which *A Room with a View* is a novel about England. As an Italian novel it invites obvious comparison with *Where Angels Fear to Tread*. Both celebrate sincerity and self-realization, both oppose convention to instinct. But the Italy of *A Room with a View* abounds in violets rather than mystery, and suffering is absent from its sunny landscape. In *Where Angels Fear to Tread*, Italy is integral to the action. The social context receives some development, and the clash between English and Italian mores has tragic implication. The motif of Philip's journey endows Italy with metaphysical value. But the Italy of *A Room with a View* is more backdrop than force, its beauties hedged with mythology and fantasy, its terrors reduced to the brief melodrama of murder in the Piazza Signoria. As in Forster's first visit, Italy remains on the surface. Italians are quaint or they are comic allegories, like Phaethon and Persephone who preside over the excursion that culminates in George's kiss. Views, depicted in the landscapes of both Italy and England, represent the truth of instinct that Lucy cannot yet perceive. Although Italy provides the context for Lucy's awakening, its major function is to illumine her England. Italy in the novel's second part metamorphoses into the Surrey countryside, which presents a continuity of moral symbolism with the earlier setting. As Lucy perceives: "Ah, how beautiful the Weald looked! The hills stood out above its radiance, as Fiesole stands above the Tuscan plain, and the South Downs, if one chose, were the mountains of Carrara. She might be forgetting her Italy, but she was noticing more things in her England" (p. 156).

In Lucy's England—the Surrey community that includes her home, Windy Corner, and the adjacent village, Summer Street, Forster has created his only image of community realized, a unity of man, society, and nature. In a sense, *A Room with a View* portrays two societies, the world of Forster's mother and her entourage, which retreats with Miss Bartlett to Tunbridge Wells, and the Surrey community over which presides Mrs. Honeychurch, who is an affectionate portrait of Forster's grandmother, Louisa Wichelo.[16] At the crux of this society, a point of stability in a world unaware of change to come, Mrs. Honeychurch is blunt, sensible, perceptive, and independent. Her virtues overwhelm such limitations as her class consciousness and indifference to culture. Her moral judgments are uncompromising: Mrs. Honeychurch's initial benignity to Cecil dissolves in the face of his condescension to Windy Corner.

The community is narrow, bounded by wealth and class. The interesting episode of Mr. Flack's villas provides its only perceptible social issue. Mr. Flack is a local resident who, following his desire with Ruskinian integrity, has constructed two vulgar and ugly semidetached houses. Mr. Flack receives authorial support, yet his villas are the first ominous sign of threat from a larger society. The apprehension surrounding the villas stems partly from their aesthetic depreciation of Summer Street but more from their converse appropriateness to a class of urban clerks, like George Emerson, to whom Surrey is increasingly accessible through improvements in train service. Technology thus facilitates an egalitarianism that Forster approves in theory but really resists. It is the same inconsistency that he admits to in the essay "My Wood," a conflict between pleasure in the exclusivity of ownership and belief in public access.[17] Such conflicts will appear in *Howards End* as part of the contradiction in the fabric of Forster's liberalism.

16. See P. N. Furbank, *E. M. Forster: A Life*, Vol. 1 (London: Secker & Warburg, 1977), p. 2.

17. E. M. Forster, "My Wood" (1926), *Abinger Harvest* (New York: Harcourt, Brace, 1936), pp. 22–26.

As with Mr. Flack's villas, the scale of the novel's world is small, its architecture domestic. Mr. Beebe's church scarcely exceeds in height the cottages around it. Nature too is domesticated, as the curtains of Mrs. Honeychurch's drawing room mediate the light: "Without was poured a sea of radiance; within, the glory, though visible, was tempered to the capacities of man" (p. 82). The scale accommodates the human: a young Edwardian lady can enter the local wood in her best clothes; the Sacred Lake at full tide holds three people. The landscape is subtle and controlled: "In the Weald, autumn approached, breaking up the green monotony of summer, touching the parks with the gray bloom of mist, the beech trees with russet, the oak trees with gold" (p. 148). Trees and a view are nature's salient characteristics here: pine trees dispel the stench of motor cars as the countryside of *Howards End* will no longer be able to do. Like cars, the suburban villas that mar Summer Street can still be incorporated into a unity that transcends them. The integrity of its residents defines the sanctity of the community: because the unaesthetic house at Windy Corner "was the home of people who loved their surroundings honestly," it suggests not "the accidental, the temporary," but seems "as inevitable as an ugliness of Nature's own creation" (p. 175). This is the microcosm of a society at peace with itself. The portrait is saved from complacency—just—by Forster's awareness of its limitations. Noting "their kindly affluence, their inexplosive religion, their dislike of paper bags, orange peel and broken bottles" (p. 109), Forster describes "a circle of rich, pleasant people, with identical foes. In this circle one thought, married and died. Outside it were poverty and vulgarity, for ever trying to enter, just as the London fog tries to enter the pine-woods" (pp. 109–110). But, he asks, "Does this very much matter?" Despite its provinciality, "Lucy had consecrated her environment by the thousand little civilities that create a tenderness in time, and . . . though her eyes saw its defects her heart refused to despise it entirely" (p. 110).

Finally, Forster knows that this world will not last. At Windy

Corner, Lucy "seemed on the edge of a green magic carpet which hovered in the air above the tremulous world" (p. 86). London hovers at its edge, a place of fog, the Hades Lucy-Persephone must enter come winter, where Cecil's "mechanical" mother entertains "the grandchildren of famous people" (p. 121). Lucy clings to paradise: "Her mother would always sit there, her brother here. The sun, though it had moved a little since the morning, would never be hidden behind the western hills" (p. 154). But Forster underlines the unreality of her hope with the symbolism of Gluck's magic garden in *Armide,* "beneath the light of an eternal dawn, the music that never gains, never wanes, but ripples forever like the tideless seas of fairyland" (p. 154). Lucy loses Eden perforce, but Forster verified its disappearance in his 1958 postscript. Windy Corner did not long survive the death of Lucy's mother, for Freddy, the heir, became "an unsuccessful yet prolific doctor" and had to sell the family inheritance. "Windy Corner disappeared, its green was built over, and the name of Honeychurch resounded in Surrey no more" (p. 211).

It is significant that in this novel, which Forster regarded as thin, the mode of dialogue should dominate, the narrative presence be comparatively effaced. The structure of plot and the organization of comic scenes is extremely intricate in *A Room with a View,* as are the rhythmic oppositions and repetitions of idea and image. Yet the coalescence of relatively narrow ambitions with the narrator's diminished presence suggests the degree to which Forster's interventions constitute the primary source of complexity in his novels, a world of implication whose richness derives from the narrator's vision. Forster presides in *A Room with a View* as the Comic Muse: he nudges the action along and extrapolates its significance, but he interprets partly through a secondary order of the commentator's creation, a world of artifice that includes the medieval lady, the Meredithean subtitles that characterize and direct the action, and the scrollwork of mythology and fantasy. The narrator's direct in-

terventions display his stage-managing propensity, metaphorical imagination, and didacticism:

> Appearing thus late in the story, Cecil must be at once described.
> He was medieval. Like a Gothic statue. Tall and refined, with
> shoulders that seemed braced square by an effort of the will,
> and a head that was tilted a little higher than the usual level of
> vision, he resembled those fastidious saints who guard the por-
> tals of a French cathedral. Well educated, well endowed, and
> not deficient physically, he remained in the grip of a certain
> devil whom the modern world knows as self-consciousness, and
> whom the medieval, with dimmer vision, worshipped as asceti-
> cism. [Pp. 86–87]

The narrator's comments place the characters in appropriate
moral hierarchies. Lucy "shoots into the empyrean" (p. 29)
when she plays the piano, Mr. Emerson "was profoundly religious" (p. 199). As in the other prewar novels, the narrator
sometimes mediates directly between characters and reader,
stepping forward here in comic exasperation to ask, "She loved
Cecil; George made her nervous; will the reader explain to her
that the phrases should have been reversed?" (p. 142).

The narrator controls the use of rhythm, leitmotifs, and repetitions in differing contexts of ideas and images, but the dominance of dialogue and the considerable use of inside views
which are partial, such as Lucy's and Mr. Beebe's, distributes
the recurrent imagery, so that the narrator's share is not central. His discriminations guide the drama of Lucy's muddle-
dom, his comments shape the irony of comic dialogues. The
dominant tone is bright. But often a tone of anxiety permeates
both dialogue and narrative comment. This anxiety radiates
most directly from Lucy and concerns her sexual dilemma, but
it also appears in the portrayal of Miss Bartlett's inhibitions
and Lucy's difficulties with her, in the apprehension Mr. Beebe's
reversal projects on the conclusion, and in Mr. Emerson who,
despite the self-assurance of his religious dissent, is always anxious about his son, an emotion in which guilt appears to play a

part. Having deprived his son of religious certainty, Mr. Emerson is prey to anxiety about man's place in the universe. By now that place is pretty small: "The twelve winds blow us—we settle nothing—" says George (p. 128). More pervasive is the sense of precariousness that underlies Forster's celebration of Windy Corner and the brief admission of tragedy that enters the novel in the narrator's description of Lucy's entrance into "the armies of the benighted," and in the accompanying imagery of decay and darkness that lifts with her rescue. But in the final chapter, which briefly chronicles the travels of the spinster Miss Alans and sweeps the reader into the narrator's world of resolution, we may see Forster's voice in its most characteristic mode: "Trembling, anxious, cumbered with much digestive bread, they did proceed to Constantinople, they did go round the world. The rest of us must be contented with a fair, but a less arduous, goal. *Italian petimus*: we return to the Pension Bertolini" (p. 205).

Amid the prevailing comedy, hints of Forster's more cosmic preoccupations emerge, motifs that will become central in the two major novels. Of these, the role of art in this novel is perhaps the most suggestive of Forster's ultimate position. Art in *A Room with a View* has a dual function: it both opposes and inspires, and Forster's attitude is not entirely consistent. Proponents such as Cecil of "the aesthetic view of life"[18] err in freezing life's spontaneity into the rigidity of a formal image, and in preferring artifacts to people. Yet visual art has a moral resonance and, as Forster notes in *Maurice,* it is impossible to separate aesthetics from desire.[19] Furthermore, despite his opposition of life and art, Forster seeks to reconcile the two, urging Lucy to live as she plays. Here art—as music, which for Forster was the most complex art and a paradigm of universal order—becomes an ideal to which life may aspire. Lucy, it is

18. See Alan Wilde, *Art and Order: A Study of E. M. Forster* (New York: New York University Press, 1964), p. 11.

19. See E. M. Forster, *Maurice* (New York: Norton, 1971), pp. 92–93.

implied, does eventually live as she plays—heroically. Her Beethoven triumphs, in contrast to Helen Schlegel's Beethoven,
which will prevail only ambiguously in *Howards End*: but even
in Lucy's victory we are left with the irony that the perceiver of
her heroic artistry, Mr. Beebe, cannot acknowledge the heroism of her life. The idea of art as the sole unity and that of the
increasing separation of art from life culminate in *A Passage to
India*, where they are demonstrated both in the novel's structure—akin to music—and its meaning.

Other presages of the complex visions of the two major
novels enter *A Room with a View*. A near-accident to the
English tourists as they return from Fiesole illustrates the preoccupation with life's fragility that becomes in *A Passage to
India* the pervasive condition of contingency. In addition, the
episode presents a partial anticipation of the Temple section of
the final novel: "the floods of love and sincerity, which might
fructify every hour of life, burst forth in tumult. They descended from the carriages; they embraced each other. It was as
joyful to be forgiven past unworthinesses as to forgive them.
For a moment they realized vast possibilities of good" (p. 71).
It is noteworthy here that, however temporary, action is still
possible. In *Howards End* and *A Passage to India*, perception
and action have been sundered.

Such a moment, in which individual consciousnesses merge
in a unity of love, finds more finite expression in Lucy's moments of epiphany, all of which, except her final insight into
love, are concerned with the harmony of family, society, and
nature, and contain within them the awareness that such harmony must pass: "And, though nothing is perfect, Lucy felt for
the moment that her mother and Windy Corner and the Weald
in the declining sun were perfect" (p. 138). In her enlightenment Lucy sees life whole—alone of Forster's characters she
experiences completion in the context of human fulfillment.
But although he allows this conclusion, Forster suggests also
the mixed nature of the universe, in the repeated metaphors of

light and darkness, sun and shadow: in this connection, George Emerson's assertion that "we cast a shadow on something wherever we stand, and . . . the shadow always follows" (p. 151) is an early and crude form of Professor Godbole's meditation on the relation between good and evil.

As bold in affirmation as it is decorous in representation, *A Room with a View* is a novel of integration and consolidation. With the split psyche healed, the humanistic ideal reaches fulfillment. Furthermore, however ephemeral the vision of harmony in society, Lucy's raison d'être transcends its context: she represents life—"the spirit of the generations had smiled through them," and her union promises "the continuance of life on earth" (p. 97). In Lucy, Forster has portrayed a Rickie without the limp, and more extraordinary, he has made her a successful artist and triumphant participant in life, whose acquisition of insight is not contingent on withdrawal. As in Rickie's novel, reality, truth, and the sacred center coalesce, but with very different implications. Poised between the personal torments of *The Longest Journey* and the apprehension of social disintegration in *Howards End*, *A Room with a View* defines a symbolic moment of near-perfection. There is no wonder it couldn't last.

4 ~

Howards End

It is time to reinterpret *Howards End,* that strange, ambitious, uneven work, which seems to mark a final affirmation of Forster's humanism and the end of his youth. Forster's fourth novel in six years and his last major piece of fiction before the appearance of *A Passage to India* fourteen years later, *Howards End* is in important respects unique. Alone among the novels it grapples head-on with the claims of the "outer" world, confronting problems of economics and social class in a society transformed by industrial growth and shadowed by approaching war. The fantasy world of *A Room with a View* yields in *Howards End* to the realities of power, money, and class as they impinge on the values of self-realization and personal relations; Forster's critique of industrialism suggests the failures alike of the business mind and the liberalism of upper-middle-class intellectuals.

The religious impulse that in all the earlier novels takes the form of a search for individual fulfillment is here directed to the social arena: the "unseen" is to be sought in right relations of the "seen." The exhortation to "connect" encapsulates an

ideal of proportion and compromise that will reconcile the
"inner" values of imagination, sensitivity, and personal relations with the "outer" energies of power, practicality, and action. Concurrently with its social application of spiritual values, *Howards End* is the novel most explicitly devoted to the
ideal of personal relations. Forster chooses, as his approved
missionary of connection, a sensitive and articulate woman, a
decision that appears to have freed him from the ambivalence
he showed to earlier male heroes, for he gives Margaret Schlegel
almost absolute moral authority. She and Henry Wilcox, the
energetic imperialist whom she marries, are terms in the hypothesis that the action tests: can the values of personal relations and connection be made to operate within the context of
social reality?

As in *The Longest Journey*, the central issue becomes the
question of England's inheritance, envisioned in the values of
rural tradition. But England's salvation, which the earlier novel
seemed to promise, has become a lost cause. The encroaching
city is a dominant menace: in the dwindling countryside Howards End itself is a brave survival. In *The Longest Journey* a
shepherd moved to London to embark on inexorable decline.
Howards End presents that decline in the career of Leonard
Bast, a dispossessed yeoman whose urban poverty allows him
to reach the life of neither body nor spirit.

Victimized both by industrial capitalism and by the well-
meaning intellectual class that is one of its beneficiaries, the
petit-bourgeois Leonard is lost, doomed to the failure of his
impulse to knowledge, condemned to early death by severance
from his rural heritage. Howards End and its shadowy guardian, the first Mrs. Wilcox, symbolize this heritage: bequest of
the farm to Margaret is intended to signify the alliance of rural
virtue with the humanistic ideal. After vicissitudes, the novel
ends with Schlegels and Wilcoxes living in harmony at Howards End, where Margaret presides as regent for the infant heir,
who synthesizes earth and intellect and embodies what hope

remains for England's survival. The diverse characters who dramatize these ideas function in a plot that must be admired for the degree to which we accept its outrageous premises and far-fetched events: the marriage of Margaret and Henry, the mating of Helen and Leonard Bast, Helen's pregnancy, Leonard's death, and the shattering and reformulation of alignments and inheritance.

Finally, the multiple themes and the action that exists to further them are interpreted by a uniquely intrusive narrative voice. The narrator of *Howards End* retains the familiar techniques of his predecessors. But *Howards End* presents more than an acceleration of earlier modes. For we encounter in this novel the most intensely personal of all Forster's narrators, of all his fictional voices the most self-conscious and dramatic. Critics have never adequately addressed the issues raised by this voice and its alterations as these define and reveal the relations in *Howards End* between Forster's narrative technique and his changing world view. They have instead focused on the novel's engagement with social issues and have accepted as Forster's intention the purpose stated in his epigraph, "only connect." Trilling, whose engaging but limited study of Forster has once again been reissued, regarded *Howards End* as "Forster's masterpiece," praising its "maturity and responsibility" and contemplating with approval its timely concern with England's fate.[1] Wilfred Stone regards the novel as "a test of the ability of Bloomsbury liberalism to survive a marriage with the great world."[2] Frederick Crews sees it as the projection of "a reasonable hope for the survival of liberalism."[3]

Most critics express a common awareness of disjunction be-

1. Lionel Trilling, *E. M. Forster* (Norfolk, Conn.: New Directions, 1964), pp. 114, 118.

2. Wilfred Stone, *The Cave and the Mountain* (Stanford: Stanford University Press, 1966), p. 235.

3. Frederick Crews, *E. M. Forster: The Perils of Humanism* (Princeton: Princeton University Press, 1962), p. 105.

tween Forster's avowed purpose of reconciliation and its accomplishment in the action. Crews sees the problem as an incompatibility between themes: "Despite [Forster's] effort to give the Wilcoxes their due, the real point of *Howards End* is the familiar individualistic one."[4] Alan Wilde formulates the issue as a "defective articulation of the symbolic and realistic levels."[5] In this view, plot, symbolism, and motif project Forster's longing for purpose and direction in life as it should be; the psychological dramatization of Margaret and Helen Schlegel's search for meaning comes closer to his vision of life as it is.[6] This split also appears in discrepancies between ideology and dramatization in the portrayals of Henry and Ruth Wilcox. Critics additionally have expressed dissatisfaction with the novel's resolution because, despite the plot's assertion of connection accomplished, the ending seems rather a victory for the Schlegels than a reconciliation between values.

However accurate, such readings are incomplete. Although they recognize that *Howards End* is more complex than its predecessors, they omit an important dimension of the novel's meaning. Critics have rightly noted the strain and failures of Forster's asserted synthesis but have wrongly regarded as causes what are really symptoms of a more fundamental difficulty. Nor do such readings explain the unusual narrator of *Howards End*. Finally, *Howards End* has been seen largely as the climax of Forster's aims in the earlier novels, dramatically separate in content and implication from its successor, *A Passage to India*. Thus, for Trilling, *Howards End* is Forster's greatest work because "it develops to their full the themes and attitudes of the early books and throws back upon them a new and enhancing light."[7] Wilde is explicit about the schism: "The gulf

4. Ibid., p. 109.
5. Alan Wilde, *Art and Order: A Study of E. M. Forster* (New York: New York University Press, 1964), p. 123.
6. Ibid., pp. 100–101.
7. Trilling, pp. 114–115.

that separates *A Passage to India* from Forster's earlier novels is far more profound than that which exists between any two others of his books."[8] Time and history define the gulf: the Great War appears to most critics an unbridgeable chasm between Georgian meliorism and modern alienation.

Important differences in content and technique do separate the prewar novels and *A Passage to India*. But we may more accurately assess *Howards End* if we recognize the degree to which it already formulates the attitudes and conceptions of the final novel. The substantial passage of time between the two books enabled Forster to structure and refine his issue: his experiences in India in 1912–13 and 1921 gave him the context for its embodiment in fiction. But the essential subject of *A Passage to India* is already present in *Howards End* as a growing sense of existential impasse, as the linguistic and thematic expression of negation. The essence of this view pervades the novel, as does a concurrent impulse toward a transcendent unity. Surely these are the ingredients that come together in the brilliantly coherent images of *A Passage to India,* in which Forster has taken the logical next and last step.

To understand the centrality in *Howards End* of preliminary versions of the vision of *A Passage to India* enables us better to locate and explain the unique qualities of this penultimate novel. It also allows us, while recognizing that *Howards End* brings to culmination important themes of the earlier novels, to define it as more than the climax of one phase in Forster's thought and art. Seen rather as part of a continuum in which it closely anticipates its successor, *Howards End* reveals the progression of Forster's thought toward the metaphysic of *A Passage to India*. Finally, comprehending the relation between Forster's expressions of cosmic apprehension in *Howards End* and his strenuous attempts to prove its values enables us to identify the sources of disjunction in the novel and to understand their consequence in the narrative voice.

8. Wilde, p. 123.

The conscious intent of *Howards End* is to resolve conflict and affirm possibility. Yet throughout the novel Forster undercuts his attempts at an optimistic synthesis by repeatedly projecting chaos. The real source of problems in *Howards End* is neither imbalance between "inner" and "outer" values nor contradiction between the aims of conciliation and victory, but rather a deeper tension that these difficulties mirror, between Forster's efforts to "prove" his humanistic values and to sustain Western society through reversion to rural virtues, and a countercurrent of disbelief, a deepening pessimism expressed through images and motifs that evoke, in a new and menacing world, a vision of cosmic disorder and loss of meaning. The rhetoric affirms connection, but the undercurrent describes collapse. This tension invades all aspects of the novel. It explains the disjunctions in theme and character; it pervades and determines Forster's narrative voice.

The case for personal relations and the inner life opens with the novel's first episode, as Helen Schlegel becomes briefly enmeshed in a disastrous romance. The retreating Paul Wilcox who, frightened by his impulsive declaration, "had nothing to fall back on," illustrates "panic and emptiness," a phrase later to suggest a more cosmic vacuum. Here it evokes Helen's credo: "I know that personal relations are the real life for ever and ever." "Amen," responds her sister.[9] A Moorean good-in-itself, personal relations form the keystone of the inner life, and Forster verifies the sisters' article of faith through his endorsement of Margaret, who articulates familiar components of the humanistic ideology: "at thirteen she had grasped a dilemma that most people travel through life without perceiving. Her brain darted up and down; it grew pliant and strong. Her conclusion was that any human being lies nearer to the unseen than any organization, and from this she never varied"

9. E. M. Forster, *Howards End*, Abinger Edition, 4, ed. Oliver Stallybrass (London: Edward Arnold, 1973), p. 25. Subsequent references are to this edition; hereafter page numbers will be indicated in the text.

(p. 28). The inner life thus comprehends a belief in the primacy of the individual and a concern with the metaphysical implications of human action. The concept also includes, as the action will demonstrate, personal integrity, the capacity for introspection, and the ability to "connect."

Seeking to vindicate the Schlegel sisters' avowal, Forster emphasizes the vicissitudes of the important relationship between them. When Margaret has decided, against Helen's advice, to marry Henry, the sisters can still maintain their relationship because, the narrator explains, "there are moments when the inner life actually 'pays,'" when years of self-scrutiny, conducted for no ulterior motive, are suddenly of practical use" (pp. 192–193). Margaret lapses temporarily from her own ideal when she participates in the deception of her husband's plan to "hunt" the sister who has mysteriously withdrawn from contact: to reestablish her credentials, "she had first to purge a greater crime than any that Helen could have committed—that want of confidence that is the work of the devil" (p. 290).

Dramatized as faith between Margaret and Helen, the inner values are more than intrinsic goods. Forster generalizes Margaret's perception of the commercialization of Christmas as "the grotesque impact of the unseen on the seen" to locate the inner life in his metaphysic. "But in public who shall express the unseen adequately? It is private life that holds out the mirror to infinity; personal intercourse, and that alone, that ever hints at a personality beyond our daily vision" (p. 79). The inner life is nothing less than the sole emblem of divinity: to affirm its primacy would seem the novel's major intent.

Yet the epigraph "only connect" suggests a competing purpose. As a plea for wholeness, this ideal does operate in personal relations and may apply both to the union of Margaret and Henry and to the reconciliation of extremes within the individual psyche whose absence Henry's schism of passion and prudery demonstrates: "Only connect the prose and the passion, and both will be exalted, and human life will be seen at its highest. Live in fragments no longer. Only connect, and the beast and the monk, robbed of the isolation that is life to either, will die" (pp. 183–184). Forster here restates the desire to bridge human incompleteness that the earlier novels rendered in the attempts of their flawed heroes to find meaning through contact with the qualities they lack. But in *Howards End,* connection transcends the individual, as Forster seeks a social contract between power and sensibility through the union of the capitalist mind with the imagination of the liberal intelligentsia. In this search he makes a real attempt, albeit within a limited spectrum, to connect imaginative vision with economic reality. The terms imply a pluralism whose goal is England's survival. A successful rubber merchant, Henry Wilcox guides the empire. His ventures provide jobs for a growing class of urban workers like Leonard Bast and guarantee the incomes of intellectuals like the Schlegels, who seek a moral distribution of economic gain. Henry's pragmatism has saved Howards End when its surviving yeoman owners could not, "without fine feelings or deep insight, but he had saved it" (p. 203); and "Henry would save the Basts as he had saved Howards End, while Helen and her friends were discussing the ethics of salvation" (p. 227).

But in the businessman's relation to social equity and national survival, Forster depicts neither successful connection nor well-meant failure. Critics have observed the limitations of Henry Wilcox and decried his emasculation at the novel's end. Forster's inability to give Henry his due reflects more than his distrust of Henry: it expresses the general despair of human possibility that undercuts the novel's formulas of hope and its rhetoric of affirmation.

The business mind offers no social synthesis. The employment Henry Wilcox gives clerks is subject to the vagaries of a system in which they have no share. The clichés of nineteenth-century liberalism provide Henry's disclaimer of responsibility:

"it is all in the day's work. It's part of the battle of life. . . . As civilization moves forward, the shoe is bound to pinch in places, and it's absurd to pretend that anyone is responsible personally" (pp. 187–188). Businessmen destroy tradition and violate the natural order. A millionaire businessman tears down Margaret's London house to build flats. Henry Wilcox owns shares in a lock that shortens the Thames. Wilcox spoliation is both personal and symbolic: dust from the Wilcox car "had percolated through the open windows, some had whitened the roses and gooseberries of the wayside gardens, while a certain proportion had entered the lungs of the villagers" (p. 16); "The Great North Road should have been bordered all its length with glebe. Henry's kind had filched most of it" (p. 331). Finally, despite Henry's service to Howards End, he has barred himself from relation to England: "the Wilcoxes have no part in the place, nor in any place. It is not their names that recur in the parish register. It is not their ghosts that sigh among the alders at evening. They have swept into the valley and swept out of it, leaving a little dust and a little money behind" (p. 246).

But Wilcoxes are not simply ephemeral. Part of "the civilization of flux," they add number without quantity. "A short-frocked edition of Charles also regards them placidly; a perambulator edition is squeaking; a third edition is expected shortly. Nature is turning out Wilcoxes in this peaceful abode, so that they may inherit the earth" (p. 182). Implicated thus in the issue of inheritance, Wilcoxes provide a pernicious apprehension of the future: "the Imperialist is not what he thinks or seems. He is a destroyer. He prepares the way for cosmopolitanism, and though his ambitions may be fulfilled the earth that he inherits will be gray" (p. 320).

Despite Forster's approval, the Schlegels' share in the national synthesis is no greater than Henry's. Margaret and her sister represent the situation of England's liberal intelligentsia in a time of economic expansion and national unease.[10] The Schlegels and their friends comprehend the economic basis of culture. Their realism extends to concern for the consequences of capitalist exploitation and for the economic and intellectual poverty of the new class of urban workers, and they spend much time discussing ways and means of achieving a more equitable distribution of money and culture. But the modern age displaces them as inexorably as it grinds down Leonard Bast. When the Schlegels' home is destroyed to make way for urban flats, it is clear that although money can save them from want, it cannot save them from the rootlessness that Forster portrays as a modern horror. Ineffective in their attempt to help the struggling classes beneath them, the liberal intellectuals present, finally, an image of liberalism's impotence to influence social change and national survival.

It is significant that although Forster exposes the ineffectuality of the liberal dialogue, he never repudiates Margaret's position. In his endorsement of Margaret's insights and didacticism, in his lack of detachment from her manipulations, Forster identifies himself not only with the intelligentsia, but also with the alienation of the outsider and the powerlessness of women. The female predicament transcends intellectual boundaries, for Ruth Wilcox, not an intellectual but a woman, cannot save her declining farm. "Things went on until there were no men" (p. 271). The eclipse of Margaret and Henry by Margaret and Helen offers additional evidence of his allegiance. *Howards End* takes its impetus from the failure of a heterosexual relationship and finds vindication in the success of a single-sex one. While this countering of the "official" ideology enacts the tension between love and friendship familiar from the earlier

10. In this respect, *Howards End* is a "condition of England" novel, expressing concerns depicted also by C. F. G. Masterman in *The Condition of England* (1909) and by such novelists as Galsworthy and Wells. For a discussion of *Howards End* in the context of England's political situation, see Peter Widdowson, *Fiction as History* (London: Sussex University Press, 1977).

novels,[11] its significance here lies in Forster's allegiance to characters who are alienated from power. Margaret triumphs over the philistines: "She, who had never expected to conquer anyone, had charged straight through these Wilcoxes and broken up their lives" (p. 339). But although women prevail at Howards End, they have no power in the public arena. Margaret does not reform Henry's politics: she only destroys the vital energy that was his chief attraction. Henry at the end is "pitiably tired" (p. 340), by his own admission, "broken" (p. 331).

The businessman retreats from the world he sought to dominate; the intellectual withdraws from hopeless debate to vanishing rural sanctities. Whatever Forster's "outsider" status contributed to his inability to conceive Wilcoxes as part of a national synthesis, his derivation of the evils of modern society from their philistinism reflects the doubt that undercuts the novel's attempts at social reconciliation. Furthermore, his displacement of focus from the social hypothesis to the privatism of affection between Margaret and Helen presents an alliance with sterility. In their limitation and disjunction, the ideologies both of personal relations and of connection imply a darker view, even though, at the same time, they represent Forster's most strenuous assertion of social possibility and human potentiality.

Amid the apostrophes to individuality and the inner life, the reader of *Howards End* becomes aware that personal relations are no longer very important. Although the values of nature and the past are posed as complementary to the human efforts to achieve harmony, ultimately these efforts are submerged in the larger question of England's fate. Well before her marriage to Henry Wilcox, Margaret begins to move beyond a concern for personal relations. She prophesies that she will end her life caring most for a place; the realization makes her "sad," but by the novel's close, Forster will describe Margaret's remote-

11. See my essay "Forster's Comrades," *Partisan Review*, 4 (1980), pp. 591–603.

ness as an approach to metaphysical insight. Like human life, personal relations are ephemeral; the agitations of personality have no effect on the rural serenity in which ultimate value resides. Margaret's attempts to introduce Mrs. Wilcox into her "set" and her aid with Mrs. Wilcox's Christmas shopping are activities inimical to the inarticulate virtues Mrs. Wilcox represents. The party talk is empty, the shopping futile, as Mrs. Wilcox signifies by her rejection of Margaret's choices. Margaret's attempts at connection are no more germane. Her ability to connect seems the moral prerequisite for her guardianship of Howards End, but as intellectual, social conscience, comrade, and artist of the imagination she is ultimately irrelevant. To assume the mantle of the first Mrs. Wilcox, a character conspicuously devoid of creative imagination, Margaret must withdraw. In spite of her dogged affection for Henry, when she begins to acquire the essential vision, "the sense of space, which is the basis of all earthly beauty" and which leads her to contemplate England as a rural sanctity, she must forget "the luggage and the motor-cars, the hurrying men who know so much and connect so little" (p. 202).

Although initially Forster presented personal relations both as intrinsic good and as the sole path to the spiritually absolute, personal intercourse depends on other values. When Mrs. Munt and Charles Wilcox quarrel, Mrs. Wilcox is able to separate the foes because "she worshipped the past. . . . and let her ancestors help her" (p. 19). In a nomadic civilization, divorced from its past, can love alone sustain personal relations? The experience of the adepts, Margaret and Helen, is instructive. The scene of their climactic reunion is Howards End, within whose farmhouse are the Schlegel possessions, unpacked by the prescient caretaker Miss Avery against Wilcox injunctions. The Schlegel movables have accrued tradition and value by their status as objects from the past and through their reinstatement in the rural context. Significantly, Margaret and Helen come to reconciliation not by talk or effort but through the past, enshrined in the rural sanctity of Howards End:

> Explanations and appeals had failed; they had tried for a common meeting-ground, and had only made each other unhappy. And all the time their salvation was lying round them—the past sanctifying the present; the present, with wild heart-throb, declaring that there would after all be a future. [P. 296]

The rural values not only transcend the claims of personal relations and the inner life: Forster posits the attainment of a universal human harmony through a vital relation to the rural tradition: "In these English farms, if anywhere, one might see life steadily and see it whole, group in one vision its transitoriness and its eternal youth, connect—connect without bitterness until all men are brothers" (p. 266). But the novel's course suggests rather the remoteness of divine unity from earthly efforts. The inheritance theme thus contains its own contradictions: nature is at once an agent of reconciliation and a nonhuman force which dwarfs human effort and which, threatened by the encroachments of the modern world, is losing potency as its kingdom diminishes. In reference to the ideals of personal relations and connection, the values of nature and tradition are similarly ambivalent, congruent in that they work together toward the possibility of earthly harmony, disjunct in that the ideologies that assert the primacy of personality and individual effort are irrelevant to the natural environment that transcends them. In its transcendence of human concerns, the natural world is linked to a concept of divine unity briefly adumbrated near the end of the novel. Restated, this idea becomes in *A Passage to India* the search for completion.

What opposes the possibility of unity in both novels is the vision of cosmic evil, rendered in *A Passage to India* through the central symbol of the Marabar caves, which in their absence of distinction suggest the negation of meaning and the absence of divinity. In *Howards End,* the suggestions of an antivision, though pervasive, are more diffuse. But their meta-physical function parallels that of the caves, and the pressure they exert similarly impels the search for a countervailing unity that will restore meaning and order to the universe. This unity is still, in *Howards End,* implied as an agnostic Christianity allied to the romantic tradition. God is no longer anthropo-morphic, but the divine existence is never in question. Nature remains the means to its apprehension, still an intermediary between man and God. In *A Passage to India,* nature is no longer visible sign or ally of man; the quest, too, has changed. In *Howards End* Forster asks whether, amid the erosion of traditional values and the emergence of new and threatening modes of existence, the Western tradition and its values can endure. In *A Passage to India* he has accepted alienation as the modern, condition and asks the ultimate question. Whether *A Passage to India* affirms or denies the existence of God, it is a far more coherent novel than *Howards End* because it confronts the problem of meaning directly. *Howards End* af-firms human potentiality and the existence of divinity, but the unacknowledged pressure of its prevision of apocalypse under-mines even its qualified optimism.

There is clearly an affinity between the goblin image of Helen's well-known reverie on Beethoven's Fifth Symphony and the vision in the Marabar caves. The goblins are an impor-tant motif. But if *Howards End* has a structural equivalent to the caves, it is not the essay on goblins but the scene at Oniton Grange, a Wilcox country house in Wales.[12] When Helen in-vades Oniton on the occasion of a Wilcox daughter's wedding, with Leonard Bast and his bedraggled wife in tow, it is dis-covered that Mrs. Bast was once Henry Wilcox's mistress. Like the caves episode, this scene centers on a sexual catastrophe and precipitates crisis. As in the caves episode, the rhythm of

12. I am indebted to James McConkey for this insight.

confrontation begins with an apparently trivial but significant accident. Forster's brief line anticipating the Oniton scene, "So the wasted day lumbered forward . . ." (p. 220), presents a compressed version of the final novel's prelude of apprehension and ennui.

The initial note of despair sounded in Helen's cry of "panic and emptiness" as her lover retreats, becomes the series of images and associations which render the cosmic apprehension that undercuts the action's strenuous efforts at reconciliation. Much of this imagery reappears in *A Passage to India*, integrated into a purposeful symbology. In *Howards End* Forster is still groping toward its formulation, but the essence of his vision is discernible in a description of King's Cross Station that considerably precedes Helen's goblins. King's Cross suggests "Infinity," its "great arches, colourless, indifferent," are "fit portals for some eternal adventure" (p. 9). This language inaugurates crucial motifs. The arch figures as gateway to a metaphysical journey whose value lies both in its destination and as the means of escape from urban horror: to which, nonetheless says Forster, "Alas! we return" (p. 9). The arch reappears as a fragment of the "rainbow bridge" that is an image of attempted completion; in *A Passage to India*, arches function in a comparable dualism as one of the symbolic paths to religious knowledge and as part of the infinite recession that questions the existence of the divine. "Colourless," "indifferent," and "Infinity" figure centrally in both novels. The motif of indifference in *Howards End* suggests the remoteness of the infinite and the indifference of the universe to man that will become the prevailing condition of *A Passage to India*. With the closely related adjective "colourless," it describes urban life, as the squalid existence of the Basts indicates, "a life where love and hatred had both decayed" (p. 112). To the cosmic indifference of the arch, Forster counterpoints the comic indifference of characters like Mrs. Munt—"To history, to tragedy, to the past, to the future, Mrs. Munt remained equally indifferent" (p. 12)—and Jacky Bast, who is "equally indifferent" to all her husband's moods (p. 51).

The colorless arches of King's Cross are linked to a pervasive gray identified with modern life and concentrated in the imagery that describes London and its residents. In *A Passage to India*, "colourless" becomes "beyond colour," and describes the Indian sky that recedes to infinity, its perspective reducing the human scale almost to nonexistence. The "colourless and indifferent" arches of *Howards End* also prefigure the indifference of the Indian environment and the culmination of cosmic indifference in the overturn of all distinctions in the Marabar caves.

Beethoven's goblins formulate the experience of meaninglessness. The mode is casual but the message is not. They "merely observed in passing that there was no such thing as splendour or heroism in the world. . . . Panic and emptiness!" (p. 31). To this void Forster opposes hyperbolic fantasies of romantic individualism and sensory imagination: "Gusts of splendour, gods and demigods contending with vast swords, colour and fragrance broadcast on the field of battle, magnificent victory, magnificent death!" (p. 31). But refuting the shallow optimism of "men like the Wilcoxes or President Roosevelt," the goblins return; this time they threaten existence itself:

> It was as if the splendour of life might boil over and waste to steam and froth. In its dissolution one heard the terrible, ominous note, and a goblin, with increased malignity, walked quietly over the universe from end to end. Panic and emptiness! Panic and emptiness! Even the flaming ramparts of the world might fall. [P. 31]

The goblins recede with Beethoven's closing affirmation. But their warning describes a vision that *Howards End* continues to reiterate and whose implications it struggles to avoid.

The portrayal of Mrs. Wilcox also provides an approach to the negative vision. A sketch for Mrs. Moore of the final novel,

Mrs. Wilcox projects a strange air of dissolution. Her voice "suggested that pictures, concerts, and people are all of small and equal value. Only once had it quickened—when speaking of Howards End" (p. 67). Mrs. Wilcox's voice, which "though sweet and compelling, had little range of expression" (p. 67), includes humanity and its artifacts in a suggestion of meaninglessness. Life—the "quickening" in her voice—remains only in the rural heritage. Conversely, Mrs. Wilcox's indistinctness, however unsuccessful as characterization, is also intended to suggest her transcendence of personality and her approach to a completion that becomes the ideal of *A Passage to India*.

The associated images of indifference, sameness, colorlessness all delineate a destructive homogeneity that renders life meaningless. London, the diabolic symbol of modern life, is evoked throughout the novel by references to the colorless color, gray. Playing thus with ideas of the absence of distinction, Forster moves in *Howards End* toward the distillation of these ideas in the master-symbol of the Marabar caves. Forster's London, like that of Dickens, is a city of fog, its atmosphere "clots of gray" (p. 78), its existence a mounting violation of the natural order:

> . . . month by month the roads smelt more strongly of petrol, and were more difficult to cross, and human beings heard each other speak with greater difficulty, breathed less of the air, and saw less of the sky. Nature withdrew: the leaves were falling by midsummer; the sun shone through dirt with an admired obscurity. [P. 106]

The "gray tides" of London proclaim the rootlessness that is the city's essence and the inner condition of its inhabitants: "emblematic of their lives, [they] rose and fell in a continual flux" (p. 106), and Margaret ponders lost continuities: "Everyone moving. Is it worthwhile attempting the past when there is this continual flux even in the hearts of men?" (p. 134). London, further, is "a tract of quivering gray, intelligent without purpose and excitable without love" (p. 106), its modern conveniences the machinery of diabolic imprisonment. The lift that takes Mrs. Wilcox up to her London flat is "a vault as of hell, sooty black, from which soots descended" (p. 83). Described early in the novel as "Satanic," London becomes, finally, the demoniac opposite of divinity: "The mask fell off the city, and she saw it for what it really is—a caricature of infinity" (p. 277).

The absent Helen, who eludes Margaret and her brother, and whose strange behavior suggests to them mental illness, seen thus is identified with the city in a vision of horror: "Helen seemed one with grimy trees and the traffic and the slowly flowing slabs of mud. She had accomplished a hideous act of renunciation and returned to the One" (p. 277). The metaphysical semantics of A Passage to India are extraordinarily similar. The grimy trees have become the indifferent Indian landscape, the traffic is transposed into the dirty city of Chandrapore, and the slowly flowing slabs of mud have become the abased inhabitants of India, described as "mud moving." The "hideous act of renunciation" in which Helen has merged into nothingness becomes Mrs. Moore's collapse of distinctions, which leads to her own renunciation of life.

Gray pervades the existence of the characters. "His was a gray life," says Forster explicitly of Leonard Bast (p. 120). Leonard swears "in a colourless sort of way" (p. 46). His wife is "descending . . . into the colourless years" (p. 48). Characters of different classes recognize the problem that is their common condition: thus, Leonard and the Schlegel sisters "had agreed that there was something beyond life's daily gray" (p. 122). And Margaret believes that "doing good to humanity was useless; the many-coloured efforts thereto spreading over the vast area like films and resulting in a universal gray" (p. 125).

Aspects of color, the distinctions of individuality oppose the gray. When, late in the novel, Margaret makes a curious last case for the variations of individual personality, she speaks of "differences—eternal differences; planted by God in a single family, so that there may always be colour; sorrow perhaps, but colour in the daily gray" (p. 336). In nature too, color opposes urban gray. At Mrs. Wilcox's funeral an observer notices "the sunset beyond, scarlet and orange" (p. 86). Howards End is edenic in its variegated hues: "There were the green-gage trees that Helen had once described, there the tennis lawn, there the hedge that would be glorious with dog-roses in June, but the vision now was of black and palest green. Down by the dell-hole more vivid colours were awakening, and Lent Lilies stood sentinel on its margin, or advanced in battalions over the grass. Tulips were a tray of jewels" (pp. 196–197). Howards End itself is illuminated by "the white radiance that poured in through the windows" (p. 96).

> Unnoticed, the sun occupied his sky, and the shadows of the tree stems, extraordinarily solid, fell like trenches of purple across the frosted lawn. It was a glorious winter morning. Evie's fox terrier, who had passed for white, was only a dirty grey dog now, so intense was the purity that surrounded him. He was discredited, but the blackbirds that he was chasing glowed with Arabian darkness, for all the conventional colouring of life had been altered. Inside, the clock struck ten with a rich and confident note. [P. 96]

The clock is in harmony with the richness that emanates from the sun. Unlike the hostile Indian sun of A Passage to India, the natural environment still has relationship to man.

In contrast to the city, with its increasing population and its "architecture of hurry," the country retains the sense of space that Margaret loses when she rides in her husband's motor car. But the drive to London brings another prevision of void: "once more trees, houses, people, animals, hills, merged and heaved into one dirtiness, and she was at Wickham Place" (p. 202). Again Forster suggests a collapse of distinctions in which the elements of life, as seen in Margaret's kaleidoscopic view from the car, achieve a negative unity—"one dirtiness." The image recurs in yet another variant as Margaret contemplates past catastrophe and future crisis. Leonard Bast's death has set in motion legal machinery that, made in the Wilcox image, will result in imprisonment for a Wilcox:

> Events succeeded in a logical, yet senseless, train. People lost their humanity, and took values as arbitrary as those in a pack of playing-cards. . . . In this jangle of causes and effects what had become of their true selves? Here Leonard lay dead in the garden, from natural causes; yet life was a deep, deep river, death a blue sky, life was a house, death a wisp of hay, a flower, a tower, life and death were anything and everything, except this ordered insanity, where the king takes the queen, and the ace the king. [P. 327]

This catalogue of chaos includes elements of life, culture, and nature. It not only links such disparate categories as card games, characters, natural phenomena, and logical and phenomological concepts, but it displaces images from their earlier contexts. Death, for example, is not elsewhere associated with flowers, hay, or the colorful sky of this novel; life is ultimately to reside not primarily in human relationships but in a house. In addition to its suggestion of cosmic negation, this passage, in some of its imagery—after her vision Mrs. Moore withdraws to her deck of "Patience" cards—and in its projection of an "ordered insanity," presages the world of *A Passage to India* at a comparable moment in its action, as Dr. Aziz's trial impends.

The chaos of Howards End resolves into a harmony of asserted reconciliation and coming harvest, but the red rust of London is already visible from the farm: "Howards End, Oniton, the Purbeck Downs, the Oderberge, were all survivals, and the melting-pot was being prepared for them. Logically, they had no right to be alive. One's hope was in the weakness of logic" (p. 337). Prophesying the dissolution of the variegated countryside into urban gray, Forster distills in the image of a melting pot that eradicates color and distinction the essence of his vision of negation.

Hope remains, but its object has shrunk from fulfillment to survival; its mode has changed from active effort to a passive reliance on default by the enemy. That Howards End and the civilization it represents will be the future as well as the past is unlikely: as Margaret admits, "all the signs are against it" (p. 337). The novel ends with Helen's call to plenty: " 'The field's cut!' Helen cried excitedly—'the big meadow! We've seen to the very end, and it'll be such a crop of hay as never!' " (p. 340). Temporarily safe in their diminished territory, the Schlegels prepare for siege.

The contradictory impulses of *Howards End* infuse Forster's narrative voice and have important implications for its quality and function. The voice contains the schism that the action also reflects, for throughout the novel the narrator strains to bring his disparate materials into congruence and the competing formulations of his own voice into compatibility. In an accelerating tension between the impassioned rhetoric of the authorial voice and the ambivalence it attempts to suppress lies the explanation of the peculiar narrator of *Howards End*. Ultimately the increasing pressure of the negative vision undercuts the voice that contains it and alters its very nature.

It seems appropriate that *Howards End*, the novel that seeks most directly to locate ultimate value within the context of human relationships, should reveal an intensely personal narrative voice. The narrator's techniques of omniscience and engagement are familiar, but his voice goes further in self-dramatization, in manipulation of the reader, in the frequency and length of intervention than in any other Forster novel. The tendency of the narrator to step out of the action to formulate its larger significance also reaches its height in *Howards End*. No other Forster narrator establishes so personal a hegemony. His use of Margaret is instrumental to his scope, for he enters her generalizing imagination so often that Margaret functions as an extension of his voice. The narrator's omniscience, his relationship with the reader, and his self-dramatization distinguish him from Margaret. Uniquely in this novel, Forster's

narrator indicates his gender, as, speculating on the difference
between male and female friendships, he notes that "when men
like us, it is for our better qualities. . . . but unworthiness
stimulates woman" (p. 240). His language defines a variety of
roles. As celebrant of England's glory he is a visionary bard, his
literary diction means to a precarious decorum. He emphasizes
his manipulations and the centrality of his function more than
he does the story itself, intervening, for example, to excoriate
Wilcox's repudiation of Mrs. Wilcox's will: "the discussion
moved toward its close. To follow it is unnecessary. It is rather
a moment when the commentator should step forward. Ought
the Wilcoxes to have offered their home to Margaret?" (p.
96). The long essay that follows displays the narrator's judicial
wisdom. But he can also present himself as a fellow-citizen,
permitting the reader a rare glimpse of domestic intimacy as
he extrapolates from Henry Wilcox's failure to mention the
mews behind Ducie Street when he hopes to sublet his flat:
"So does my grocer stigmatize me when I complain of the
quality of his sultanas, and he answers in one breath that they
are the best sultanas, and how can I expect the best sultanas at
that price?" (p. 178).

Through diction and tone, the narrator seeks control of his
structure and reader. With deceptive self-effacement he casts
himself as the mind behind the action: "one may as well begin
with Helen's letters to her sister" (p. 1). As the narrator continues, his grammatical emphases imply reader agreement—
"Certainly Margaret was impulsive. She did swing rapidly from
one decision to another" (p. 8). He moves toward fuller control of the reader through frequent mediations between reader
and characters, in which he often furthers intimacy by direct
address. Thus, defending Leonard Bast's reticence about the
adventure of his all-night walk, Forster admonishes the reader:
"You may laugh at him, you who have slept nights out on the
veldt, with your rifle pat beside you and all the atmosphere of
adventure pat. And you may also laugh who think adventures

silly. But do not be surprised if Leonard is shy whenever he meets you, and if the Schlegels rather than Jacky hear about the dawn" (pp. 121–122). This passage is singular in the degree to which it defines reader as well as character and commenting voice; its hostility to the imagined reader is perhaps Forster's coy attempt to produce sympathy appropriate to his character. But the passage is also noteworthy for its erosion of the boundary between experience and fiction. The rhetorical nature of Forster's narrative technique is not new, but the frequency in *Howards End* of conflations like this is unique in his fiction.

As he intrudes into a comic scene between Margaret's Aunt Juley and Charles Wilcox, the narrator interrupts his narrative to suggest its irrelevance: "Young Wilcox was pouring in petrol, starting his engine, and performing other actions with which this story has no concern" (p. 14). The narrator's qualification, itself an aside, renders the action he excludes parenthetical also. Yet, in a comic anticipation of *A Passage to India*, his very exclusion includes. For his distinction implies the existence of his characters in a realm of reality that is not the story, a world in which the reader may be presumed to function also. More directly, the narrator identifies Margaret with "others who have lived long in a great capitol," a classification that implies her shared reality with potential readers. Like these city-dwellers, Margaret has "strong feelings" about railway stations, emotions that become the narrator's truth: "They are our gates to the glorious and the unknown" (p. 9). From Margaret the narrator moves to the implied reader who coexists with her in the world outside his fiction, with the judgment that "he is a chilly Londoner who does not endow his stations with some personality, and extend to them, however shyly, the emotions of fear and love" (p. 9). The use of direct address intensifies the reader's participation in the narrator's rhetoric. Hoping that Margaret's connection of King's Cross Station with infinity "will not set the reader against her," he intrudes further to insist on Margaret's insight: "If you think this is ridiculous, remember that it is not Margaret who is telling you about it; and let me hasten to add that they were in plenty of time for the train" (p. 9). The assumption of potential conversation between Margaret and the reader merges the double fiction of character and narrator with the reader's world of experience, for it is the narrator who, ostensibly in the character's behalf, confronts the reader. The commentary has become not only a direct conversation but an argument, in which the narrator disarms potential opposition, assumes responsibility for his characters' perceptions, and buttresses his case with apparent considerations of common sense. These techniques are significant because they reveal the intensity of Forster's need in this novel to persuade, and suggest the degree of his extremity.

For despite the narrator's brilliance, his persuasion must ultimately be regarded as unsuccessful. He does not achieve a harmonious integration of ideology and dramatic representation, of content and form. His reflections are often disconnected from the action, so that the novel appears to present an uneven alternation between essay and scene, comment and action. To a degree found in no other Forster novel, the narrator's diction is abstract, metaphorical, hyperbolical; the anxiety and inflation of his tone suggest the desperation of his attempt to harmonize and persuade. The prominence, the intimate tone, the rhetorical techniques of this narrator are evoked by the impossibility of his task. Equal intensity seems to attend each exhortation. Nowhere does he acknowledge incompatibility among contending values. It is as if Forster is trying to bridge the gap between desire and disillusion by the insistence of his presence, to cover his inconsistencies of attitude and the unlikeliness of character and action by the sheer weight of his rhetoric as narrator. Consequently he is eloquent and hysterical, strained, elaborate, evasive, intimate, familiar, powerful, and unconvincing as he attempts to impose on the world of the novel a coherence that action and voice alike belie.

The narrator's rhetoric thus embodies its own limitations, which appear in all the novel's contexts. The portrayal of Mrs. Wilcox, for example, is an attempt to establish the mythic significance of an unsubstantial character. First seen by Helen, Mrs. Wilcox wears a long dress, she "trails," she picks up a piece of hay, she smells flowers, she is tired, she is "steadily unselfish." The corroborating narrator assures that Mrs. Wilcox is "just as Helen's letter had described her, trailing noiselessly over the lawn, and there was actually a wisp of hay in her hands" (p. 19). But in the absence of dramatic context, Forster asserts a larger significance: "One knew that she worshipped the past, and that the instinctive wisdom the past can alone bestow had descended upon her—that wisdom to which we give the clumsy name of aristocracy" (p. 19). Mrs. Wilcox, described throughout as shadowy, is too shadowy to bear this weight. To the degree that her behavior is recorded, she is rather a caricature of the traditional wife and mother, naive, submissive, and insular. The preciosity of Margaret's guests at a luncheon she gives for Mrs. Wilcox is balanced by the parochiality of the lady herself. Margaret's brief experience of Mrs. Wilcox doesn't warrant her belief that she and her family "are only fragments of Mrs. Wilcox's mind," and that Mrs. Wilcox "knew everything" (p. 311). Nor does the characterization support the narrator's direct claim that Mrs. Wilcox is "nearer the line that divides daily life from a life that may be of greater importance" (p. 74). Assertion seeks unsuccessfully to bridge the gap between intention and presentation.

Forster's relation to Leonard Bast is at best uneasy, a mixture of compassion and condescension. The significance of Leonard Bast is in his origin, in his pivotal position as cause célèbre for the liberal intellectuals and victim of the capitalists, and in his sentimental apotheosis into England's future. An uncertainty of narrative tone pursues Leonard throughout. Initially Forster demythifies him: "he was inferior to most rich people, there is not a doubt of it. He was not as courteous as the average rich man, nor as intelligent, nor as healthy, nor as lovable" (p. 43). Leonard has a half-baked mind; his conversation is querulous and banal; he is "one of the thousands who have lost the life of the body and failed to reach the life of the spirit" (p. 113). Margaret's assessment contains no hint of irony, although it catches her in violation of her own individualistic credo: "She knew this type very well—the vague aspirations, the mental dishonesty, the familiarity with the outside of books" (p. 113). Leonard's capacity for spontaneity and his questing spirit redress the balance, but even in this Forster undercuts his praise: "Within his cramped little mind dwelt something that was greater than Jeffries' books—the spirit that led Jeffries to write them" (p. 118). When ultimately Forster transfigures Leonard, his invocation does not create heroic significance: "Let Squalor be turned into Tragedy, whose eyes are the stars, and whose hands hold the sunset and the dawn" (p. 328).

In comparable interventions the narrative voice asserts dimensions that the action cannot substantiate, as when Forster tries unsuccessfully to cover Margaret's crisis with sister and husband by a rhetoric of benediction: "For the present let the moon shine brightly and the breezes of the spring blow gently, dying away from the gale of the day, and let the earth, who brings increase, bring peace" (p. 309). The inflation and unease of these assertions is compounded in many of the essaylike passages that stud the novel. Forster's evocation of a rainbow bridge is replete with questionable images:

> . . . she might yet be able to help him to the building of the rainbow bridge that should connect the prose in us with passion. Without it we are meaningless fragments, half monks, half beasts, unconnected arches that have never joined into a man. With it love is born, and alights on the highest curve, glowing against the gray, sober against the fire. Happy the man who sees from either aspect the glory of these outspread wings. The roads

of his soul lie clear, and he and his friends shall find easy going. [P. 183]

How is the reader to interpret the implied parallel between prose and passion and monk and beast, the location and meaning of fire, the literal and metaphorical discrepancy of gray, the location and condition of the man "who sees from either aspect" and to incorporate into all this the sudden appearance of roads in the man's soul? One has only to contrast this jumble with the powerful and coherent imagery of arch and echo of *A Passage to India*. Groping in *Howards End* for the way to embody his thought, Forster too often substitutes preachiness for the integrated imagery of a coherent position.

The narrator presides over the survival theme, and most of the passages that celebrate England emanate from his voice. Elegiac and passionate, sentimental and unabashed, they transcend the focus on personality even as they represent a desperate attempt to retain the civilization for which it was a primary value.

> Branksea Island lost its immense foreshores and became a sombre episode of trees. Frome was forced inwards toward Dorchester, Stour against Wimborne, Avon towards Salisbury, and over the immense displacement the sun presided, leading it to triumph ere he sank to rest. England was alive, throbbing through all her estuaries, crying for joy through the mouths of all her gulls, and the north wind, with contrary motion, blew stronger against her rising seas. What did it mean? For what end are her fair complexities, her changes of soil, her sinuous coast? Does she belong to those who have moulded her and made her feared by other lands, or to those who had added nothing to her power, but have somehow seen her, seen the whole island at once, lying as a jewel in a silver sea, sailing as a ship of souls, with all the brave world's fleet accompanying her towards eternity? [P. 172]

F. R. Leavis cites this passage to note that Forster "lapses into such exaltations quite easily," and he criticizes the vagueness that Forster's use of "somehow" creates in the last sentence.[13] But do we not react more to the inflated diction of "leading it to triumph ere he sank to rest," to the frenetic personifications of "England was alive," "throbbing," and "crying"? Besides the hyperbole, of which one can find in *Howards End* surpassing examples, the passage is noteworthy for revealing Forster's ambivalence of preoccupation and uncertainty of mode. The rhetorical question about England's fate leads not to concern with "the brave world's fleet" but to an expression of conflict between power and the creative imagination. In this it reflects the disjunction between the goals of reconciliation and victory seen in the action and implies the ascendancy of those who see life whole, who have "seen the whole island at once." These, of course, are the Schlegels, and, as the only voice capable of the rhetorical question, the narrator himself. Thus while appearing to transcend the concern with personality, Forster displays the superiority of the mind whose insight includes but discounts "those who have moulded her and made her feared by other lands." Yet Leavis's uneasiness with "somehow" ought to have extended to the literary echoes and secondhand images, which suggest limitation or, as I. A. Richards put it, a "forcing" of the creative imagination.[14] Again to contrast the ungrounded abstraction of this language with the concrete diction and integrated imagery of *A Passage to India* is to envision the distance Forster still has to travel.

The inner tensions that these "forcings" imply may also be seen in direct expressions of ambivalence within the narrative voice. Noteworthy here is the degree to which Forster's apprehension contains something other than concern for the civil-

13. F. R. Leavis, "E. M. Forster," *The Common Pursuit* (London: Chatto & Windus, 1952), reprinted in *Forster,* ed. Malcolm Bradbury (Englewood Cliffs, N.J.: Prentice-Hall, Inc., 1966), p. 42.

14. I. A. Richards, "A Passage to Forster: Reflections on a Novelist," *The Forum,* 78 (December 1927), 914–920, reprinted in *Forster,* ed. Bradbury, p. 19.

ization he loves, for underlying the exhortation to human relations is a striking sense of recoil from humanity.

> Their house was in Wickham Place, and fairly quiet, for a lofty
> promontory of buildings separated it from the main thorough-
> fare. One had the sense of a backwater, or rather of an estuary,
> whose waters flowed in from the invisible sea, and ebbed into a
> profound silence while the waves without were still beating.
> Though the promontory consisted of flats—expensive, with
> cavernous entrance halls, full of concierges and palms—it ful-
> filled its purpose, and gained for the older houses opposite a
> certain measure of peace. These, too, would be swept away in
> time, and another promontory would rise upon their site, as
> humanity piled itself higher and higher on the precious soil of
> London. [P. 5]

The narrative voice discriminates between house and city and,
more significantly, between human life and nature. Noise, vulgarity, meaningless aggregation cover simultaneously the flats
of a burgeoning city and the ephemeral but continuous flow of
humanity they enclose.

This ambivalence may also be seen in Forster's treatment of
characters. It is curious that this most personal narrator should
display so little real sympathy for the characters of whom he
claims such profound knowledge. But the intimacy of his rhetoric obscures the indifference or hostility that underlies his
professions of concern. To the gap between Forster's theory
and his practice with Henry Wilcox and his condescension to
Leonard Bast we must add the overt repugnance he feels for
Jacky Bast: "A woman entered, of whom it is simplest to say
that she was not respectable. . . . Yes, Jacky was past her
prime, whatever that prime may have been" (p. 48). Even the
Schlegels, though in a more disguised manner, receive a share
of this ambivalence. Helen is passionate and truthful, the only
character to act on the doctrine of personal responsibility that
Margaret and the narrator espouse. But Forster's disapproval
of Helen's excesses and his fear of her enticements undercut his

support of her perceptions. On Margaret the narrator renders little judgment, but whether from unconscious intention or inability to separate himself from her characteristics, Forster has produced a character whose stridency evokes a certain recoil. And the narrator's impulse to protect himself from the vulgar crowd and the less comfortable realities of existence is mirrored in Margaret, to whom the appearance of Leonard Bast's wife, "Mrs. Lanoline," causes an anxiety that is not solely concern for the Basts: "She feared, fantastically, that her own little flock might be moving into turmoil and squalor, into nearer contact with such episodes as these" (p. 112).

Thus, even as Forster describes with some compassion the consequences for Leonard Bast of his entrapment in class (Mrs. Lanoline is such a consequence), he draws back from contact with the imperfectly washed. Concerned though he is with social equity and social cost, Forster shrinks from humanity in the aggregate. His ideology may be seen partly as an expression of this ambivalence: the individual is nearer to the "unseen" than any organization, humanity as a concept is associated with isms and programs. The consequences of this position engender what has been described as Forster's critique of liberalism. But although he dramatizes the impotence of the liberal intelligentsia to solve the problems of modern society, there is little evidence of Forster's separation from liberal values.

Portrayed as inhabitants of a feminine culture and divorced from power, the intelligentsia are dilettantes. While Forster yearns for masculinity, he can conceive it only as Henry Wilcox, whom he repudiates, or as Leonard Bast, who is so disadvantaged he doesn't signify. With apprehensions about the feminization of culture, expressed in his criticism of Margaret's effeminate brother Tibby and in the sisters' awareness of the need for balance, he nevertheless places his moral weight behind the Schlegels. To women as a group he is less generous. Margaret and Helen's all-female discussion club presents something of a parallel to the Apostolic session of *The Longest*

Journey. But the women discuss social questions whereas the men engaged in metaphysical speculation, a Forsterian estimate of their relative capacities, as the narrator's misogynistic comment that "the female mind, though cruelly practical in daily life, cannot bear to hear ideals belittled in conversation" (p. 125) suggests. One should note, however, that both discussion groups are equally ineffectual.

Although Forster treats Leonard Bast more as representative of a class than as an individual, he does not conclude that social or economic action to improve the situation of Leonard Basts is desirable. On the contrary, the members of the debating society avoid the issue by bequeathing their fictional millionaire's legacy within their own class. Margaret wishes to help only the individual, but the very values of integrity and honor that comprise the "inner" ideal nullify this possibility in the novel itself. For when Helen undertakes to realize Margaret's ideal of personal philanthropy, the near-starving Leonard Bast declines her offer. His refusal, "very civil and quiet in tone" (p. 252), aligns him with the gentlemanly standards of Forster's own class. One could wish that Forster had shown here the hardheaded sophistry of his contemporary Shaw, whose Mr. Doolittle is concerned only about his translation to gentility.[15] At any rate, Leonard's "higher" instincts doom him even more effectively than the indifferent machinations of capitalism. Nice guys finish last, as the contrast of his honorable behavior to Jacky with Henry's sexual opportunism also demonstrates. But although Forster dramatizes these ironies, he clings to the old formulations of honor. For him, the only alleviation of the modern condition lies in escape from the encroaching mass and its urban hive.

Forster's authorial voice itself expresses the conflicts that character and action embody. More than in any other novel Forster directs, exhorts, emphasizes, and seeks to harmonize,

15. See Bernard Shaw, *Pygmalion* (New York: The Modern Library, 1953), p. 288.

as the realities he presents become increasingly intractable to his hopes. Attempting for the last time to demonstrate a hopeful synthesis, straining to bring recalcitrant materials into conformity with his ideology, Forster's voice projects an anguish that moves us but does not solve the novel's problems. The narrator's intense rhetoric is a last, desperate exercise of personality, a final attempt to celebrate the creed of individuality through the colorful tonalities of a highly personal voice.

But *Howards End* demonstrates the limits of the personal, and Forster's movement away from the values of individual fulfillment and personal relations engenders the eventual effacement and withdrawal of his narrator. A valedictory persona, the narrator spends himself in a last violent effort to sustain, through his intense relationship with the reader and through characters in whom he no longer believes, his commitment to individual effort and personality. As the action converges upon Howards End, the narrator begins to withdraw. This is not a dramatic movement, but as his presence diminishes, the narrative voice abandons its exhortations and its intimate tone: in the final pages it appears only to validate Margaret's ominous apprehension of the end of rural civilization and to underline briefly the last revelations of plot, as Margaret discovers that Mrs. Wilcox had bequeathed her Howards End long ago. With this withdrawal the novel approaches the mode, the insights, and the austere voice of *A Passage to India*.

The movement of Forster's narrative voice in *Howards End* from the celebration of personality to a near-detachment from worldly concerns, a progression mirrored in the course of his central character, may be seen as the expression of exhaustion and defeat. But it also represents the impulse to a larger unity that has been present, though in less complex forms, from the first novel. A search for human wholeness and for the perception of cosmic unity underlies the efforts and adventures of all Forster's protagonists, except Maurice, whose depiction presents a special case. The novels that precede *Howards End* focus on the metaphysical resonances of individual self-realization, dramatized in Philip's progress to salvation, Rickie's search for the meaning of reality, and Lucy Honeychurch's acceptance of her sexuality. As we have seen, Philip begins as incomplete both in character and vision. The price of Philip's eventual insight, his withdrawal from participation in life, is a paradox whose implications Forster does not explore. But completion remains both as the ideal for the individual and as a metaphysical condition to be perceived in the universe. Thus Forster insists in *Where Angels Fear to Tread* on the coexistence of opposing qualities. In the world some of these are separate from Philip, but they are what, to approach wholeness, he must come to see.

Forster urges Rickie Elliot to engagement with life and reiterates the moral value of Rickie's participation. Forster's equivocal treatment of Rickie undermines his conception of wholeness in *The Longest Journey*. But Rickie's incompleteness is submerged in the greater capacity of his half-brother, Stephen, and the novel suggests a more or less complete world in the alliance of Cambridge and Wiltshire, which forms a symbolic connection of mind and body, the creativity of intellect and the spontaneity of a not-yet-lost primal paradise. Simpler than its predecessors, *A Room with a View* defines wholeness both as happy sexual union and as the spiritual comradeship of man and woman.

The formulation of an ideal of completeness is far more complex in *Howards End,* and all the novel's themes partake of its conception. In *Where Angels Fear to Tread* the suburban ethos was domestic, the issue formulated simply as a clash between convention and instinct, safely played out across the Channel. The contemporary context enters with the Pembrokes of *The Longest Journey,* whose "public" values threaten the life of imagination, and with the first depiction of a technological progress that threatens the values of nature and tradition. In *Howards End* Forster extends his examination of these issues to the whole of society, seeking an application of the humanistic values that will bring the disparate elements of the social order into harmony. Because the novel asserts harmony and presents conflict, because its efforts to vindicate personal relations and social connection collide with each other and with the increasingly dominant theme of inheritance, the movement it describes appears more impasse than development. But for all its strains, *Howards End* gropes toward what becomes in *A Passage to India* the controlling idea of completion. Personal, social, and metaphysical, the attempts to connect in *Howards End* are all expressions of a single impulse to unity, whose avenue of fulfillment alters significantly in the course of the action.

Margaret herself enacts this alteration. That she has been moving toward a new definition of value is suggested quite early. As a result of Mrs. Wilcox's death, Margaret "saw a little more clearly than hitherto what a human being is and to what he may aspire. Truer relationships gleamed. Perhaps the last word would be hope—hope even on this side of the grave" (p. 101). This language, which hints at ultimates, recurs in association with Howards End and its wych-elm, which, in transcending sex, transcend the personal: "to compare either to man, to woman, always dwarfed the vision. Yet they kept within limits of the human. Their message was not of eternity, but of hope on this side of the grave. As she stood in the one, gazing at the other, truer relationship had gleamed" (p. 203). House and tree project a sense of man's insignificance in time:

> The present flowed by them like a stream. The tree rustled. It had made music before they were born, and would continue after their deaths, but its song was of the moment. The moment had passed. The tree rustled again. Their senses were sharpened, and they seemed to apprehend life. Life passed. The tree rustled again. [P. 312]

Notable here is the effacement of personality, as the narrative voice sharply distances the characters. Forster's reiterations emphasize the power, continuity, and creative expression not of man but of nature. The human characters have a moment of perception, "their senses were sharpened and they seemed to apprehend life," but its transitoriness is immediately asserted in the short, bold, declaratory two-word sentence, "Life passed." The tree has the last word. The moment of apprehension is a moment of peace, both timeless and ephemeral.

> The peace of the country was entering into her. It has no com-
> merce with memory, and little with hope. Least of all is it
> concerned with the hopes of the next five minutes. It is the
> peace of the present, which passes understanding. Its murmer
> came "now", and "now" once more as they trod the gravel,
> and "now" as the moonlight fell upon their father's sword. They
> passed upstairs, kissed, and amidst the endless iterations, fell
> asleep. [P. 312]

This passage presents a significant anticipation of *A Passage to India,* in which humanity is dwarfed by the vast Indian landscape and distanced by the Marabar hills, "older than anything in the world."[16] In the final novel, nature is no longer redemptive, but there, as here, Forster develops man's subordination to a timeless and powerful nature and fixes a visionary moment at once permanent and transitory.

Howards End retains the possibility of redemption through nature, clinging to the romantic tradition and an agnostic Christianity in which, although no longer anthropomorphic, God still exists. Margaret, although "not a Christian in the accepted sense," because "she did not believe that God had ever worked among us as a young artisan" (p. 79), lectures to Helen on "eternal differences, planted by God in a single family" (p. 336). She believes in immortality for herself: "An eternal fu-

16. E. M. Forster, *A Passage to India,* Abinger Edition, 6, ed. Oliver Stallybrass (London: Edward Arnold, 1978), p. 116.

ture had always seemed natural to her" (p. 330). But although, in contrast to the contingency of the final novel, *Howards End* clings to belief, its conceptions of negation and harmony are closely analogous to the symbolic chaos of the caves and the precarious harmony of the Indian Krishna celebration. In a passage quoted earlier, Margaret adumbrated a catalogue of chaos, a "jangle" of arbitrary values and their negation. Amid this collapse of distinctions that presages the vision of the caves, motifs associated with Mrs. Wilcox suggest an ultimate harmony:

> Ah, no; there was beauty and adventure behind, such as the man at her feet had yearned for; there was hope this side of the grave; there were truer relationships beyond the limits that fetter us now. As a prisoner looks up and sees stars beckoning, so she, from the turmoil and horror of those days, caught glimpses of the diviner wheels. [P. 327]

As in *A Passage to India,* turned the other way out, the vision is one of inclusion in God's plan, an affirmation of cosmic unity.

In the novels before *Howards End,* the potential attainment of harmony on earth is not in doubt. Although the equivocal heroes of *Where Angels Fear to Tread* and *The Longest Journey* are permitted only a glimpse of possibility, their fertile comrades, Gino and, more directly, Stephen, are candidates for fulfillment. In the triumph of Lucy Honeychurch, Forster comes closest to the depiction of earthly harmony. But although Lucy's accomplishment mirrors a cosmic wholeness, it is self-contained. Perhaps because there is no discrepancy between earthly possibility and divine unity, the latter is assumed within the terms of Lucy's struggle and victory. There is no significant context beyond her.

But in *Howards End* the search for wholeness becomes implicated in a changing world view, as an intrusion of cosmic evil threatens the entire fabric. Imaged as goblins, gray, city, melting pot, the approach of a disintegrative vision lurks be-

neath the action, casts in doubt human possibility, and anticipates the apocalyptic symbolism of *A Passage to India*. The
pressure of this vision undercuts and nearly effaces worldly
hope—in the inner life, in personal and social connection, in a
last desperate embrace of nature and the past. Despite the suggestions of divine order, *Howards End* presents more forms of
negation than of unity, seen in its recurring imagery of indifference and collapse, in Forster's recoil from the proliferating
human scene, in the strained solutions of action, in the shaky
optimism of the ending, and finally, in the loss of energy of the
narrative voice.

Confronting such negation, the search for meaning acquires
new urgency. Forster's insistence and desperation in *Howards
End* express his reluctance to admit the insufficiency of the old
values, and as we have seen, the problems of the novel arise
from Forster's inability to face the issue directly, to confront
the implications of his own presentation. His apprehension of
cosmic disaster engenders a network of allusion to infinity,
eternity, the unseen—a machinery behind the action, invoked
throughout the novel by the narrative voice to suggest the discrepancy between human flux and divine stasis. This discrepancy points the way toward a resolution that only the final
novel articulates fully. But Margaret's development in *Howards End* shows the direction. As crisis descends, she accepts
the subordination of human effort to the forces beyond it:
"No, there was nothing more to be done. They had tried not to
go over the precipice, but perhaps the fall was inevitable" (p.
329). But to approach an intuition of ultimate harmony, Margaret must withdraw: "At such moments the soul retires within,
to float upon the bosom of a deeper stream, and has communion with the dead, and sees the world's glory not diminished, but different in kind to what she has supposed. She
alters her focus until trivial things are blurred" (p. 329).

In her detachment Margaret moves toward the vision and
mode of Mrs. Wilcox, in which "daily life appeared blurred."

The "trivial things" that Margaret's new insight enables her to blur are the very values she has heretofore been at pains to assert and reconcile. The condition for Margaret's enlarged vision is withdrawal. It is doubtful that Forster intended that the dramatization of this movement should render Margaret as unattractive as she appears. The visible signs of her increased insight are indifference, irritation, and a proprietary concern for Howards End that focuses on matter rather than spirit. But whatever Margaret's deficiencies, her situation is significant because it expresses a dualism inherent from the beginning in Forster's fiction and paves the way for the insights of the final novel.

As she withdraws from worldly effort, Margaret reenacts the paradox seen in Forster's removal of Philip and Rickie from participation in life at the very moment of their real or potential acquisition of crucial insight. But Margaret's situation represents a new development. For her acceptance of limitation is itself an attempt to articulate a new synthesis, to penetrate to a new metaphysic. Paradox remains, in that withdrawal from the values she championed throughout the novel is the condition for Margaret's insight of divine harmony. But *Howards End* has begun the movement, developed fully in *A Passage to India,* beyond the paradox of action to the more complex paradox of implication: Margaret's eventual position hints at the condition of Professor Godbole of the final novel, for whom the abnegation of personality and withdrawal from action are the conditions necessary to the insight of metaphysical unity.

Forster's creation in *Howards End* of a universe that must accommodate evil as well as good suggests that the negative vision must inevitably be included in any assertion of cosmic unity. Although in much of the novel Forster has seemed primarily concerned to test his humanistic philosophy in the social arena, preoccupation with the metaphysical implications of his values underlies the action more thoroughly here than in any earlier novel. *Howards End* still presents the most comprehensive expression of Forster's liberalism. But although we may find irritating the aura of sanctity that surrounds Margaret Schlegel, Forster's message in *Howards End* is that even the saved are not safe. England's decline is not averted, only postponed. Profound and irrational forces threaten the survival alike of individual and society. In *Howards End* Forster fights the implications of the personal and social failures that his novel dramatizes. In *A Passage to India,* he accepts the consequences of human inadequacy and takes as subject the limitation he sought earlier to transcend.

5 ～

Maurice and Fictions
of Homosexuality

MAURICE is a painful book. We must respect the suffering it reveals, but the novel is otherwise distinguished largely by an absence of the eloquence and depth that make Forster a novelist of distinction. Forster wrote *Maurice* to set his creative impulses free by confronting the situation he could not treat in the "publishable" novels.[1] The irony, as with so much about Forster, is double. He did write another novel—his greatest—after *Maurice*. But *A Passage to India* derives rather from the darkening vision of *Howards End* and from Forster's second visit to India in 1921 than from any identifiable aspect of *Maurice*.[2] The second irony is that, for all its depiction of a forbidden subject, *Maurice* is a study in restriction.

The novel's most significant limitation is its lack of the metaphysical dimension that underlies the actions of the other novels,

1. See P. N. Furbank, *E. M. Forster: A Life*, Vol. 1, *The Growth of the Novelist (1879–1914)* (London: Secker & Warburg, 1977), p. 259.
2. For the history of this visit, see Furbank, *E. M. Forster: A Life*, Vol. 2, *Polycrates' Ring (1914–1970)* (London: Secker & Warburg, 1978), p. 67 and *passim*.

in which characters seek through personal and social connections to apprehend an ultimate reality. *Maurice* is likewise deficient in social texture and sustained characterization; the limitation of its authorial voice amounts almost to absence. The two Forster novels with which *Maurice* invites comparison, *A Room with a View* and *The Longest Journey*, both expose the poverty of the homosexual novel. *A Room with a View* and *Maurice* share the subjects of passion and fulfillment, and as Maurice o'erleaps class to live with his gamekeeper-lover, so Lucy crosses the social boundaries of Summer Street to marry a railway clerk. Yet compared to *Maurice*, *A Room with a View* is profound. *Maurice* includes neither the rich ironic comedy of its predecessor, nor the patriotic idyll of an English Eden. More important, Lucy's acceptance of her sexuality occurs in a context that transcends her personal fulfillment. In gaining her soul she gains something for the world and approaches the Arnoldian ideal articulated in *Howards End*, the ability to see life steadily and see it whole. Personal and social worlds demonstrate a spiritual unity, an organic whole to which the homosexual fable cannot aspire.

Maurice presents a more direct parallel to *The Longest Journey*, and in a "Terminal Note" written in 1960, Forster identifies these novels as similar both in atmosphere and in the historical moment they record.[3] Furthermore, each has as its protagonist a young man homosexually inclined, who experiences two intense friendships. The first love in both cases is a Cambridge classmate of the protagonist, the second a rough hero of lower-class origins, and in each novel the second liaison is intended as redemptive. But here the resemblances cease, for the meaning of Rickie Elliot's education far exceeds its homosexual origin. For Rickie, as for Philip Herriton of *Where Angels Fear to Tread*, education is the means to insight into meta-

---

3. Printed in E. M. Forster, *Maurice* (New York: Norton, 1971), p. 254. Subsequent references both to the "Terminal Note" and to *Maurice* will be indicated in the text.

physical truth: as Rickie and Philip battle themselves and a world of convention, they struggle toward the consciousness of a larger framework. *The Longest Journey* explores the meanings of art, imagination, truth, and ultimate reality, and its rough hero is the touchstone of a larger value than the protagonist's sexual or moral needs. Homosexual energies create a strong undercurrent in these novels, but *Where Angels Fear to Tread* and *The Longest Journey* pursue absolutes with a depth and assurance of authorial presence that establishes their complexity.

In contrast, *Maurice* explores only the condition of its protagonist. Between Maurice and his society there is little dialogue and no real dialectic. Maurice is not a rebel: only when sexual attraction forces him does he seek to cross class barriers. Nor is his lower-class lover a Lawrentian idealogue. On the contrary, Alec Scudder is an opportunist who exploits the class system for his advantage. Whereas in the other novels the relation between conventional and natural man is imbedded in a world of symbolic values, Maurice and Alec have only the pitiful significance of their story. The story is univocal and belongs to Maurice: it recounts his recognition and acceptance of homosexuality. Maurice is a young man "average" and "normal" in all respects except for his sexuality. His education proceeds in two stages. The first, through an intense but unconsummated affair with a fellow undergraduate, Clive Durham, provides the revelation that Maurice is homosexual. Clive's rejection of Maurice inaugurates the second stage of Maurice's education, which defines as the primary condition of his sexuality its urgent physical nature. He achieves consummation with the gamekeeper of his former friend and becomes aware of the inadequacy of a society built on class distinctions. At the novel's end, Maurice and his lover escape to the greenwood, an undepicted rural paradise in which their liaison takes on the permanence of fiction if not of art. In his "Terminal Note" Forster admitted that *Maurice* was a tract: "A happy ending was imperative. I shouldn't have bothered to write otherwise. I was determined that in fiction anyway two men should fall in love and remain in it for the ever and ever that fiction allows" (p. 250).

But not only does *Maurice* suffer from its limitation as a thesis novel: at the heart of the thesis is a contradiction that prevents even its narrow purpose from being realized. For despite his assertion of fulfillment, Forster cannot overcome his ambivalence about the homosexual condition, and throughout the novel an inner schism undermines the brave ideology of his postscript. In *Maurice* Forster expresses two objections to homosexuality, the first of which appears elsewhere in his fiction as well. First, male lovers are excluded from literal and symbolic continuance because they cannot procreate (Forster was less concerned over the fate of their female counterparts, retaining despite his support of Radclyffe Hall's *Well of Loneliness* a special aversion to lesbians).[4] Barred thus from what Forster saw as nature's central glory, his homosexual heroes are always peripheral: they cannot approach the "spirit of life"—Ansell in *The Longest Journey* cannot understand the mystery of birth, concluding, when he hears of Agnes's pregnancy, that such matters are beyond him—and they can never achieve the wholeness that in the novels before *A Passage to India* is contingent on a right relationship to nature. Thus, Rickie laments his sterility, but in *The Longest Journey*, as in all the other novels except *Maurice*, Forster was able to evade the full implications of that condition by giving the homosexual love-object heterosexual powers. Stephen does not suffer the limitations of Ansell or Rickie. The primitivist heroes of the novels before *A Passage to India* are all fertile: the instinct they symbolize is harmonious with nature's purpose and provides a source of hope for the future of the West.

In *Maurice*, Forster seeks to acknowledge the sexuality he

4. Furbank, *Forster: A Life*, 2:155.

must submerge in the other novels, but the homosexual condition precludes celebration, for even as he depicts the idyll of Maurice and his Cambridge friend Clive, he laments the condition that bars them from the fulfillment of nature. As Maurice realizes,

> An immense sadness had risen up in his soul. He and the beloved would vanish utterly—would continue neither in Heaven nor on Earth. They had won past the conventions, but Nature still faced them, saying with even voice, "Very well, you are thus; I blame none of my children. But you must go the way of all sterility." The thought that he was sterile weighed on the young man with a sudden shame. [P. 97]

It is no accident that nature in *Maurice* is not only minimal but, in a passage significant for its obvious analogy to Maurice, nature is described as blighted, in its cankered state an emblem of its own human sports.[5]

Thus, the homosexual ideal is not only barred from nature's pantheon, it is tainted from within and here Forster's second "objection" emerges. For the cankered blossom, the crippled hero—Forster's oblique signification in *The Longest Journey*—suggest what *Maurice* shows: that despite his pleas for passion and wholeness, for the integration of body and spirit, faced with the only love he can attest directly, Forster cannot accept sexuality without shame. Not only the sterility that is its consequence, but the very condition evokes this response. His equivocation pervades the portrait of Maurice, and his confusions beset the novel's two love affairs. The result is a novel whose interest lies not in its artistic claim, which is slight, but rather in its expression of an inner conflict whose psychological and

5. "Blossom after blossom crept past them, draggled by the ungenial year: some had cankered, others would never unfold: here and there beauty triumphed, but desperately, flickering in a world of gloom. . . . the failure irritated him. Scarcely anything was perfect. On one spray every flower was lopsided, the next swarmed with caterpillars, or bulged with galls. The indifference of nature! And her incompetence!" (*Maurice*, p. 179).

social implications reflect their historical context and reveal heretofore hidden aspects of the man. As a kind of reverse phenomenon, *Maurice* also illumines Forster's better fiction. It indicates the narrow origin of some of his themes; its lacunae suggest that only through omission of social context, natural environment, and ultimate values could Forster confront his subject, and this implies further that Forster could not envision the coexistence of social and metaphysical value with homosexual love. The limitations of *Maurice* do not explain the complex structure of idea, image, and voice of the other novels. *Maurice* does, however, show that Forster's evasions and suppressions in the published novels were less a bar to his creativity than he believed.[6]

But let us consider the ways in which Forster's ambivalence to the homosexuality he purports to celebrate emerge in *Maurice*. His decision to remove Maurice from too personal an identification with himself initiated an authorial problem of distance and sympathy: "In Maurice I tried to create a character who was completely unlike myelf or what I supposed myself to be: someone handsome, healthy, bodily attractive, mentally torpid, not a bad business man and rather a snob" (p. 250). Forster at once presents Maurice's ambiguous mixture of characteristics as innate and blames them on family and society. He locates the Halls in the suburban world of consumerism, "a land of facilities, where nothing had to be striven for, and success is indistinguishable from failure" (p. 16). Its "presiding genius" is Maurice's mother, whose capacities may be illustrated by her comment, "There is nothing like home, as everyone finds" (p. 17). Supporting a neighbor's disdain, Forster agrees, "No one could be deeply interested in the Halls" (p. 19).

Yet this verdict must include Maurice, who is repeatedly likened to his passive and undistinguished father (who is, like

6. For a fuller account, see my essay "Forster's Comrades," *Partisan Review*, 4 (1980), pp. 591–603.

most Forster fathers, dead). Progressing through adolescence, Maurice becomes "a mediocre member of a mediocre school" (p. 21). His limitations are innate: he is "constitutionally lazy" (p. 29), "indifferent to beauty as a rule" (p. 35), and one "not dowered with imagination" (p. 56). Yet on vacation from Cambridge, Maurice finds that "home emasculated everything" (p. 52); "He was less alert, he again behaved as he supposed he was supposed to behave" (p. 56). Of the "insincerity" that leads him to flirt with a young woman, Forster says, "His family were the main cause of this" (p. 56). Of his announced atheism, "no one took any notice, for the suburbs no longer exact Christianity. This disgusted him; it made him look at society with new eyes" (p. 53).

In a letter to Forrest Reid, a fellow writer and homosexual, Forster confirms this view of society:

> Are these "perverts" good or bad like normal men, their disproportionate tendency to badness (which I admit) being due to the criminal blindness of Society? Or are they inherently bad? . . . The man in my book is, roughly speaking, good, but Society nearly destroys him, he nearly slinks through his life furtive and afraid, and burdened with a sense of sin.[7]

Striking here is Forster's belief that homosexuals are characterized by a "disproportionate tendency to badness." To his assertion that Maurice escapes the burden of sin we may oppose the continuing evidence of Forster's ambiguous attitude to the character and the novel's air of fastidious guilt, which show that Forster and Maurice, however defiant, are never at ease with their situation.

The ambivalent assessments of Maurice continue as the narrator supports Clive Durham's perception of his friend as "bourgeois, unfinished and stupid" (p. 71), and makes Maurice aware of his "thick brown hands" and thick brown mind (pp. 48–

7. Furbank, *Forster: A Life*, 2:14.

49). At times Maurice transcends his advertised limitations. When he encounters the clever undergraduate Risley, Maurice perceives the accuracy of the latter's Stracheyan self-estimate: "It had struck him at once that Risley was serious" (p. 32). Similarly, Maurice "saw that Durham . . . had a tranquil and orderly brain" (p. 38), a judgment of greater acumen than Forster's outline suggests as appropriate. At other times Maurice performs in consonance with the narrator's reduction: his belief collapses because he cannot formulate an opposition to Clive's arguments; he cannot follow Clive's reflections about the relation between aesthetics and desire; his political opinions (like Clive's) are reactionary—and here it is unclear whether Maurice's conservatism is a stigma that indicts his suburban heritage or the uninflected sign of his "normality."

The repugnance implied in Clive Durham's estimate and in Maurice's own sense of coarseness becomes overt when the problem of sex arises. But Forster participates without irony in hints of Maurice's "brutality" and sadomasochism. Of the sexual issue I will speak at length, as Forster's attitude toward Maurice reveals a larger conflict about the meaning of homosexual love. I wish here to indicate the many aspects of Forster's uneven distance from his character. Forster equivocates about Maurice's condescension to women and servants. Whereas he generally approves bullying of the former, he sometimes shares Maurice's patronization of the lower classes, sometimes uses it to expose Maurice. The obverse of his condescensions to Maurice is a sentimental hyperbole, which seeks unsuccessfully to redress the balance and to generalize the action's significance. For example, of Maurice's suffering after Clive has withdrawn, he asserts, "struggles like his are the supreme achievements of humanity, and surpass any legends about Heaven" (p. 144). Having withstood a blackmail attempt from his gamekeeper-lover, Maurice approaches a kind of apotheosis: "Not as a hero, but as a comrade, had he stood up to the bluster, and

found childishness behind it, and behind that something else"
(p. 226). He has found "the greatest triumph ordinary man can
win" (p. 226).

With the account of Maurice's sexual development, Forster's
guilt and repugnance become direct. The narrator summarizes
Maurice's adolescence as "obscene" and tersely catalogues his
sexual world: "Thoughts: he had a dirty little collection. Acts:
he desisted from these after the novelty was over, finding that
they brought him more fatigue than pleasure" (p. 23). The
passionate but technically chaste relationship with Clive Durham escapes this castigation, and of the implications of this
affair I will have more to say. With Clive's rejection, Maurice's
physical nature asserts itself. But the brief series of episodes
that describe his awakening to sexual need begin in horror and
move toward degradation. For what Maurice awakens to both
he and his creator identify as "lust." Forster presents the outcome of Maurice's brief infatuation with a schoolboy as the
narrow escape of victim from predator:

> "I'm above," panted Maurice, not daring. "In the attic over
> this—if you want anything—all night alone. I always am."
>   Dickie's impulse was to bolt the door after him, but he dis-
> missed it as unsoldierly, and awoke to the ringing of the break-
> fast bell, with the sun on his face and his mind washed clean.
> [P. 149]

Maurice's self-revulsion is even more direct: "What a stoat he
had been! . . . He saw the boy leaping from his embrace, to
smash the window and break his limbs, or yelling like a maniac
until help came. He saw the police—" (p. 150). Subsequent
temptations come to Maurice as "odours from the abyss" (p.
150), Forster's term in *Howards End* for the lower classes and
a significant association.[8] Maurice retreats from a French business colleague, and there follows a frightening episode on the

8. See Wilfred Stone, "Overleaping Class: Forster's Problem in Connection," *Modern Language Quarterly*, 39 (1978), 389.

train, in which Maurice responds to a sexual overture from an older man and then assaults him. Unbelievably, Forster asserts that all this is leading to a fortunate fall, that Maurice's suffering is "the flesh educating the spirit . . . developing the sluggish heart and the slack mind against their will" (pp. 151–152). The next step is Maurice's intercourse with Clive Durham's gamekeeper, a connection that bravely violates both sexual and class taboos. But despite Forster's assertion that this is love, the liaison does not resolve the ambivalence of author or protagonist. Maurice's reaction to "the precise facts of the situation" (p. 203) is to become violently sick, as Clive Durham had done in revulsion from him. He compares the sexual episode tellingly to the circumstances of his first love: "Cambridge had left him a hero, Penge a traitor" (p. 206). Forster's attitude to the hypnotist whom Maurice has consulted in an effort to change his sexuality is ironic, but he does not repudiate the hypnotist's judgment: "By pleasuring the body Maurice had confirmed— that very word was used in the final verdict—he had confirmed his spirit in its perversion, and cut himself off from the congregation of normal man" (p. 214). Finally, although the equivocal relationship between Maurice and Alec culminates, we are told, in a permanent union, Forster never challenges Maurice's assessment: "Oh, the situation was disgusting—of that he was certain, and indeed never wavered till the end of his life" (p. 204).

That Maurice has fallen we cannot doubt, nor can we doubt that the serpent in the garden is the longed-for consummation. The ambivalent characterization of Maurice's awakening sexuality, the equivocal relationship between Maurice and Alec and the inferior relation to this liaison to the earlier unconsummated affair between Maurice and Clive all show that beneath Forster's commitment to homosexual love is an inability to reconcile the idea of such a love with the fact of sexuality. This schism appears in the terms which Maurice must integrate, aspects of love prefigured in his childhood dreams and illus-

trated in his love for Clive, "idealism" and "brutality." And, as
Alan Wilde has noted in a recent essay that charts the increasing divergence between love and sex in Forster's homosexual
fiction, the affair with Alec represents not a fulfillment but a
falling-off in which the original terms undergo reduction, as
Maurice "twists sentimentality and lust together into love" (p.
218).[9] Unredeemed by authorial irony, the transports of the
lovers illustrate their triviality. To Alec, " this was 'oliday, London with Maurice, all troubles over, and he wanted to drowse
and waste time, and tease and make love" (p. 228). Similarly,
for Maurice, "Yes, he was in luck, no doubt of it. Scudder had
proved honest and kind. He was lovely to be with, a treasure, a
charmer, a find in a thousand, the longed-for dream" (p. 229).

These inside views expose Forster's lack of distance and the
embarrassing awkwardness of his attempt to render a passion
he had not by 1911 experienced, but the greater interest lies in
their representation, however crude, of the class distinction
between the lovers. This difference is crucial, for more to the
point than the sentimental idyll is Maurice's postcoital horror
at his embrace of a butcher's son, and his accurate apprehension that the situation "contained every promise of blackmail"
(p. 207). Wilfred Stone's recent comments on the association in
Forster's homosexual fiction between sexual consummation and
lower-class lovers are pertinent here. Stone notes that "the gentleman, with his puritan inheritance, does not know how to
appease the conscience if the appetites, particularly the sexual appetites, are indulged; for the appetites tend to connect
with what is 'low'; low in class as well as low in morals."[10]
Thus, Maurice's intercourse with a lower-class man becomes a
measure of "his descent, morally and socially, into the lower
depths."[11]

9. Alan Wilde, "Desire and Consciousness: The 'Anironic' Forster," *Novel*,
9 (Winter 1976), 120.
10. Stone, "Overleaping Class," p. 390.
11. Ibid., p. 393.

Maurice presents much evidence that this is so: it remains to develop the implications of Forster's unconscious use of lower-class status as symbol for social depravity. Alec's negative characteristics are tied to his class status, as his anticipation of the attempt to blackmail Maurice illustrates: "When the victim drove up he became half cruel, half frightened. . . . He was waiting for signs of fear, that the menial in him might strike" (p. 220). Maurice withstands the threat because he plays by gentleman's rules—"he determined not to strike until he was struck" (p. 220): his victory thus manifests his class superiority. Authorial perception reinforces Maurice's view of the lowness of Alec. As the lover departs for morning chores after spending the night in Maurice's room at Penge, "Maurice called, 'Scudder,' and he turned like a well-trained dog" (p. 197). When, retreating from his blackmail threat, Alec talks with Maurice in a London square where railings encircle the trees, Forster describes the gamekeeper as a caged animal: " 'I wouldn't take a penny from you, I wouldn't hurt your little finger,' " he growled, and rattled the bars that kept him from the trees" (p. 226). Maurice's fantasies about Alec are inseparable from his perception of the class distinction: "when he got out to his new life he would forget his escapade with a gentleman and in time he would marry. Shrewd working-class youngster who knew where his interests lay . . ." (pp. 232–233). Even after copulating, the lovers are "Mr. Hall" and "Scudder."

As additional evidence, we may note the beginning of Maurice's sexual awareness, like Forster's, in his childhood experience with a garden boy, who in the novel is clearly a forerunner of Alec. Maurice's dream of "brutality," focuses on a naked figure, "a nondescript whose existence he resented," and who "turned into George, that garden boy" (p. 22), disappearing to punish the dreamer for his desire just as he is about to touch him. Sexual play is thus connected with a lower-class object. When, finally, Maurice achieves the consummation that was the goal of his education, his success has engendered a double degradation. For not only is homosexual love illicit, sexual connection with a lower-class person is not a social deviation but a moral descent—as Maurice puts it, "The feeling that can impel a gentleman towards a person of lower class stands self-condemned" (p. 151). A person who believes that sex is bad is likely to choose as partner one who is "unworthy" rather than vent his desire on an equal. Perhaps Maurice's rejection by Clive (who was modeled on Forster's bisexual Cambridge friend, Hugh Meredith)[12] proved to him that he could not fulfill his unspeakable desires with someone "worthy": in this connection, Forster's dual identification of the "abyss" with sexual depravity and the lower classes becomes meaningful.

It is thus impossible to regard Maurice's attempt to overleap class, a brief and belated coda to his sexual adventure with a servant, as a search for social justice or a conversion to universal brotherhood. No social significance can legitimately be wrung out of what is so clearly motivated by sexual desperation and accompanied by sexual guilt. In this connection, we may contrast the comparative ease with which Forster pursues cross-class friendships, whether single-sex or heterosexual, in the other novels. The reason why Alec is the only lower-class hero in the novels whose class origin explains his inferiority is clear also: Forster did not in those other novels confront the sexual problem, the sine qua non of overt homosexual love. Stephen's illegitimacy, and the horror it arouses in the conventional characters and Rickie's limp, are the nearest hint of what Alec represents. As Forster need not vent his unconscious horror at homosexuality in the other novels, he presents the romance or the pity of class: Stephen and the dispossessed shepherd Fleance in *The Longest Journey*, Leonard Bast in *Howards End*—alienation transposed into a more acceptable context.

That ideology does not motivate Maurice may be seen in the novel's evidence that his homosexuality becomes incompatible

12. See Furbank, *Forster: A Life*, 1:98.

with his acceptance of convention only when Clive's rejection forces him out of the comfortable routine in which their homosexual friendship had proceeded without disturbance. At the apex of his relationship with Clive, Maurice and his life as a broker are in tune: "Maurice's habits became regular. He ate a large breakfast and caught the 8:36 to town. In the train he read the *Daily Telegraph*. He worked till 1:00, lunched lightly, and worked again through the afternoon. . . . But every Wednesday he slept at Clive's little flat in town. Weekends were also inviolable" (p. 102). In the privacy of Clive's flat the couple even shares the same bed, on occasion, though chastely. Society seems to present no impediments. It is only when Maurice breaks the gentlemanly code that he must become an outlaw.

Nor does Maurice's awakening rapprochement with the lower classes extend beyond his passion for Alec. When, seeking his lover at the boat on which Alec is to embark for Argentina, Maurice instead meets Alec's relatives, he is repelled by "Mr Scudder, an unattractive, middle-aged man, a tradesman, a cad—" (p. 234). The source of the inducement of democracy is single and sensual, as we see when Maurice compares brother Fred with his own lover: "Alec's main charm was the fresh colouring that surged against the cliff of his hair: Fred, facially the same, was sandy and foxlike, and greasiness had replaced the sun's caress" (p. 234). Forster provides no authorial correction of Maurice's condescension: "a morbid fascination kept him among the Scudders, listening to their vulgarity, and tracing the gestures of his friend in theirs" (p. 235). Love does not level all ranks.

The other characters are as imbedded in convention as Maurice. We know from the time Maurice meets him as an undergraduate at Cambridge that Clive is to inherit the estate at Penge and stand as a Tory for Parliament, although it is only after Clive's sexual *volte-face* that Forster attacks the restrictiveness of his life and views. Alec, the "natural man," is as class-bound as the others: "He sprang, as he had boasted, of a respectable family—publicans, small tradesmen—and it was only by accident that he had appeared as an untamed son of the woods" (p. 219). As jealous of his reputation as his upperclass friend, Alec in his complaint sounds the note of Maurice's degradation: "I've always been a respectable young fellow until you called me into your room to amuse yourself. It don't hardly seem fair that a gentleman should drag you down" (p. 221). When he meets Maurice, Alec is on his way out of the woods, which "contain no 'openings'" (p. 219). His response to Maurice's plea that they elope rings with a common sense that is in abeyance elsewhere in this novel: "'Yours is the talk of someone who's never had to earn his living,' he said. 'You sort of trap me with I love you or whatever it is and then offer to spoil my career. Do you realize I've got a definite job waiting for me in the Argentine?'" (p. 232).

Rather than confront the social or sexual contradictions that beset *Maurice,* Forster withdraws his heroes to a mythical greenwood, and the novel concludes with a lapse into the fantasy of "Other Kingdom." But *Maurice* ends in banishment, not transcendence, for the fantasy-wood is no longer, as in the short stories, a place of festival or freedom, but represents instead an exile from which the apprehension of pursuit is never absent.[13] Forster has been unable to connect the classes. Nor could he resolve the conflict between brutality and idealism that Maurice's dreams of garden boy and radiant "friend" symbolize.[14] Neither in himself nor in his affair with Alec Scudder does Maurice accomplish the integration of mind and body, of spiritual and passional natures. Yet one of the most curious aspects of *Maurice* is that it comes close to this achievement. Forster presents and then repudiates a near-ideal because it could not be made to accord with the imperative of his thesis.

13. Elizabeth Wood Ellem, "E. M. Forster's Greenwood," *Journal of Modern Literature* 5 (1976), pp. 89–98.
14. *Maurice,* pp. 22–23.

For the novel's real center of interest is not Maurice but Clive, whose inner harmony and moral superiority Forster unambiguously endorses. Moreover, the idyll of the two Cambridge undergraduates presents, for its duration, an ideal fulfillment of homosexual love. Here, as in the presentation of Maurice and Alec, Forster's inner conflict between love and sex is determining. Since the affair between Maurice and Clive does not reach physical consummation, it is insufficient to the thesis of a full homosexual love. Yet two aspects of this relationship are significant because they dramatize the ambivalence the novel cannot resolve. First, despite Forster's insistence on the Platonic love of Clive and Maurice, their love is patently sexual, its expression limited only by technical chastity. Second, Forster views that restraint as inseparable from the conception of Clive's wisdom and his moral ascendancy over the grosser Maurice.

The affair between Maurice and Clive presents a refashioning of the friendship between Ansell and Rickie and includes many of the same elements. There is an intellectual and an intuitive partner, a physically dominant and a weak one, although *Maurice* presents some transposition of these roles. To the moral and intellectual dominance of Clive, Forster opposes the physical dominance of Maurice, and this contrast is significant, for Clive receives the greater authorial approval. At the same time, as in *The Longest Journey*, Forster takes distinct pleasure in the playful brutality of his characters, and the sexual nature of their energy is unmistakable. Just as Ansell forcibly held Rickie in the grass to prevent his keeping an appointment with Agnes, Maurice joyfully dramatizes his first rapprochement with Clive by pulling out a handful of his friend's hair, forcing him between his knees, and fitting his head into the waste-paper basket. Comments Forster, "It was the first time he had dared to play with Durham" (p. 45). An increase in intimacy follows this incident: "They walked arm in arm or

arm around shoulder now. . . . Maurice would stroke Durham's hair" (p. 45).[15]

Clive's declaration comes after a scene that begins as

> Maurice stretched out a hand and felt the head nestle against it.
> . . . Very gently he stroked the hair and ran his fingers down
> into it as if to caress the brain. . . . [Soon] he had accomplished
> a new tenderness—stroked it steadily from temple to throat.
> . . . Now Durham stretched up to him, stroked his hair. They
> clasped one another. They were lying breast against breast soon,
> head was on shoulder, but just as their cheeks met someone
> called "Hall" from the court. [Pp. 57–58]

Reflecting that "You love and are loved. . . . You are strong, he
weak and alone" (p. 66), Maurice leaps through Clive's window as later Alec Scudder will leap into his. Together at Penge
the lovers exchange kisses and endearments, and Clive uses the
analogy of heterosexual courtship to articulate their love: "I
feel to you as Pippa to her fiancé, only far more nobly, far
more deeply, body and soul, no starved medievalism, of course,
only a—a particular harmony of body and soul that I don't
think women have even guessed" (p. 90).

This harmony is the keynote in Forster's characterization of
Clive. Unlike Maurice's, his friend's emotion "was not split
into the brutal and ideal, nor did he waste years in bridging the
gulf" (p. 69). The authorial voice approves Clive's "sincere
mind, with its keen sense of right and wrong" and explains
that, "deeply religious, with a living desire to reach God and to
please Him" (p. 69), Clive repudiates Christianity not from
desire—"He came of a family of lawyers and squires, good and
able men for the most part, and he did not wish to depart from
their tradition" (p. 70)—but because Christianity rejects homosexual love. Clive is aware of his sexual attraction for Mau-

15. The most bizarre illustration of Maurice's connection of power and
humiliation with tenderness occurs when, against Clive's will, Maurice attends
him in illness and cleans his chamber pot. "Now that Clive was undignified
and weak, he loved him as never before" (p. 107).

rice, and the authorial voice endorses his progress: the integration he achieves in love mirrors his own virtue.

> . . . he liked being thrown about by a powerful and handsome boy. It was delightful too when Hall stroked his hair. . . . He was under no illusion on those occasions. He knew what kind of pleasure he was receiving, and received it honestly. . . . Once certain that Hall loved him, he unloosed his own love. Hitherto it had been dalliance, a passing pleasure for body and mind. How he despised that now. Love was harmonious, immense. He poured into it the dignity as well as the richness of his being, and indeed in that well-tempered soul the two were one. [Pp. 71–72]

Clive's self-discipline dominates the relationship and guides the less profound partner. When Maurice, who has been sent down from Cambridge after cutting college with Clive, regrets that they did not make love, Forster adduces Clive's greater wisdom: "Maurice did not know that they had thus spent it [a day's illegal holiday from classes] perfectly—he was too young to detect the triviality of contact for contact's sake. Though restrained by his friend, he would have surfeited passion. Later on, when his love took second strength, he realized how well Fate had served him" (p. 82). We may note the ambivalence of "contact for contact's sake" in a situation that Forster has already defined as love. Despite his inclusion of the body in Clive's love, Forster's schism continues to manifest itself.

But it is clear that Clive is the architect of the ideal homosexual love, and Forster emphasizes Clive's superiority through his account of the affair: "Clive knew that ecstasy cannot last, but can carve a channel for something lasting, and he contrived a relation that proved permanent. If Maurice made love it was Clive who preserved it, and caused its rivers to water the garden." Clive, finally, represents the acme of "love passionate but temperate, such as only finer natures can understand" (p. 98), and Forster's summation is a paean to the virtue, central in the other novels, of proportion:

> . . . he found in Maurice a nature that was not indeed fine, but charmingly willing. He led the beloved up a narrow and beautiful path, high above either abyss. It went on until the final darkness—he could see no other terror—and when that descended they would at all events have lived more fully than either saint or sensualist, and would have extracted to their utmost the nobility and sweetness of the world. . . . Love had caught him out of triviality and Maurice out of bewilderment in order that two imperfect souls might touch perfection. [Pp. 98–99]

What follows perfection cannot be other than a falling-off, and Forster attempts to bolster the claims of Maurice's second affair by denigrating his first lover. With Clive's sexual change comes a sudden alteration in character, but nothing in the action justifies his swift reduction to a decadent country squire. Clive indeed does not choose his course, and his new awareness includes a sense of helplessness that in the major novels delineates a cosmic condition. Forster's voice supports Clive's fatalism and evokes the identification of man with mud and slime that becomes integral to the vision of limitation in *A Passage to India*: "He descended the theatre wearily. Who could help anything? Not only in sex, but in all things men have moved blindly, have evolved out of slime to dissolve into it when this accident of consequences is over" (p. 116). This is the nearest *Maurice* comes to metaphysical speculation: that Clive undergoes the experience reinforces his centrality and makes Forster's subsequent treatment of him less believable. Forster's ambivalence about the meaning of Clive's "change" is patent throughout the episode. Horror at homosexual love takes the form of nausea in *Maurice,* and Clive expresses his new revulsion from Maurice by becoming violently ill, in a scene that begins as Clive asserts that "is" and "ought to be" may be the same. Moving toward what he "ought to be," Clive is clearly approaching the preferred state; Maurice remains the undesirable reality. When the crash comes between Maurice and Clive, Forster's sympathy suddenly shifts to Maurice, but the narrator's description expresses the envy of those who are barred from the mainstream: Clive "too suffered and exclaimed, 'What an ending!' but he was promised a dawn. The love of women would rise as certainly as the sun, scorching up immaturity and ushering the full human day, and even in his pain he knew this" (p. 130).

With Clive gone, the problem of sexuality emerges for Maurice. What was earlier the desideratum achieved through Clive's wisdom now becomes a limitation Maurice must transcend. "It had been understood between them that their love, though including the body, should not gratify it" (p. 151), but Maurice translates Clive's philosophy of temperate love as "the less you had the more it was supposed to be" (p. 184). Gratification is the object, and as consummation becomes a possibility, the idea of sexual passion undergoes reduction. Thus, Maurice, contemplating "those jolly scents, those bushes where you could hide, that sky as black as the bushes," longs only for "wild oats," for "a fling," for "fun in the damp" (p. 187).

The novel's strange finale suggests that, despite the "happy ending," Clive remains the object of Maurice's desire, a continuing obsession which has determined the course of his behavior. For in the last scene Maurice confronts Clive to throw in his former lover's face his affair with Clive's gamekeeper. Maurice's choice has enabled him to shock Clive with the extremity of his violation of the gentleman's code—as Maurice himself reflected, "He had abused his host's confidence and defiled his house in his absence" (p. 206). Significantly, Maurice defines his affair with Alec not in its relation to himself but to Clive: "It's miles worse for you than that: I'm in love with your gamekeeper" (p. 242). He next announces that they have slept together in Clive's house, provoking in Clive the same nausea he himself had experienced after that event. Finally, Maurice reveals the source of his action: "You care for me a little bit, I do think, . . . but I can't hang all my life on a little

bit. You don't hang yours on Anne. . . . I can't hang mine on to
the five minutes you spare me from her and politics. You'll do
anything for me except see me. That's been it for this whole
year of Hell" (p. 245). Surely this lover's complaint shows that
Maurice's "fulfillment" is the revenge of the rejected lover.
Despite Forster's attempt to undermine Clive by authorial judgment on "his thin, sour disapproval, his dogmatism, the stupidity of his heart" (pp. 243–244), Clive and the initial valuation
of his "dignity and richness" provide the novel's only real affirmation. Forster's awareness of incongruity—he admits in the
postscript to *Maurice* that after his sexual change "Clive deteriorates, and so perhaps does my treatment of him—" (p.
251)—did not enable him to resolve the inner contradiction
between love and sexuality that the portrayals of Clive, Maurice, and Alec all manifest. His only solution is the factitious
greenwood into which Maurice disappears in a final evasion of
the reality *Maurice* purported to confront.

The contradictions of *Maurice* permeate the authorial voice
whose resonance scarcely extends beyond the ambivalent com-
mentaries it provides on Maurice and his loves. Absence of
both the metaphysical implication and the social texture that in
the other novels create a complex interaction between character and value marks the narrative voice of *Maurice,* whose
world exists only as an insubstantial background to the tormented progress of its protagonist. The England of *Maurice* is
unrecognizable as the country of *Howards End,* whose celebration so closely preceded it. We have only to compare the narrative imagination that in the *The Longest Journey, Maurice*'s
nearest counterpart, creates a rich texture of symbolic and social implication in its loci of Sawston, Cambridge, and Wiltshire, to the flat voice that in *Maurice* nods briefly at a London suburb, Cambridge, and Penge. Passive and colorless, the
narrative voice sketches Maurice's world in brief and reductive
statements about his suburban origin. Its evocation of Cambridge is transient and undeveloped. London exists only as

Maurice's business destination or as the brief mecca of Clive's flat. Politics does not transcend the common conservatism of Maurice the broker and Clive the squire; class is, as I have noted, not a social but a psychic issue. The despair of shame that underlies Forster's bravado about his unpublishable subject seems to drain the authorial voice of energy and reference. Here is Penge:

> The house lay among woods. A park, still ridged with the lines of vanishing hedges, stretched around, giving light and air and pasture to horses and Alderney cows. Beyond it the trees began, most planted by old Sir Edwin, who had annexed the common lands. There were two entrances to the park, one up by the village, the other on the clayey road that went to the station. There had been no station in the old days, and the approach from it, which was undignified and led by the back premises, typified an afterthought of England's. [P. 86]

The passage is flat in tone, minimal in implication. Tradition and nature benefit only the lower orders of creation and imply the indifference of county society to its vanishing heritage. Old Sir Edwin's activities reflect Forster's ambivalence about ownership and class[16] and suggest the mixed nature of good and evil that is a major preoccupation in *A Passage to India*. The undignified back road figures briefly as a social issue between the owners and the British public when Clive's mother closes the road to access. But the action never develops these hints of a world beyond the dilemma of Maurice.

To Penge we may contrast the narrator's description of Cadover in *The Longest Journey*:

> Cadover was not a large house. But it is the largest house with which this story has dealings, and must always be thought of with respect. . . .
> It was a comfortable but not very attractive place, and to a certain type of mind, its situation was not attractive either.

16. See also E. M. Forster, "My Wood" (1926), *Abinger Harvest* (New York: Harcourt, Brace, 1936), pp. 22–26.

From the distance it showed as a grey box, huddled against evergreens. There was no mystery about it. You saw it for miles. Its hills had none of the beetling romance of Devonshire, none of the subtle contours that prelude a cottage in Kent, but proffered its burden crudely, on a huge bare palm. "There's Cadover," visitors would say. "How small it still looks. We shall be late for lunch." And the view from the windows, though extensive, would not have been accepted by the Royal Academy. A valley, containing a stream, a road, a railway; over the valley fields of barley and wurzel, divided by no pretty hedges, and passing into a great and formless down—this was the outlook, desolate at all times, and almost terrifying beneath a cloudy sky. The down was called "Cadbury Range" ("Cocoa Squares" if you were young and funny), because high upon it—one cannot say "on the top," there being scarcely any tops in Wiltshire—because high upon it there stood a double circle of entrenchments. A bank of grass enclosed a ring of turnips, which enclosed a second bank of grass, which enclosed more turnips, and in the middle of the pattern grew one small tree. British? Roman? Saxon? Danish? The competent reader will decide. [Pp. 114–115]

The richness of this voice inheres in the narrative personality it reveals, in its diversity of concern, its discriminations, and in the accumulation of details whose dramatic and symbolic meaning will develop from this introduction. The voice of *Maurice* nowhere attains this complex intention. On the contrary, that voice everywhere reflects the novel's limitations of significance. Forster's generalizations, like his evocations of setting, are fragmentary and brief. Where he is inhibited or unsure, the abstractions lack reference. Thus of the protagonist's adolescence, Forster notes, "Maurice had fallen asleep in the Valley of the Shadow, far beneath the peaks of either range, and knew neither this nor that his school-fellows were sleeping likewise." Having become aware of his homosexual nature, Maurice "stood upon the mountain range that overshadows youth, he saw" (p. 62). Forster provides no explanation or context for these images, nor do they reappear. Inadequate substitutes for dramatization, such generalizations reveal the narrator's participation in the novel's confusions. Often such statements are didactic; for example, of Clive's decision to end his affair with Maurice, Forster comments, "when love flies it is remembered not as love but as something else. Blessed are the uneducated, who forget it entirely, and are never conscious of folly or pruriency in the past, of long aimless conversations" (p. 120). The trappings of aphorism and biblical diction here do not cover the ambiguity of these assertions, for which the action provides no basis. To be "conscious of folly or pruriency" implies the existence of these qualities, not faulty recollection by the perceiver. Moreover, Clive's embrace of "the life spirit," described in the same passage, implies the superiority of his future to the past with Maurice, of heterosexual love to homosexual romance. Yet the raison d'être of *Maurice* is to celebrate the homosexual future of Maurice. The contradiction is inescapable, and the authorial voice only augments the novel's confusions.

From the limitations of *Maurice* to the vision of limitation that informs *A Passage to India* is a giant step, and *Maurice* provides no evidence that Forster's best energies, seen as *ave atque vale* in *A Passage to India,* owe anything to his homosexual novel. On the contrary, *Maurice* demonstrates that the necessity for suppression and indirection of which Forster complained when he wrote novels of conventional sexual reference cannot be adduced as inhibitions to his achievement in those books. His homosexuality no doubt partially explains the unease of his fictional love relationships, although the constrictions of his Edwardian childhood account as well for the decorous evasions of his romantic encounters. The idealization of "elemental" men in the novels bespeaks Forster's peculiar class-ridden homosexual nostalgia: but although his orientation appears as a strong undercurrent in the novels, it does not vitiate them or detract from the universal nature of their concerns. Rather, the suppressed message, the necessary subversion, is

part of their energy. Forster's personal secret, now acknowledged, gives an added poignancy to his depictions of loneliness
and alienation and to his search for an inclusive vision. But
Maurice has no part in that search. Concerned with a narrow
freedom, it does not achieve even the liberation of confession.
Where the other novels approach metaphysical paradox in their
relation of engagement to vision, *Maurice* attempts neither to
confront the world nor to comprehend it. Forster's homosexual
novel presents the lesser paradox that in his protected attempt
at candor Forster has created his work of greatest inhibition.
Perhaps the act of writing *Maurice*—though certainly not its
content—was an exorcism for Forster that helped him to the
achievement of his final novel. At any rate, from *Maurice* to *A
Passage to India* we pass from shadow to substance.

Forster began *Arctic Summer* after *Howards End,* abandon-
ing it after several draft fragments to write *Maurice.*[17] The covert
homosexuality of this unfinished novel perhaps helped make
possible his directness in *Maurice*. *Arctic Summer* also represents in its apparent repudiation of Martin Whitby's civilized
doctrines, an opposition to *Howards End.*[18] Because the novel
fragment constitutes a comment on the twilight of civilization
in prewar England, it provides an addendum to *Howards End.*
But *Arctic Summer* never approaches the thoughtfulness and
complexity of its predecessor, nor do its value-antitheses, de-

17. For an excellent discussion of the genesis of *Arctic Summer,* see E. M.
Forster, *Arctic Summer and Other Fiction,* Abinger Edition, 9, ed. Elizabeth
Heine and Oliver Stallybrass (London: Edward Arnold, 1980), pp. vii–xxxv.
All subsequent references are to this edition; hereafter page numbers will be
cited in the text.

18. As Furbank notes, Forster seems to wish his protagonist to unlearn the
aesthetic doctrines of Roger Fry: see Furbank, *Forster: A Life,* 1:207. Like Fry
also (and like Ruth Wilcox), Martin Whitby is of Quaker origin. His wife's
tolerance and intellectuality, unlike Margaret Schlegel's, are intended as judgments on her: but the hostility to Venetia and concomitant approval of her
reactionary mother, Lady Borlase, do not strike me as subtle explorations of
the point of view they endorse.

spite Forster's sense of their similarity, accord with the formulations of *Howards End*.[19] Whereas in its attempted synthesis of prose and poetry *Howards End* designates Margaret Schlegel as "poetry," the character in *Arctic Summer* who most closely approximates Margaret's values represents "prose." Nor is the concept well defined. The tepid professionalism of Martin Whitby may render him prosaic, yet a difficulty in *Arctic Summer* is the indistinctness of Forster's attitude to Martin. While castigating the tedium of Martin's work, Forster rewards him for his honesty and discipline: "Beauty did not vanish, as he had feared; it transferred itself . . . to his work, and dwelt in the masses of the hills" (p. 131). Despite Martin's weaknesses—the most specific being his lack of physical courage, seen when he flees a fire without rescuing his lame chauffeur—the many encomiums of Martin and his dramatization render him not only sympathetic but far more believable than his heroic antithesis, Clesant March, who is intended to serve Martin's education.

Forster's antithesis in *Arctic Summer* is between "the civilized man, who hopes for an Arctic Summer, and the heroic man who rides into the sea" (p. 162). But even with allowance for the novel's fragmentary status, the opposing categories do not achieve realization in the characters who embody them. The authorial attitude to Martin, the "civilized" protagonist, is a confused mixture of approval and condescension, and the contrary elevation of Clesant presents a curious regression to the primitive romanticism of the early fiction. Martin Whitby becomes a more sophisticated version of the young protagonist in need of redemption, and as in *Where Angels Fear to Tread* and *The Longest Journey*, the redeemer is a heroic man of action.

Clesant March, however, is a Stephen Wonham with far less to recommend him. Forster admitted that "where conditions are unfavourable" Clesant is "dazed, trite and sour" and justi-

19. Said Forster in 1913, "The only book I have in my head is too like *Howards End* to interest me" (quoted in *Arctic Summer*, p. xxi).

fied these traits by the warrior-idealist's contact with the negative character of modern life—"the hero straying into the modern world which does not want him and which he does not understand" (p. 161). But as dramatized, Clesant is petulant, infantile, and cruel. His stiff chivalry is only a form of hostility to women; his gesture of repudiation in tearing up the "permesso" by which he can view the self-portrait at Tramonta that brought him to Italy comes through merely as a tantrum. Furthermore, the explosion of moralism that causes his brother's suicide is inconsistent with the very ideal of romantic heroism: it violates the primal loyalty between man and man that is, in other contexts, the crux of Forster's ethic of male comradeship.

Especially disturbing about *Arctic Summer* is the degree to which worship of the romantic hero seems inextricable from the romantic glorification of violence and war. Tellingly, Forster himself compares his hero to T. E. Lawrence,[20] and he not only reincarnates in Clesant the passionate warrior of Tramonta, but further, he connects Clesant's bloodlust for the hunt with a valuation of war that is especially shocking as it issues from Forster's narrator: "[The otter's] death stamped the morning with peculiar splendour, and was recalled by Clesant in after years. On they rode, full of the gay chivalry that purified medieval warfare, and is said to purify war today" (p. 174). Nor is this the only expression of such a view, which may be seen also in Forster's portrait of Mr. Vullumy, the uncle who repudiates his nephew, Clesant's brother. In the novel's single description of the relation between good and evil, a concept directed elsewhere in the novels to the formulation of a compassionate and inclusive vision of the human condition, Forster notes approvingly of Mr. Vullumy that "the belief of the coexistence of good and evil underlay his religious life as well as his political" (p. 178). The application of this belief is Mr. Vullumy's desire for Armageddon as a corrective to the laxities of modern society.

20. Forster said of his conception of Clesant March, "T. E. Lawrence, whom I did not then know, offers a hint" (p. 161).

Elizabeth Heine, its editor, would have us judge *Arctic Summer* by criteria other than the nature of its "major public themes" (p. xxiii). I cannot agree that these are irrelevant and must conclude that, whatever its private significance for Forster, and however it may have helped him toward the mature characterizations and complex themes of *A Passage to India, Arctic Summer* presents, and fortunately, an achievement of minor significance in the progress of Forster's fiction.

Of Forster's thirteen surviving homosexual stories, seven followed *A Passage to India* and one, "The Life to Come," closely preceded it. This group is of interest because it constitutes Forster's only fiction after *A Passage to India*, concludes the implications of homosexual union depicted in *Maurice*, and presents, however reductively, a coda to Forster's artistic career. The most striking characteristics of these stories are their almost invariable association of sex and violence, and, in the more serious tales, the inevitable ending of their homosexual unions in death. Whereas in *Maurice* Forster tried, however unconvincingly, to assert a love that encompassed more than sex, the homosexual stories define love solely as the joy of consummation. Within this context there is some range, from the protagonist's play in "Arthur Snatchfold" with a jolly milkman, to the obsessive fidelity of the duped native, Vithobai, in "The Life to Come," to the more complex nuances of passion and conflict between the lovers of "The Other Boat." The symbolic moment of recognition that precedes salvation in such covertly homosexual Forster stories as "The Story of a Panic," "Albergo Empedocle," "The Curate's Friend" and in the brief rapproachement of Rickie and Stephen in *The Longest Journey,* is no longer a vision of truth. The epiphany is only, the homosexual stories reiterate, the moment of sexual pleasure, for which the participants will inevitably pay. With the disappearance of the greenwood, Forster's homosexual lovers have nowhere to retreat. Attitudes to class and sex in the stories continue the pattern of *Maurice*. The sexual act is both salvation and damnation, as an upper-class Englishman experiences rapture and retribution for his connection with a lower-class lover. In his conflict, he inflicts punishment on his partner; the lovers are sacrificial objects, born to die or face imprisonment for the salvation of their upper-class consorts. Yet, in the more serious tales they are tempters as well as martyrs, luring their partners to a fulfillment which is also doom.

Associations of sexuality, violence, and death, implicit or disguised elsewhere in Forster's fiction, become explicit in the homosexual stories. "The Life to Come" and "The Other Boat" dramatize the pleasures of violence, for which the provocation of the lower-class lover affords permission: Vithobai's murder of Pinmay is an act of emotional release, and in biting his lover, Cocoa of "The Other Boat" liberates Lionel's latent aggression, which issues in an orgy of rape, murder, and suicide. The stories express hatred both as hostility to the upperclass protagonists who deflect or deny their impulses, like Paul Pinmay, the repressed missionary of "The Life to Come" and as self-hatred, in the portrayal of Clesant in "Dr. Woolacott." The protagonists also embody the inner conflict of selves who desire a freedom that both society and their psyches deny: they can neither defy society nor overcome their self-disgust. Significant also in the stories is Forster's animus against women, seen, for example, in his portrait of Perpetua, the self-righteous virgin of "The Torque" and, with greater breadth, in Mrs. March of "The Other Boat," who represents the underside of the semi-deified mother figures in the novels. This last of Forster's fictional mothers may suggest something of the complex emotions in his long filial relationship with "Lily."[21]

For the homosexual missionary of "The Life to Come" (1922), sexual love is guilt and despair. The story turns on his pagan lover's conflation of physical and religious love, a merging of distinctions that the missionary rejects. Converted through

21. See Furbank's sensitive account in the biography. It is interesting also that Mrs. March does not appear until after the death of Forster's mother.

sex to Christianity, Vithobai declines under the yoke of Western religion and progress as the story moves toward double catastrophe. The defeat of passion becomes victory through death, as dying, the pagan chief takes his reluctant lover with him into the life to come. Although the native lover achieves a consummation of revenge, the story emphasizes a process of torment and the ruin of an innocent; despite its bitter comedy, action and tone dramatize the impossibility of homosexual union.

"Dr. Woolacott" (1927) continues the direction of "The Life to Come," this time with a protagonist who resembles Rickie Elliot in his weakness and despair. As in *Maurice*, Clesant's summons brings the fantasy-lover who redeems him from falsity. Clesant seeks liberation not only from the hypocrisy of society, symbolized in the repressive Dr. Woolacott, but from the solipsism of his own consciousness, which itself creates the death-in-life Dr. Woolacott protracts. This fantasy of self-hatred presents the familiar motif of a maimed protagonist who seeks freedom from self in sexual union with a lower-class lover. Clesant betrays his lover and repudiates himself as his diseased consciousness labels the lover "an illusion whom you created in the garden because you wanted to feel you were attractive."[22] Desire and resistance war: "There was always a barrier either way, always his own nature" (p. 95). Giving in at last to love, Cleasant finds that love and death are one. The point of the story seems to be that death is more desirable than the death-in-life that awaits the rationalist who cannot accept his impulses. As in "The Life to Come," homosexual passion can prevail only through death.

"Arthur Snatchfold" (1928) presents the scapegoating of the homosexual life force and the cynical victory of society, as a

22. E. M. Forster, *The Life to Come and Other Stories*, Abinger Edition, 8, ed. Oliver Stallybrass (London: Edward Arnold, 1972), p. 94. Subsequent references are to this edition; hereafter page numbers will be indicated in the text.

Wilcox-like businessman sacrifices his lower-class lover: the socially prominent protagonist escapes detection, while society sends the vital young milkman to jail. The story illustrates Forster's remark in the "Terminal Note" to *Maurice* that "Clive on the bench will continue to sentence Alec in the dock. Maurice may get off" (p. 255).

"The Other Boat" (1957–58), Forster's last story, is a painful and remarkable narrative. Its strong characterizations of the Englishman and his half-caste lover and its signification of the psychic power of the mother in Forster's mind give it greater artistic interest than the other homosexual stories. Lionel March, a British officer en route to Bombay, is seduced by Cocoa, a young but sophisticated half-caste, into an affair that ends in violence and catastrophe. Cocoa's native status, appearance, perceptiveness, and opportunism a little recall Aziz, but March is no Fielding; rather he is like Maurice, an unintellectual, physically attractive Anglo-Indian, unaware of his charms or his nature. Once drawn into sexual relations, March faces the conflict between sexuality and convention; in the crisis, he denies his deepest impulses and chooses society. The outcome presents Forster's final and most explosive depiction of the defeat of homosexual passion.

To the love affair Forster counterpoints March's relationship with his mother, on whom he blames Lionel's predicament, and whose symbolic and emotional influence receive extraordinary development. March is the center of a triangle composed of lover and mother, and Mrs. March correctly identifies Cocoa as the agent of subversion in a prologue that pairs Lionel and Cocoa as childhood playmates on an earlier voyage. Similarly, although Mrs. March is not present during the story's major action, Cocoa's fear of her influence on his lover looms large in the plot.

What is significant is the mother's importance as influence and threat. She resembles the Anglo-Indian ladies of *A Passage to India* whom Forster repudiates with efficient astringency.

But in this story the Anglo-Indian mother is a major figure. Whereas in the novels such mothers as Mrs. Honeychurch, Mrs. Wilcox, and Mrs. Moore are objects of affection or awe, Mrs. March, antithetically valued, is equally potent. She represents, both in character and in her presence in March's mind, the inhibitions and conventions he cannot overcome in his attempt to bridge the sexual and social chasms that separate him from Cocoa. As daughter of a clergyman and wife of an officer, the mother not only symbolizes British ruling institutions; she embodies for her son the taboo against sexuality. Sexual temptation is punishable by death, and, as the perceptive half-caste realizes, this principle underlies the mother's hatred of him. For, deserted by her husband for a native lover (presumably male), Mrs. March has relaxed her vigilance over the children with whom she is returning to England, to flirt on board with an English officer. The youngest child dies subsequently, and Mrs. March identifies the cause as the seductions of Cocoa, which her neglect has permitted. Thus, the mother's sexual guilt informs her hostility to natives, both as they deflect her from duty and as they represent a sexuality she lacks. The story's ultimate significance seems to lie in the rebound of these guilty sexualities on their creator.

The figure of the mother assumes symbolic dimension as fate, an incomprehending, unaware, all-powerful force: She is "another power, . . . blind-eyed in the midst of the enormous web she had spun—filaments drifting everywhere, strands catching. There was no reasoning with her or about her, she understood nothing and controlled everything" (p. 193). Lionel sees her both as the source of all his conflicts and the ideal from which he has fallen through indulgence of his sexuality. Her control comes from his reverence and anxiety rather than from any action she performs. His falling away, finally, from the internalized ideal of feminine purity is the cause of his self-execution. Lionel's sin has been no less than the violation of his mother. His murder and suicide expiate a sexuality whose ambiguous manifestations have additional implications. For carnality and brutality unite in this story, and from start to finish the blossoming of sexuality in Lionel presents a final testimony to Forster's admiration of violence.

Forster's attitude to the lovers mixes attraction and condescension. Cocoa is nicknamed "Monkey" and portrayed as predatory. Initiating Lionel into experience, the half-caste seeks to subjugate March to his sexual desires. Cocoa's destruction occurs because he provocatively tries to assert his dominance, first by disregarding the secrecy that permits the Englishman to violate sexual and class taboos, then by a symbolic move into the forbidden reaches of the Englishman's upper bunk. Neither sexual nor class connection can be accomplished, and the Götterdämmerung that follows Cocoa's final provocation, an attempt to seduce March by violence, obliterates both protagonists and ends Forster's explorations of homosexuality in fiction.

The homosexual stories concern themselves not with the meaning of life but with a byway of experience, the thrills and punishments of homosexual passion. As Alan Wilde recently noted, Forster moves here from depths to surfaces, and the stories are striking in their loss of the authorial distance and irony that characterize Forster's best fiction.[23] Despite Forster's description of them as recreation,[24] these stories are noteworthy also for the sense of despair they project. Love and sex now exist only in discontinuity. The fantasy of the greenwood has become a chance roll on the sward of a country estate; homosexual unions have no place in the world, and Forster's protagonists can escape the prison of solipsism and the repressions

23. See Alan Wilde, "Depths and Surfaces: Dimensions of Forsterian Irony," *English Literature in Transition,* 16:4 (1973), 257–274; and "Desire and Consciousness."

24. "They were written not to express myself but to excite myself" (Forster's diary for 8 April 1922, quoted by Oliver Stallybrass, *The Life to Come,* p. xii).

of society only through death. In their repudiation of the solution of *Maurice,* the more serious stories make final acknowledgment of the incompatibility of homosexual unions both with Forster's contemporary social and legal codes and with his divided self. Their orgies of rape, mutilation, and death project anguish, but also a questionable pleasure in violence, self-punishment, and destruction. Ultimately the significance of these stories is private, in whatever personal solace they gave their author. Their minor status should also, I hope, free them from the burden of their temporal position, which has caused so astute a critic as Alan Wilde to place them implicitly on the same conceptual level as *A Passage to India.* In their reversion to surface, their narrow concern with sexual pleasure and torment, these stories display Forster's artistic fragmentation after *A Passage to India.* The creative impulse that achieved integration there seems in a sense to split into rational and psychic components, a schism between mind and impulse, expressed on the one hand through the urbane intelligence and moral passion of Forster's nonfiction, on the other in these private fantasies, whose limitations of both form and subject debar them from consideration or judgment with the mainstream of Forster's fiction. Thus, despite their greater contemporaneity, the homosexual stories close the byway opened in *Maurice* with a no-exit sign and direct our attention to the culmination of Forster's art in *A Passage to India.*

6 ~

A Passage to India

A PASSAGE TO INDIA moves toward catastrophe and symbolic
revelation with the visit of two English ladies and their Indian
host to the famous Marabar caves. As Mrs. Moore, Adela
Quested, Aziz, and their entourage of servants enter the first
cave, Forster describes their passage:

> The small black hole gaped where their varied forms and colours
> had momentarily functioned. They were sucked in like water
> down a drain. Bland and bald rose the precipices; bland and
> glutinous the sky that connected the precipices; solid and white,
> a Brahmany kite flapped between the rocks with a clumsiness
> that seemed intentional. Before man, with his itch for the seemly,
> had been born, the planet must have looked thus. The kite
> flapped away. . . . Before birds, perhaps. . . . And then the hole
> belched, and humanity returned.[1]

Perhaps the most startling aspect of this description is the remoteness of its perspective. For the cave entrance to appear as

1. E. M. Forster, *A Passage to India,* Abinger Edition, 6, ed. Oliver Stallybrass (London: Edward Arnold, 1978), p. 138. All subsequent quotations are
from this edition; hereafter page numbers will be indicated in the text.

"a small black hole" the speaker must be quite far away. Moving toward the cave, the party had "climbed up over some unattractive stones" (p. 138). The small black hole is similarly uninviting; those who enter it are reduced to its scale. The diction projects a sense of ominous foreboding. The combined effect of perspective and diction is to emphasize the insignificance of the human actors. The rhythmic inversions and repetitions enlarge the importance of setting. Every word contributes to the impression of man's pettiness, to his helpless lack of dignity before the most elemental forces of the universe. From the narrator's distant perspective, the human beings are merely forms and colors; even as these their agency in the scene is transitory—they have "momentarily functioned." Their entrance into the black hole places them in the grip of powers beyond their control and beyond their ken; Forster's verb and simile—they are "sucked in like water down a drain"—reduce their dignity still further. When the people return, they are expelled from the caves, again as if by an overwhelming force: "the hole belched"; in the context of this personification, mankind is merely an unpleasant excretion.

With *A Passage to India* the reader moves into a world that, however implied in the earlier novels, shares less with those worlds than they did with each other. Though fraught with apprehensions about the encroachments of modern society, though occasionally hysterical in tone and hollow in its affirmations, Forster's voice maintained a hopeful tone in that prewar era which saw the composition of five of his six novels. But the dregs of Edwardian optimism vanished in the abyss of the Great War. When Forster came to his last novel, he turned his narrative techniques to the expression of a vision more distinctly modernist than anything seen in his earlier work. The foreboding of apocalypse rendered in the imagery of *Howards End* has become a statement of humanity's potential doom. The novel's central symbol of caves that generate evil not because of their own attributes but because of the human inadequacy which they echo is explicitly the metaphysical abyss that confronts contemporary man.

But to describe *A Passage to India* as modernist in subject and symbolistic in method is to give a very partial impression. For Forster, continuing the practice of omniscient narration derived from an earlier tradition, is no less present here than in his early works; in fact, his narrative voice is more pervasive. Yet it differs in important ways from the narrative voices of the earlier novels. In *A Passage to India,* Forster has created a voice that is controlling, from the opening phrase of the first chapter, "Except for the Marabar caves," to the concluding statement, "No, not there."

Forster's unique achievement in *A Passage to India* lies in the union of a narrative voice that speaks in new accents with the cumulating reiterations of phrase and image that E. K. Brown and others, following Forster's own terminology in *Aspects of the Novel,* have called "rhythm." The combination of Forster's voice with his rhythmic use of image and symbol, his control of the variations that reveal his major themes in their complexity, give *A Passage to India* its extraordinary sense of structural coherence. The narrator's interventions are both integral and primary to the expression of theme and to the context that engenders the novel's complex symbolism. That the narrative voice and the developing symbols project a vision in which chaos and disorder dominate the faint glimpses of an ordered universe in no way reduces the quality of verbal and artistic order in the novel itself.

To study authorial presence in *A Passage to India* is both to define the quality of Forster's narrative voice and to view the effect of its relationship to the rhythmic repetition of words, phrases, and images that infuse the novel with symbolic implication. Such consideration should correct the view, implied or directly stated by some critics, that because Forster develops an intricate symbolism in *A Passage to India,* he does not comment significantly in his own voice. E. K. Brown, for example, distinguished between "the interweaving of themes" through rhythm that he considered Forster's prevailing mode and "a much blunter instrument, comment" that is "the usual Victorian means." Brown's demonstration of Forster's command of rhythm was meant to imply Forster's fortunate abandonment of the "blunter instrument."[2] Wilfred Stone asserts directly that "*A Passage to India,* unlike earlier books, is almost totally lacking in editorial or didactic comment."[3] Brown's view that narrative commentary is crude does injustice to the complexity and subtlety of Forster's narrative interventions, and his belief that Forster does not significantly employ these does not reflect the reality of Forster's practice in *A Passage to India.* I would take even more direct issue with Stone's statement. To begin with, the opening chapter of *A Passage to India,* one of three in all the novels devoted entirely to the narrator's language, dramatically refutes the idea that Forster is neither editorial nor didactic.

The first chapter is an extraordinary achievement. Simple and concentrated, it encapsulates the major thematic polarities that inform the novel, includes the central concepts whose symbolic importance Forster will develop, projects the novel's salient and startling view of man, and through diction, tone, and perspective creates the narrative voice that evokes and controls all the important terms of meaning.

Forster's first sentence reads, "Except for the Marabar Caves —and they are twenty miles off—the city of Chandrapore presents nothing extraordinary." Frank Kermode has noted the inversion of principal and subordinate clauses that makes caves the initial object of the reader's attention and associates them, as future references will, with the adjective "extraordinary"— "The excepted is what must be included if there is to be mean-

2. E. K. Brown, *Rhythm in the Novel* (Toronto: University of Toronto Press, 1967), pp. 63, 86.
3. Wilfred Stone, *The Cave and the Mountain* (Stanford: Stanford University Press, 1966), p. 340.

ing."[4] But more than this, the narrator's first sentence effectively suggests the novel's major polarity. For action and comment will assert that human life is a condition of exclusion: living in invidious separation from his fellows, man is isolated from meaning and from God. The "passage to India," a complex and somber transformation of the title of Whitman's poem, is a voyage of the soul, a search for meaning, the attempt to discover a unity that includes man, the natural world, and all matter in a transcendent vision of divine love.

Kermode's analysis indicates the rhetorical function of so apparently casual an arrangement of clauses and suggests the profundity of implication that underlies the deceptively simple concreteness of Forster's description of Chandrapore. But his characterization of Forster's words as "easy, colloquial, if with a touch of the guide-book,"[5] does not represent the substance or suggest the bleak and detached tone of the opening chapter. For Forster conveys, within the framework of exclusion and inclusion, the terrifying vision of human insignificance that demonstrates itself as the novel's most basic assumption.

Far from presenting a travelogue, the opening chapter suggests a view of man whose emphases are outlined in the first paragraph.

> Except for the Marabar Caves—and they are twenty miles off—the city of Chandrapore presents nothing extraordinary. Edged rather than washed by the river Ganges, it trails for a couple of miles along the bank, scarcely distinguishable from the rubbish it deposits so freely. There are no bathing-steps on the river front, as the Ganges happens not to be holy here; indeed there is no river front, and bazaars shut out the wide and shifting panorama of the stream. The streets are mean, the temples ineffective, and though a few fine houses exist they are hidden away in gardens or down alleys whose filth deters all but the invited guest. Chandrapore was never large or beautiful, but

4. Frank Kermode, "Mr. E. M. Forster as a Symbolist," in *Forster*, ed. Malcolm Bradbury (Englewood Cliffs, N.J.: Prentice-Hall, 1966), p. 92.
5. Ibid.

two hundred years ago it lay on the road between Upper India, then imperial, and the sea, and the fine houses date from that period. The zest for decoration stopped in the eighteenth century, nor was it ever democratic. In the bazaars there is no painting and scarcely any carving. The very wood seems made of mud, the inhabitants of mud moving. So abased, so monotonous is everything that meets the eye, that when the Ganges comes down it might be expected to wash the excrescence back into the soil. Houses do fall, people are drowned and left rotting, but the general outline of the town persists, swelling here, shrinking there, like some low but indestructible form of life. [P. 2]

Forster's careful discriminations in this paragraph are microcosms of the themes he will develop. It will later be seen that the fundamental characteristic of the Marabar caves is that "Nothing, nothing attaches to them" (p. 117). The conjunction in the first sentence between "nothing" and "extraordinary" presents a highly condensed suggestion of the caves' significance. That it is an active suggestion is not evident on first reading; as Kermode says, the words "lie there, lacking all rhetorical emphasis, waiting for the relations which will give them significance. . . . but they are prepared for these relations."[6]

The first sentence implies more than the importance of including the excepted. In distinction to the caves, the city is "nothing extraordinary." In contrast to the caves, which have no attributes and are in any case not described here, the city has many, none of which is extraordinary. The attributes of the city share two major characteristics. They are abased, and they reveal an indistinction of city from rubbish, man from city, and man from rubbish. The reduction of distinctions anticipates the climactic message of the caves, in which everything is characterized by a negative sameness, in which the smallness of the universe becomes embodied in an echo that says "ou boum" to whatever is said.

6. Ibid.

In the second sentence Forster separates nature's work from man's and suggests that between humans and garbage there is little difference. Nature forbears to cleanse man—the Ganges edges rather than washes the city. The ensuing sentences of this paragraph develop the degraded associations of man and his works and intensify the implication that humanity is too loathsome or insignificant even for nature's purifying attention.

With an implied contrast between the "panorama of the stream" and the bazaars that shut it out, the third sentence hints at the haphazard quality of man-made distinctions and categories—the Ganges "happens" not to be holy at this place. Forster introduces another major theme by suggesting the elusively changing quality of reality, the difficulty of clear-cut identification. Not only is the view "wide and shifting," the initial observation that there are no bathing-steps on the river becomes the assertion that "indeed there is no river front." Later in the novel Forster claims that "nothing in India is identifiable, the mere asking of a question causes it to disappear or to merge in something else" (p. 78). The constant alteration of matter, illustrated frequently in the novel, is connected with those changes that move constantly from one apparent absolute to the next, seeking an answer to the fundamental question of which all other questions and appeals are but a version: "Beyond the sky must not there be something that overarches all the skies, more impartial even than they? Beyond which again . . ." (p. 34).

The fourth sentence details the city's degradation. The "mean" streets, the "ineffective" temples, the "filth" of the alleys specify and support the earlier identification with "rubbish." This sentence also begins the important metaphor of invitation. The alleys of Chandrapore ironically exclude most of the humanity they presumably exist to accommodate; only the "invited guest" may penetrate the filth. The fatuity of man's invitations and exclusions is suggested here, and Forster will develop a view of the futility of man's attempts to exert control over his destiny through assertions of will in a series of variations on the idea of invitations. This reference places the concept of invitation in the context of the repugnant character of man's offerings.

If a guide-book quality can be said to characterize any part of the opening chapter, it appears in the next three sentences, but even here Forster's meaning transcends the apparent simplicity of description. Sentence five explains the largely excluded: the paucity of beauty or decoration in the city is historically conditioned. The next sentence enlarges an implication of the "invited guest" who figures in sentence four. The activity of decoration was temporary, its beneficiaries were few. Most of the population was excluded—the little art that existed was not "democratic" in its application. The next sentence illustrates this contention: as the seat of common humanity, the bazaars are characterized by the absence of art. The uncarved wood is scarcely distinguishable from mud, the lack of differentiation extends from man's works to man himself, "mud moving." The ninth sentence passes specific and general judgment: "abased" derives from the primitive lowness of mud, "monotonous" from the monochromatic similarity of wood and man; the statement is also a comment on all that has gone before—the adjectives culminate in "everything," the remainder of the sentence defines all of Chandrapore as an "excrescence." The speaker's observation that the river "might be expected" to wash the city back into the soil is an enlargement of the initial hint provided by the "edged rather than washed" of the second sentence. Rather than presenting a harmony, man and nature are in tension: so repelled is nature by man's abasement and filth that her forbearance to purge herself of the "excrescence" surprises. The last sentence of the paragraph suggests small movements of flux within a primordial continuity. The context is death and decay—"houses do fall, people are drowned and left rotting." Apathy, not agency, characterizes man; at the very bottom of the scale of life, his sole activity is to "persist." The final image of the city with its rotting dead is that of an amoeba, "swelling here, shrinking there." Its lowness is matched only by its capacity to survive: beyond this, Forster does not accord man a single positive characteristic.

From this extraordinarily bleak picture of human incapacity, Forster moves in the second paragraph to develop the comparison between nature and man. Viewed from the rise of the civil station above the city, "Chandrapore appears to be a totally different place." The languid river that shrinks from contact with humankind has become a "noble river" and washes "a tropical pleasaunce." Water imagery is associated in all the Forster novels with fecundity and regenerative power. The narrator has already suggested that for the river to exercise its cleansing function would be to rid itself of man altogether. But for the vegetation, water performs its accustomed services. Beside the river, "ancient tanks nourish" the tropical trees. Nature asserts itself: the trees hide the bazaars as the bazaars hid the view of the river. Forster contrasts the energy of the natural world with the limitations of man. "Endowed with more strength than man and his works," the trees are motivated also by their desire to escape from the inglorious confines of man's world: they "rise," they "burst out of stifling purlieus and unconsidered temples," they "soar above the lower deposits" to find light and air, to greet each other, and "to build a city for the birds." From this perspective, the city is "a city of gardens," "a forest sparsely scattered with huts," finally, "a tropical pleasaunce." This view is possible only because the works of nature hide the works of man. Only as a city for the birds can Chandrapore be seen as beautiful. Forster suggests again the illusory quality of reality by the conjunction of the conditional verb "appears" with Chandrapore, and he reminds that nature's glorification does not present the "real" city, by noting the "disillusionment" of the newcomer, once driven down from the rise.

With a brief description of the civil station whose roads

"intersect at right angles," a triumph of sensible planning that will not take man far into the realms of spirit, Forster reiterates the suggestion of separations and exclusions: the civil station "shares nothing with the city except the overarching sky" (p. 3). Again the idea of exclusion and the concept of "nothing" mean more than the apparently straightforward statement seems to say. In sharing nothing except the sky, the civil station shares all, for the chapter's final paragraph asserts the dominion of sky: "the sky settles everything." Anglo-Indians and natives have nothing in common: the exclusions are man-made.

The final two paragraphs move from consideration of the nature that is more beautiful and powerful than man but yet shares a sense of scale with him to the larger aspects of nature that dominate both: earth, sun, and sky. Earth is vast but like man helpless, dependent on sun and sky. To the image of the "prostrate earth" is contrasted the phallic energy of the "fists and fingers" of the Marabar Hills. In Forster's final sentence, the inversion with which he began the chapter culminates in the reintroduction of the caves, emphasized further by their reiterated association with the adjective "extraordinary."

Diction, tone, and perspective create a controlling narrative voice. Detached and impartial, the speaker seems to regard all he sees as unsurprising. But what his diction develops as "nothing extraordinary" is a view of humanity as degraded. Verbs describing the city are low in energy, as in "it trails along the bank," or as in the frequent forms of "to be" that, coupled with adjectives or verbal participles, reveal the city as "mean," "ineffective," "abased," "monotonous," "rotting." The nouns similarly reiterate the negative character of Chandrapore, a rare strong verb is attached to "filth"—"filth deters," and Forster offers in summary the intensely repellent noun "excrescence."

The deliberately impassive tone combines with a perspective that moves from near to far. The inclusion of the cosmic intensifies the insignificance of man, and in the increasing remoteness of the narrator's point of view, the human scale is reduced

further. The speaker bounds Chandrapore by size and shape;
the city, not its inhabitants, is the object of initial consideration, and they are not mentioned until after rubbish, filthy
alleys, and inartistic bazaars have been noted. Barely differentiated from these, even at the point of the narrator's focus
upon it, humanity is low and small.

The perspective withdraws to include civil station and city in
the cosmos, then farther still, to contemplate the distance between sky and stars and thence between stars and infinity.
Seen from here, man is almost incongruously tiny. As the perspective recedes, it can be seen that change is the only constant. In the second paragraph, "the prospect alters." The third
paragraph discusses the "changes" of the sky and moves to
consider the distance behind the stars, by implication beyond
change, "beyond colour, last freed itself from blue." Each change
in perspective engenders a different view of reality, and each
such change identifies the alteration of matter not only with
the idea of appearance and reality—viewed through trees, the
city's illusory beauty hides the grim truth of Chandrapore—but
with an ever enlarging series that moves from one apparent
absolute to the next. In the systematic movement from city to
infinity, structure and perspective become aspects of the narrative voice in rendering Forster's preoccupation with the nature
of reality and the existence of God.

A *Passage to India* moves between polarities of exclusion
and inclusion, separation and unity, discord and harmony,
negation and affirmation, the emptiness of the caves and the
fullness of a universe animated by divine presence, the reductive vision and the inclusive vision. The novel's burden is the
demonstration of discord, the search for unity its motive power.
Bridging the oppositions is a continuous appeal, an invocation
of divine presence that seeks to transcend the prevailing chaos
and isolation of human existence. The first chapter reveals
Forster's narrative voice as it defines these informing concepts
and categories whose full meanings arise as they appear and

reappear in changing contexts. The chapter also demonstrates the novel's crucial unity of voice with theme and setting. As the means by which India—at once the most fragmented and the most inclusive concept in the novel—is rendered, Forster's voice assumes a major role.

Early in the action, Aziz regales his Moslem cronies with a recitation of poetry. As they listen entranced, the narrator moves beyond their limited perceptions to note the ironically disparate attitudes of man and nature, to contrast appearance and reality, and to suggest the human longing for unity: "India— a hundred Indias—whispered outside beneath the indifferent moon, but for the time India seemed one and their own, and they regained their departed greatness by hearing its departure lamented, they felt young again because reminded that youth must fly" (p. 10). The moment is fleeting as well as illusory, and the themes of Aziz's poetry—"the decay of Islam and the brevity of love"—suggest the ephemerality of man's powers.

The human fragments of India see unity in terms of their own exclusions. Aziz, buoyed and exhilarated after his meeting with Mrs. Moore, "seemed to own the land as much as anyone owned it. What did it matter if a few flabby Hindus had preceded him there, and a few chilly English succeeded?" (p. 18). But India is far from unitary. The Collector's invitations to a "Bridge Party" "caused much excitement and was discussed in several worlds" (p. 30). And the narrator invokes those whom Mr. Turton's invitation had not reached:

> . . . clients, waiting for pleaders, sat in the dust outside. These had not received a card from Mr. Turton. And there were circles even beyond these—people who wore not even that, and spent their lives in knocking two sticks together before a scarlet doll—humanity grading and drifting beyond the educated vision, until no earthly invitation can embrace it. [P. 32]

The discriminations of the "educated vision" exclude most of humanity: it is an infinitesimal fragment of the world it seeks to dominate, and its invitations are meaningless acts of will. The "circles" repeat the series of the opening chapter whose ever enlarging perspectives move toward infinity. The circles widen beyond the confines of earthly vision to some hinted at but undefined absolute.

From the limitations of the human, the narrative voice moves to the only potential source of unity: "All invitations must proceed from heaven perhaps; perhaps it is futile for men to initiate their own unity, they do but widen the gulfs between them by the attempt" (p. 32). Mr. Sorley, the "advanced" missionary, fails to consider the inclusion of oranges, cactuses, crystals, mud, and bacteria in his Father's mansions. "We must exclude someone from our gathering, or we shall be left with nothing" (p. 32) refers to Mr. Turton's invitations as well as to the missionary's inability to contemplate a heaven for any form of life lower than mammals. The irony is comic, but the subject foreshadows the vision of the caves.

The "indifferent" moon presided over Aziz's conviviality. At the Bridge Party, this indifference is generalized to all nature, and the figure of a series reappears, along with the translucent sky of the opening chapter, that in its transcendence of individual colors suggests the unity that may reside with infinity.

> Some kites hovered overhead, impartial, over the kites passed the mass of a vulture, and, with an impartiality exceeding all, the sky, not deeply coloured but translucent, poured light from its whole circumference. It seemed unlikely that the series stopped here. Beyond the sky must not there be something that overarches all the skies, more impartial even than they? Beyond which again . . . [P. 34]

As in the opening chapter, Forster's perspective and diction combine to dwarf humanity. The birds that watch the human scene—they hover, rather than fly—are birds of prey, eaters of carrion. Their "impartiality" obliterates the distinctions on which the variously conflicting human characters insist and reduces the pretensions and aspirations of human will. Moving through the ascending series of kite, vulture, sky, and the "something that overarches all the skies," the speaker's perspective progressively diminishes the earthbound characters, as the "Drink Me" elixir shrank Alice.

Forster has posed the question directly here. What is behind all the skies? Is there a God in the universe? The unity that men seek suggests the possibility of good, as exclusions and conflict express the existence of evil. For most of the characters, the absence of good signifies the absence of God. The novel represents an appeal for his presence, a search for the unity that would imply his existence, a passage toward revelation. But revelation of what? For the prevailing imagery, as these brief exegeses suggest, emphasizes the impotence, even the loathsomeness of human beings. Moreover, in its vast and varied world, India includes the Marabar caves, and Forster impels his actors toward a shattering vision of nothingness that some readers view as the novel's essential meaning.

The problem of India becomes explicit as characters ask "what is India?" and offer partial answers. Adela Quested, fresh from England, demands to see "the *real* India" (p. 19). Her inexperienced fiancé, pompous and brash, "places" the educated Indians: "But these people—don't imagine they're India" (p. 34). The more perceptive characters have portions of the truth. Fielding, the intuitive and humanistic schoolmaster, approaches Forster's inclusive view when he asserts that those who would see India should see Indians (p. 21). Mrs. Moore feels, "quite illogically," that her administrator son's toughminded sincerity "was not the last word on India." The narrative voice that attributed illogic to Mrs. Moore belies it in describing Ronny and his words, "the self-satisfied lilt of them . . . the mouth moving so complacently and competently beneath the little red nose" (p. 44). Mrs. Moore, contemplating the ingredient missing from Ronny's recital, identifies the "one touch of regret" that might have redeemed, if not justified, the

British Empire's presence in India. To Mrs. Moore, India is
"part of the earth" (p. 45), and as such the proving ground of
God's design of love and unity among people.

The implications of India pervade the novel. The "proportion" that Margaret Schlegel so earnestly sought is impossible
of fulfillment in India, where the environment seems to nourish
the petty animosities of men. "It was as if irritation exuded
from the very soil" (p. 71), says Forster, and Fielding, contemplating the disordered conclusion of his tea party, observes,
"There seemed no reserve of tranquillity to draw upon in India.
Either none, or else tranquillity swallowed up everything, as it
appeared to do for Professor Godbole" (p. 71). When shortly
after this Ronny and Adela quarrel, it is as much as anything
else because "they were both in India, [that] an opportunity
soon occurred" (p. 74).

In this setting, man is a minor element, whose pretensions to
dominion are belied by the power of the Indian climate and
ignored by the greater population of India.

> It matters so little to the majority of living beings what the
> minority, that calls itself human, desires or decides. Most of the
> inhabitants of India do not mind how India is governed. Nor
> are the lower animals of England concerned about England, but
> in the tropics the indifference is more prominent, the inarticu-
> late world is closer at hand and readier to resume control as
> soon as men are tired. [P. 105]

While Aziz and his friends discuss the existence of Providence,
the hot weather advances: "The heat had leapt forward in the
last hour, the street was deserted as if a catastrophe had cleaned
off humanity during the inconclusive talk" (p. 105). The narrator's language reiterates his earlier identification of man with
rubbish and nature as a purgative agent. The efficiency of the
heat contrasts with the "inconclusive talk" of the human beings,
who seem united only in their helplessness before the torments
of the sun, which mock the concept of individuality.

When the seven gentlemen who had held such various opinions inside the bungalow came out of it, they were aware of a common burden, a vague threat which they called "the bad weather coming." . . . The space between them and their carriages, instead of being empty, was clogged with a medium that pressed against their flesh, the carriage cushions scalded their trousers, their eyes pricked, domes of hot water accumulated under their headgear and poured down their cheeks. Salaaming feebly, they dispersed for the interior of other bungalows, to recover their self-esteem and the qualities that distinguished them from each other. [P. 105]

This obliteration of distinctions echoes in Forster's characterization of most of human life as "so dull that there is nothing to be said about it" (p. 125). The reductions of individuality and significance here prefigure the message of the caves, as "dull" and "nothing" reappear in changing contexts, all of which imply negation. The Indian setting echoes the dullness of life: "Trees of a poor quality bordered the road, indeed the whole scene was inferior, and suggested that the countryside was too vast to admit of excellence" (p. 79). And although Adela misses its message, India is like "the train half asleep, going nowhere in particular and with no passenger of importance in any of its carriages, the branch-line train, lost on a low embankment between dull fields" (p. 128).

India, finally, is beyond rational apprehension.

How can the mind take hold of such a country? Generations of invaders have tried, but they remain in exile. The important towns they build are only retreats, their quarrels the malaise of men who cannot find their way home. India knows of their trouble. She knows of the whole world's trouble, to its uttermost depth. She calls "Come" through her hundred mouths, through objects ridiculous and august. But come to what? She has never defined. [P. 128]

From their condition of exclusion and alienation, men seek the reassurance of divine presence. But vast, irrational, anticlimactic, inconclusive India is not that presence. Rather, India is a metaphor for the human condition, in herself a denial of unity. Thus, Aziz insists, "Nothing embraces the whole of India, nothing, nothing" (p. 136).

That nothing is the only thing that does, is the message of the caves. As Peter Burra noted, the caves "are the keynote to the symphony to which the strange melody always returns."[7] *A Passage to India* begins with caves, and all the action moves the characters to the Marabar. In the "passage" to India they are a crucial stop, but their ultimate significance must be sought not only in terms of the beliefs they represent but in their relation to the novel's total structure, to the attitude toward men revealed there, and to Forster's central question about the existence of God. The caves may be the keynote, but more important, they are part of a process, and their meaning must be understood as such. The reiteration of the keynote reminds us that they do not vanish—but it is essential to remember that other things do not vanish as well.

After their introduction in the opening chapter, the caves remain dormant, as the characters slowly move toward them. The caves motif appears briefly as at sunset Adela is struck by their beauty. Even this early, Forster connects the caves with the girl's problem. "But she couldn't touch them. In front, like a shutter, fell a vision of her married life" (p. 41). "Touch" is a physical, instinctive means by which humans explore the realities of their environment. But Adela cannot have this direct contact with whatever reality the caves may represent, for the falsity of her anticipated marriage intervenes. This brief episode prefigures Adela's experience in the caves, when her inability to confront an instinctual truth will produce the collapse of her rational categories.

When at Fielding's tea party, Aziz, motivated not by the impulse to give pleasure but rather by irritation at Adela's persis-

7. Peter Burra, "The Novels of E. M. Forster," in *Forster*, ed. Bradbury, p. 27.

tence, invites the English ladies to the Marabar caves, he is, like all the characters, in the grip of forces beyond his power to comprehend. His invitation responds, in a sense controlled only by Forster's manipulation, to Adela's earlier desire to "touch" the caves and initiates a sequence which will include all that has gone before. As the tea party breaks up in squabbling and pettiness, and Professor Godbole appeals for the return of good, the scene provides a prevision of the evil that awaits at the Marabar caves.

In the second chapter devoted entirely to the narrator's commentary, Forster describes the caves in negative superlatives. They are "unspeakable," "without proportion," "like nothing else in the world," "they bear no relation to anything dreamt or seen." Nothing distinguishes the caves from each other, and "nothing, nothing attaches to them" (p. 117). They are older than humanity, and "their reputation—for they have one—does not depend on human speech" (p. 117). The narrator's description of a match lit in the caves implies something of their symbolic meaning. The chamber is circular, the flame reflected in the rock is "like an imprisoned spirit." The flames "approach and strive to unite, but cannot" (p. 117). The moment closest to unity engenders death: "the flames touch one another, kiss, expire" (p. 118). The match lit by a human hand is like the human ego itself, striving for union with other egos, seeking an awareness of meaning. The caves without entrances are said to "exceed in number those that can be visited, as the dead exceed the living" (p. 118). This comparison intensifies the sense of the ineffectuality of those humans who presently live, so insignificant are they compared to those who have already lived. In this context also, the dead extend their emptiness to the living: the sealed caves are as empty as the ones that can be explored. Forster reiterates their nullity in a diction whose significance began with the novel's first phrase. "Nothing is inside them, they were sealed up before the creation of pestilence or treasure; if mankind grew curious and excavated, nothing, nothing would be added to the sum of good or evil" (p. 118).

The Kawa Dol collapses man-made distinctions: it "has neither ceiling nor floor, and mirrors its own darkness in every direction infinitely" (p. 118). The description implies what Mrs. Moore will encounter in the caves; as the ever-ascending arches that move toward the overarching sky are partly visual versions of the aural echo, so the infinitely mirroring darkness of this cave is a version of Mrs. Moore's echo, that will mirror her own darkness thus. The conception of the cave if it should fall, as "empty as an Easter egg" (p. 118), implies the fate of Mrs. Moore's Christian faith, which will undergo not the resurrection associated with Easter but rather the fate of an Easter egg—an object already emptied of its contents, hollowed out, filled with nothing, and, finally, shattered.

The approach to the caves intensifies the view of man as small, impotent, and unattractive that began with Forster's description of Chandrapore. The visitors are in a state appropriate to the vision that awaits them: they are at "half pressure" (p. 228), in a cocoon, existing without enthusiasm. Forster's language conveys a sense of indifference and fatalism. The characters are without control of their destinies: "no one was enthusiastic, yet it took place" (p. 120). The apathy is part of a general phenomenon, a condition of human life.

The environment echoes the apathy of the characters, as Forster interprets the general disappointment and connects the scene with ultimate value:

> It was as if virtue had failed in the celestial fount. The hues in the east decayed, the hills seemed dimmer though in fact better lit, and a profound disappointment entered with the morning breeze. Why, when the chamber was prepared, did the bridegroom not enter with trumpets and shawms, as humanity expects? The sun rose without splendour. He was presently observed trailing yellowish behind the trees, or against insipid sky, and touching the bodies already at work in the fields. [P. 129]

The reader who immediately notices the difference between this view of nature and the English landscapes and sunrises of the earlier novels finds the comparison made explicit, as Mrs. Moore invokes Grasmere and the narrator comments: "Romantic yet manageable, it sprang from a kindlier planet" (p. 130). Forster's diction conveys a sense of anticlimax that maintains the tone of his earlier description of the caves, where "the visitor returns to Chandrapore uncertain whether he has had an interesting experience or a dull one or any experience at all" (p. 117). Here the rhetorical question "Why . . . did the bridegroom not enter . . . ?" generalizes the characters' experience of the sunrise to the expectations of all people. Following his characterization of the scene as the failure of virtue in the celestial fount, Forster's question links the disappointed hope of humanity to the absence of divinity.

The narrator's language maintains the sense of anticlimax and foreboding. The approach to the caves rings with "a spiritual silence": "Life went on as usual, but had no consequences, that is to say, sounds did not echo or thoughts develop. Everything seemed cut off at its root, and therefore infected with illusion" (p. 132). Such words as "confusion," "capriciously," "dead and quiet," "unhealthily" seem premonitory. Irregular and inexplicable phenomena accompany the travelers and increase the sense of insecurity: films of heat radiate from the precipices and jump, the plain suddenly "quietly disappeared" (p. 133). The narrator's similes again suggest the generalized significance: "It was as if the contents of the corridor had never been changed" (p. 133). But the characters themselves either notice nothing, like Aziz, or translate their unease into general doubt about the project and longing for the concrete—specifically, they desire something with attributes, like a mosque.

Forster renders the antivision of the caves through an echo that returns the same sound, dull and hollow like the prevailing atmosphere, to all that is said. To Mrs. Moore, such an echo obliterates the distinction between good and evil and subjects

every generous belief and every human misery alike to universal reduction:

> . . . it had managed to murmur, "Pathos, piety, courage—they
> exist, but are identical, and so is filth. Everything exists, nothing
> has value." If one had spoken vileness in that place, or quoted
> lofty poetry, the comment would have been the same—"ou-
> boum." If one had spoken with the tongues of angels and pleaded
> for all the unhappiness and misunderstanding in the world, past,
> present, and to come, for all the misery men must undergo
> whatever their opinion and position, and however much they
> dodge or bluff—it would amount to the same, the serpent would
> descend and return to the ceiling. Devils are of the North, and
> poems can be written about them, but no one could romanticize
> the Marabar, because it robbed infinity and eternity of their
> vastness, the only quality that accommodates them to mankind.
> [Pp. 140–141]

The narrator's gloss develops Mrs. Moore's perception and
generalizes her response. The impersonal pronoun "one" implies that the echo and its obliteration of distinctions exists for
persons more articulate than Mrs. Moore, who can scarcely be
envisioned either speaking vileness or quoting poetry. Similarly, Mrs. Moore's compassion would not extend to past,
present, and future suffering: in enlarging the categories beyond
her capacity, Forster implies the Christian view. His paraphrase
of Saint Paul reiterates, in the context of the negative vision,
Mrs. Moore's earlier admonition to her son to have "Goodwill
and more goodwill and more goodwill. Though I speak with
the tongues of . . ." (p. 45).

The descending serpent derives from the narrator's immediately preceding description of the echo: "Even the striking of
a match starts a little worm coiling, which is too small to complete a circle, but is eternally watchful. And if several people
talk at once an overlapping howling noise begins, echoes generate echoes, and the cave is stuffed with a snake composed of
small snakes, which writhe independently" (p. 139). The connection of snakes with the striking of a match recalls the little

flames that strive to meet but are forever incomplete, balked by the imprisoning stone walls of the cave. The flames make an incomplete circle, an image that suggests ideas of separation and limitation. The flame is specifically associated with the idea of the human ego; as such it has appeared earlier as the "little ineffectual unquenchable flames" that represent the individual egos of Aziz's friends, alternately benevolent and quarrelsome, who group about his bed expressing themselves "each according to his capacity" (p. 98), before they disperse to lose their individuality in the common menace of the Indian climate. Worms and snakes, then, connect with flame: they represent the limitations and separations of individual personality. That this is so the aural counterpart of the flames emphasizes: human speech creates snakes also, the many voices become "a snake composed of small snakes, which writhe independently" (p. 139). Forster's image reduces the importance of individuality, even as he emphasizes the existence of many petty egos that guard their separations by being "eternally watchful" (p. 139).

As the snake metaphor continues, Mrs. Moore's "boum" is the serpent that descends from the ceiling. And in contrast to the ideas of eternity and infinity, which the images of arch and echo seek to define as they create an ever enlarging series, the Marabar makes everything small. Infinity and eternity alike reduce to the same dull sound, are transmuted into the "serpent" that arises from the expression of any sound in a Marabar cave.

Christianity falls in the general melee, and the cause of Mrs. Moore's disturbance seems understandable enough. Whether or not the caves, devoid of attributes as Forster emphasizes, represent the absolute Brahman is less important than the fact that the echo returns the same sound to whatever is proffered and comes through to Mrs. Moore as the collapse of all distinctions. If good and evil are the same, then, as she perceives it, "everything exists, nothing has value" (p. 140).

From Genesis to the crucifixion, "boum" obliterates the significance of Western religion. Although Mrs. Moore has been predisposed to this insight by age and illness, its reality does not depend on her limited perceptions. Not only she, but "no one could romanticize the Marabar." Furthermore, although the cave symbology expresses Mrs. Moore's despairing insight, Forster suggests that it is a more general contemporary phenomenon.

> She had come to that state where the horror of the universe and its smallness are both visible at the same time—the twilight of the double vision in which so many elderly people are involved. If this world is not to our taste, well, at all events there is Heaven, Hell, Annihilation—one or other of those large things, that huge scenic background of stars, fires, blue or black air. All heroic endeavour, and all that is known as art, assumes that there is such a background, just as all practical endeavour, when the world is to our taste, assumes that the world is all. But in the twilight of the double vision a spiritual muddledom is set up for which no high-sounding words can be found; we can neither act nor refrain from action, we can neither ignore nor respect Infinity. [Pp. 197–198]

Mrs. Moore had sought unity, but the collapse of distinctions has increased her own separateness from her fellows and from God. Her own smallness intensified, her condition finds expression in egotism.

> What had spoken to her in that scoured-out cavity of the granite? What dwelt in the first of the caves? Something very old and very small. Before time, it was before space also. Something snub-nosed, incapable of generosity—the undying worm itself. . . . The abyss also may be petty, the serpent of eternity made of maggots. [P. 198]

Reiterating the writhing snakes and the descending serpent of the caves, the imagery of worm, maggot, and serpent associates Mrs. Moore herself with the pettiness of evil.

E. K. Brown has amply described the double function of the echo symbol, which both expresses the quest for an absolute and symbolizes the evil consequences that issue from the caves.[8] It remains to emphasize what Forster has so carefully elaborated in the action: that, as Godbole notes, all participate in the evil, and the echo is only a reverberation of what the characters themselves have brought to the caves. Thus Mrs. Moore, old, ill, already predisposed to a negative insight, reads the echo as a denial of all her values and retreats into egocentric self-absorption. Adela, insistently rationalizing the prospect of a loveless marriage, experiences the psychic reduction of love in a church to love in a cave, and projects her repressed feelings onto Aziz. Until she can clear herself of delusion, the echo remains in her head.

Like the echo, the characters' visions, insights, distortions, and failures of imagination produce evil consequences. Adela's hysteria sets in motion the jingoism of the Anglo-Indian rulers; the Indian resistance resounds with an equal force of suspicion and hatred. Fielding, whose humanistic Western virtues are not equal to the powers of irrational evil, is nevertheless aware of what he faces: "the evil was propagating in every direction, it seemed to have an existence of its own, apart from anything that was done or said by individuals" (p. 178). The echo circulates among the minds of the characters. Adela's reflections on it reproduce Fielding's observation on the madness that is abroad—"Evil was loose . . . she could even hear it entering the lives of others. . . ." (p. 185). Fielding generalizes the echo's significance to the social and political situation, encompassing a world from which the "invisible power" that once checked evil is absent: "in the old eighteenth century, when cruelty and injustice raged, an invisible power repaired their ravages. Everything echoes now; there's no stopping the echo. The original sound may be harmless, but the echo is always evil" (p. 264).

The vision of the caves influences the action to the end.

8. Brown, *Rhythm in the Novel*, pp. 98–103.

Although Aziz is cleared of the charges against him, his unity with Fielding is doomed. The decency that impels Fielding, after the trial, to protect Adela from the quixotic behavior of the mob results in Aziz's groundless belief that Fielding intends himself to marry her for her money. Aziz and Fielding can ultimately be reconciled only because they both come to recognize that their friendship has no place in the world. Thus the novel's major attempt at "connection," at the triumph of personal relationships that in earlier novels was Forster's path to ultimate value, ends in failure. Mrs. Moore's death signifies, in this substantial way at least, the finality of her vision.

The separations increase as the lines re-form. Adela gives up her attempt to see the "real" India and returns to the West. A new and equally obtuse imperial administration replaces the old. English and Indians are politically and personally as isolated as before, and although after the trial Indians make attempts to preserve the precarious unity they have attained in opposing the British, by the novel's end these are as ephemeral as any of the other human efforts. The action itself offers little ground for hope, provides small counterweight to the vision of meaninglessness that the caves imply as the prevailing condition of contemporary life.

Is this, then, Forster's final message? Does the negative vision provide the only answer to the pervading quest for divine order? Does an opposing view supersede the nullifying insight of the Marabar, or does it merely raise other possibilities? In the continuing controversy over readings of *A Passage to India*, what evidence and what means suggest the nature of Forster's intention? Several aspects of the novel provide a limited redemption from despair. In the culmination of the rhythmically developed ideas and images that have animated the novel, Forster presents some resolution of his metaphysical problem. Controlling both the description and the thematic implications of setting, his narrative voice combines with the accumulating repetitions of idea and image, to extend and counter the significance of the caves with an alternative vision.

In its evocation of the multifarious aspects of the Indian setting, Forster's narrative voice extends the actual cast of characters. The inclusion of vivid and disparate forms of life suggests a unity that counters Aziz's perception of the disunity of India and transcends Mrs. Moore's negating vision. Forster includes in this world the water-chestnut gatherer in Fielding's tank, who experiences with delight what produces confusion and foreboding in the Western characters; he celebrates also the punkah wallah, whose inarticulate sexuality rebukes the frenetic appellants who share the courtroom with him; he limns the missionaries, rejected for their unconventionality by the official British and despised by the Indians for their ineffectiveness; to these he adds unnamed characters who enlarge the frame of reference and show the global nature of his purview, the people who awake as Mrs. Moore and her household go to sleep. Then there is the natural world of squirrels and birds, participants also in the universal quest, reliant for expression of their existence and claims on the narrator. The mangy squirrel who clings to a tree is "in tune with the infinite" (p. 105). The unnamed bird that piques the categorizing curiosities of Ronny and Adela is part of the Indian condition, which foils definitive answers: he is "unidentifiable" (p. 78). Brahmany bulls, elephants, "impartial" kites, wasps, the fish who wriggle into the mud and survive the hot season better than men—all these are part of the Indian universe.

Despite nature's indifference and hostility to man, despite the absence of harmony, the Indian setting nevertheless represents a whole, a cosmos that includes birds, snakes, men, stars, railways, caves, and stones. The animation of the natural universe which the olive trees of *Where Angels Fear to Tread* suggest has become explicit in *A Passage to India*, and Forster as narrator directs its dramatization. "The air felt like a warm bath into which hotter water is trickling constantly, the temperature rose and rose, the boulders said, 'I am alive,' the small stones answered, 'I am almost alive'" (p. 142). This dialogue of the stones sheds light on a later passage in which Fielding and Hamidullah commiserate rather lukewarmly on the death of Mrs. Moore. The passage, which deserves quotation for its pertinence in illustrating a concept of the oneness of the universe, has acquired some notoriety as a result of F. R. Leavis's misunderstanding.[9] "If for a moment the sense of communion in sorrow came to them, it passed. How indeed is it possible for one human being to be sorry for all the sadness that meets him on the face of the earth, for the pain that is endured not only by men, but by animals and plants, and perhaps by the stones?" (p. 235). The appearance of plants and stones in this catalogue in conjunction with the idea of pain implies the inclusion of all matter in a common fate. This attribution of feeling to plants and particularly to stones (which disturbed Leavis) is a logical extension of the stones' earlier assertion that they are alive. The inclusion of stones implies the transcendence of categories and distinctions, exlusions and separations, and these extend to matter as well as applying to the separations among men. Although God can comprehend all matter in his divine love, man's reason balks at the incongruities. Thus, although stones appear in both passages, the little stones of the first description are not quite alive. Their qualified claim indicates that man cannot quite transcend his rational faculties to accept the unity of all matter. Similarly, the "perhaps" with which Forster hedges the stones in the later passage indicates the uncertainty of man's capacity to comprehend such a unity as well as the vision's conditional nature.

That "stones" figure in such a conception, however, is suggested throughout. Stone is an elemental form of matter. The Marabar caves are made of stone and represent a primal reality. Prehistoric, "older than all spirit" (p. 117), stone shells, devoid of attributes, they enclose nothing. But the terrifying vision they engender must figure in any comprehensive view of reality. Stones are also part of the Indian environment, and as

9. F. R. Leavis, "E. M. Forster," in *Forster*, ed. Bradbury, pp. 44–45.

such they are sometimes hostile to man. They are the little "surprises" that impede walkers; they "exhaust" vulnerable humanity (p. 13). Thus Aziz, the more hindered because he is wearing pumps, stops to rest at a mosque. As a consequence he meets Mrs. Moore, and the results of this encounter illustrate another aspect of the oneness of the universe, the participation of all in good or evil actions. Here the stones, in creating discomfort, help engender a crucial friendship. Later Mrs. Moore herself participates in Aziz's evil fate by staying behind when he and Adela enter the caves.

Stones are associated with emptiness and aridity, with the absence of civilization. Fielding, disappointed at the apparent failure of his burgeoning intimacy with Aziz, is about to leave the Indian's bungalow, when Aziz suddenly recalls him to show Fielding a portrait of his dead wife. The older man is "astonished, as a traveller who suddenly sees, between the stones of the desert, flowers" (p. 107). When later Adela makes a tactless remark to Aziz, her error breaks up "their civilization, it almost had been—which scattered like the petals of a desert flower" (p. 137).

Aziz's party toils over "unattractive stones" as they climb to the caves. A stone is implicated in Adela's sudden moment of vision—her realization that she does not love Ronny: "as she toiled over a rock that resembled an inverted saucer, she thought, 'What about love?'" (p. 143). The footholds in the rock have impelled Adela's question. They signify, Forster tells us, the patterns made by the Nawab Bahadur's tires as his car hit an unknown animal. The instinctual, subconscious awareness of truth that this connection implies is an implacable obstacle to Adela's rationalization, a counter to the spurious unity that the accident caused between her and Ronny, a fundamental, disagreeable reality. Adela tries unsuccessfully to exclude the message of the stone from her life; the consequence is hallucination and echo.

On the approach to the caves, Adela has expressed her troubled preoccupation with love and sex by asking Aziz if he has more than one wife. Forster couples her loneliness and isolation with the setting—Adela asks her offensive question, "having no one else to speak to on that eternal rock" (p. 144). Stone is also in this connection a timeless, unyielding reality, of which a view of the universe must take account.

The effect of India's climate on the capacity of man to arrange his own destiny is to paralyze his efforts: "The triumphant machine of civilization may suddenly hitch and be immobilized into a car of stone" (p. 201). Stone here symbolizes the implacable reality of nature, against which man's will is a feeble exercise. Forster also suggests the impotence of man's creation, the machine, by comparing it with and then translating it into the impervious natural element.

Stones, finally, reappear in the Temple section, where they are absorbed into suggestions of reconciliation and unity. In a much discussed passage, Professor Godbole includes Mrs. Moore and a wasp in his love, impelling them "by his spiritual force to that place where completeness can be found" (p. 277). The wasp is perched on a stone, but here Godbole's human limitations intervene: "—could he . . . no, he could not, he had been wrong to attempt the stone, logic and conscious effort had seduced" (p. 277). Godbole's capacity to comprehend a vision of cosmic unity is the greatest of any character, yet he balks at the stone. The complete vision is beyond human capacity. But the narrator implies the inclusion of stones in his description of the ceremonial moment of Krishna's birth:

> Infinite Love took upon itself the form of SHRI KRISHNA, and saved the world. All sorrow was annihilated, not only for Indians, but for foreigners, birds, caves, railways, and the stars; all became joy, all laughter; there had never been disease nor doubt, misunderstanding, cruelty, fear. [P. 278]

However impossible of analysis, however evanescent, the momentary apprehension of a world united through divine love requires all matter (the caves being stone) in its catalogue to achieve "completeness, not reconstruction" (p. 277). As the divisions of the daily world return, stones resume their intractability to man's efforts at unity. At the novel's end, stones help thwart the possibilities for friendship between Fielding and Aziz: "But the horses didn't want it—they swerved apart; the earth didn't want it, sending up rocks through which riders must pass single-file" (p. 312). The setting of India, dominant in its influence, personified and dramatized by Forster's narrative voice, has the last word:

> . . . the temples, the tank, the jail, the palace, the birds, the carrion, the Guest House, that came into view as they issued from the gap and saw Mau beneath: they didn't want it, they said in their hundred voices, "No, not yet," and the sky said, "No, not there." [P. 312]

With this we seem returned to Mrs. Moore's negating vision in the cave. Her own course, however, suggests that although her weakened frame could not sustain the effects of the nullifying echo, the vision was not final. For after she leaves Chandrapore, Mrs. Moore begins to move out of her solipsism toward a new objectivity: "She watched the indestructible life of man and his changing faces, and the houses he has built for himself and for God, and they appeared to her not in terms of her own trouble but as things to see" (p. 199). The hundred Indias, the reappearing scenes that insist "I do not vanish" imply an inclusive vision, and Mrs. Moore's beginning apprehension of this seems clear. As Forster animates the landscape in disavowal of the finality of her negative vision, Mrs. Moore indicates in her curiosity the distance she has traveled from despair to hope.

> "I have not seen the right places," she thought. . . . she longed to stop, though it was only Bombay, and disentangle the hundred Indias that passed each other in its streets. . . . thousands of cocoanut palms appeared all round the anchorage and

climbed the hills to wave her farewell. "So you thought an echo
was India; you took the Marabar Caves as final?" they laughed.
"What have we in common with them, or they with Asirgarh?
Good-bye!" [Pp. 199–200]

Mrs. Moore's vision remains incomplete, for she does not
long survive her movement toward reconciliation. Forster must
use other means, and, as with the stones, he moves toward
resolution by the development of recurring motifs whose meanings increase with the evolving action. One such is the echo,
which continues to function in a complex manner. Symbolic of
the quest for a divine reality behind ever-receding forms of
appearance, the echo has emerged from the Marabar caves as a
symbol of evil. As answer to the cosmic question, it offers the
annihilation of meaning. But even as jingoism and hostility
spread through Chandrapore in the wake of the Marabar incident, countermovements begin that will ultimately vanquish
the echo from the caves. Forster's repetitions, themselves echoing earlier usages, develop a meaning made greater through its
connections. When Mrs. Moore, sunk in depression, asserts
Aziz's innocence, "her mind seemed to move towards them
from a great distance and out of darkness" (p. 195). Even here
her instinctive knowledge begins to combat Adela's delusion:
Mrs. Moore's belief has an alleviating though temporary effect
on the echo that resounds in Adela's head. But in the courtroom, Mrs. Moore herself becomes an echo: invoked as a witness, she reappears as "Esmiss Esmoor." The chanting of her
name in the courtroom impels Adela to a similar place of vision: "A new and unknown sensation protected her, like magnificent armour. She didn't think what had happened, or even
remember in the ordinary way of memory, but she returned to
the Marabar Hills, and spoke from them across a sort of darkness to Mr. McBryde" (p. 216). In the presence of truth,
Adela is able to dispel her echo. The waves of evil recede, although not without their toll of "the residue of the Marabar."

In the final section of *A Passage to India,* Mrs. Moore reappears, again as an echo when Aziz hears her name in the interstices of the Krishna chant. Here the echo participates in a synthesis of all the earlier elements into a momentary vision of completion. Caves are included in the reconciliation, and the cycle in which they figured so destructively ends. Like the God, Mrs. Moore comes. As she seeks the God, Godbole comes to her. The earlier echoes that asked about divine presence are stilled in the momentary assurance of unity, and matter is comprehended in a transcendent vision of divine love. The Hindu celebration reaches a climax with the immersion of Fielding, Ralph and Stella Moore, and Aziz in the water of Mau's tank. The moment is accompanied by "an immense peal of thunder, unaccompanied by lightning, [that] cracked like a mallet on a dome" (p. 305). The "dome" recalls the overarching sky of the quest for an absolute, and the sound is significantly devoid of an echo. This is as final a suggestion as Forster makes, and it is tempered as always by the conditional: "That was the climax, as far as India admits of one" (p. 305).

Linked to the echo symbolism is the motif of appeal that voices the pervading desire for divine presence and seeks to bridge the prevailing chaos with hope of a divine order. Moving between the polarities of Mrs. Moore's nihilistic vision and the affirmation embodied in the Krishna ceremony, the appeals demonstrate above all that the prevailing condition of life on earth is contingency. Thus, of what use, Forster asks, are light, bell, or brake to a cyclist "in a land where the cyclist's only hope is to coast from face to face, and just before he collides with each it vanishes?" (pp. 10–11). The association of "only hope" with "land" suggests India's need. She entreats relief from her chaos: though practiced in an existence that depends on forces outside human will, her inhabitants have no control over their destinies. To a degree this is Forster's point, seen elsewhere, about the insecurity of life, but India is at once the context and symbol of a helplessness that has become the dominant characteristic of existence. Luck, not virtue, provides the only hope.

When early in the action Aziz stands by a mosque and contemplates "the complex appeal of the night" (p. 14), the array of smells and sounds that calls to him encompasses man and nature, East and West, life and death. The calls that resound through the novel usually bring no response. All versions of appeal have in common the elusiveness of the object. Thus Aziz tries to recall his dead wife, "not realizing that the very fact that we have loved the dead increases their unreality, and that the more passionately we invoke them the further they recede" (p. 50). More centrally, man's appeal to deity goes unanswered, as Godbole's song illustrates.

Godbole's entreaty at the tea party is premonitory: occasioned by the coalescence of caves and human muddle, the appeal to the absent God permeates the developing action. Godbole has announced that his song is "composed in a raga appropriate to the present hour, which is the evening" (p. 72). When, shortly, Ronny and Adela talk, Adela finds "no point in being disagreeable to him and formulating her complaints against his character at this hour of the day, which was the evening" (p. 75). Forster's language echoes Godbole's remark about the "appropriateness" of his appeal. The song has been followed by a moment of total silence, a moment of nothingness. Ronny and Adela are heavy in spirit, the sun is "declining" (p. 75), the trees hold a "premonition of night" (p. 75). Ronny and Adela's confused course, which will end in their misconceived engagement, is "appropriate" (p. 85) to a situation from which the god is absent.

When, moments later, Ronny and Adela ride without enthusiasm in the Nawab Bahadur's car, the theme of Godbole's raga reappears. The vast and inferior landscape mirrors the prevailing human inadequacy and similarly entreats divine presence; "In vain did each item in it call out, 'Come, come.'

There was not enough god to go round" (p. 79). With the accident on the Marabar road that results in Ronny and Adela's spurious unity, Forster again invokes the language of Godbole's raga, reiterating the "appropriateness" of divine absence in such a circumstance: "Neither had foreseen such a consequence. She had meant to revert to her former condition of important and cultivated uncertainty, but it had passed out of her reach at its appropriate hour" (p. 85).

Appeals appear in comic variation, permeating the Indian environment. Thus, Ronny summons his servant:

> "Krishna!" Krishna was the peon who should have brought the files from his office. He had not turned up, and a terrific row ensued. . . . Servants, quite understanding, ran slowly in circles, carrying hurricane lamps. Krishna the earth, Krishna the stars replied, until the Englishman was appeased by their echoes. [P. 88]

Though the context appears trivial, Forster's symbols reiterate the major themes, and the incident itself follows the pattern of other appeals to the god. The servants run in circles—a recurring image that implies the search for completion, they carry lamps, which recall the stars of the opening chapter and imply a firmament that in fact appears in the next sentence. Ronny's calls echo outward to infinity, and like the god, the absent Krishna does not respond.

India is a land where masters can call and not call, servants hear and not hear (p. 92), where everything is ambiguous, indefinable, constantly altering, and illusory or real, depending on one's perspective. In such a context, appeals reflect the prevailing conditionality. Aziz, beseiged by his friend Hamidullah's wife's insistence that he marry, responds, " 'Perhaps . . . but later . . .' his invariable reply to such an appeal" (p. 9).

Appeal figures in the familiar context of human invitations and rejections. The different church bells call respectively to Anglo-India and to mankind. To the Moslems, Godbole becomes tinged with political miasma when he seeks another Hindu as physician. "Everybody looked and felt shocked, but Professor Godbole had diminished his appeal by linking himself with a co-religionist. He moved them less than when he had appeared as a suffering individual. Before long they began to condemn him as a source of infection" (p. 96).

Art expresses the human need for divine reassurance. Aziz's recitation to his friends is such an appeal.

> The poem had done no "good" to anyone, but it was a passing reminder, a breath from the divine lips of beauty, a nightingale between two worlds of dust. Less explicit than the call to Krishna, it voiced our loneliness nevertheless, our isolation, our need for the Friend who never comes yet is not entirely disproved. [P. 97]

This passage moves to the heart of Forster's concern. The narrator combines a triple series of nouns, "loneliness," "isolation," and the culminating "need" with the concept of the deity: the "Friend," as Aziz elsewhere informs Fielding, is "a Persian expression for God" (p. 265). Again one is left with the overwhelming sense of the conditional: the only thing certain is uncertainty, yet this enables one to continue calling for the God.

Thus, aware that the God will remain absent, Godbole continues to entreat His presence. His serenity rests on two major premises. The first is that "nothing can be performed in isolation. All perform a good action, when one is performed, and when an evil action is performed, all perform it" (pp. 168). Following from this, "When evil occurs, it expresses the whole of the universe. Similarly when good occurs" (p. 169). By such an account, all are implicated in the events of the Marabar, as the action itself demonstrates. The second tenet of Godbole's religious belief is expressed in his ability to distinguish between good and evil and yet to comprehend both.

"Good and evil are different, as their names imply. But, in my own humble opinion, they are both of them aspects of my Lord. He is present in the one, absent in the other, and the difference between presence and absence is great, as great as my feeble mind can grasp. Yet absence implies presence, absence is not non-existence, and we are therefore entitled to repeat, 'Come, come, come.' " [P. 169]

Bridging absence and presence, the appeals continue. An appeal to Mrs. Moore presents a muted and ironic counterpoint to Aziz's trial. The British are responsible for her invocation, an action that contravenes their own interest in convicting Aziz. Mrs. Moore as Hindu goddess is a not inappropriate "travesty," because she has been closest of any Western character to the Hindu identification of divine love with all matter. Mrs. Moore herself cannot come, not only because she is on a ship bound for England, but because she is dead, a fact known only to Forster, who withholds it here from characters and reader alike. Now summoned by the Indian populace, she "comes" to rescue her friend. The powers of love and truth have prevented a travesty of justice.

But Esmiss Esmoor cannot prevent the effects of the residue of the Marabar—a near riot at the Minto hospital, in which "the spirit of evil again strode abroad" (p. 224), continuation of a supercilious English officialism, and most important, the disintegration of the friendship between Aziz and Fielding. Ironic and thwarted appeals accompany the process. Forster places his characters in the position of the God, a role they are unable to assume—illustrating once again the human separation from meaning. Meeting Adela after the trial, Hamidullah is cold, even cruel to her, and Forster explains that if Adela had appealed to him, had "shown emotion in court, broke down, beat her breast, and invoked the name of God . . . ," Hamidullah would perhaps have placed himself in the position of the Divinity, for "she would have summoned forth his imagination and

generosity—he had plenty of both" (p. 233). When Ronny
arrives, Hamidullah's sardonic exclamation, "He comes, he
comes, he comes" (p. 234), repeats the religious summons.
Fielding influences Aziz to let Adela off paying compensation
money by appealing to the memory of Mrs. Moore, a deliberate manipulation that produces the desired result but also
furthers Aziz's suspicion that Fielding wants to marry Adela
himself.

The appeals that sound through the novel culminate in the
Temple section, where without deliberation or volition—and
part of Forster's message is that man cannot will his own salvation—Godbole sees the entreating image of Mrs. Moore. She
"happened to occur among the throng of soliciting images, a
tiny splinter" (p. 277). Transcending in his religious ecstasy the
limitations of his daily humanity, Godbole answers the appeal.
His response both echoes and completes his earlier explanation
of the legitimacy of appeal.

> He was a Brahman, she Christian, but it made no difference, it
> made no difference whether she was a trick of his memory or a
> telepathic appeal. It was his duty, as it was his desire, to place
> himself in the position of the God and to love her, and to place
> himself in her position and to say to the God, "Come, come,
> come." [P. 281]

It has already been noted that although Godbole includes in his
love both Mrs. Moore and a wasp she had previously blessed,
his human limits balk at the stone on which the wasp is seated.
But that his act implies some measure of resolution, the repeated associations and images suggest, the action demonstrates, and Forster's comments on the genuine if evanescent
unity achieved by the Krishna festival, imply.

Thus, where the original wasp "clung" to a peg, Mrs. Moore
has "round her clinging forms of trouble." Reiterated and amplified, the original association finds embodiment in the action.
Ralph Moore and Aziz meet as Ralph is stung by bees. Their

relationship begins with trouble, for Aziz is hostile and cruel; but Ralph's challenging directness, similar to his mother's insight, allows the cycle that began at the Chandrapore mosque to find completion in the meaning of the temple at Mau, to which Ralph himself becomes, as Aziz recognizes, a "guide."[10] For the characters, the Marabar is wiped out in the mutual understanding of Aziz and Ralph and the renewed though valedictory friendship of Fielding and Aziz. In the jubilation of the Hindu festival, the Marabar is drowned, and the actual immersion of Aziz, Fielding, and the younger Moores in the Mau tank marks the disorganized culmination of an affirmed unity that can exist only in the paradox of its temporary nature, and can be expressed only in itself. Of the moment of Krishna's birth that unites all matter in a vision of divine love, Forster says: "not only from the unbeliever are mysteries hid, but the adept himself cannot retain them. He may think, if he chooses, that he has been with God, but, as soon as he thinks it, it becomes history, and falls under the rules of time" (p. 178). Finally, in the symbolic sacrifice of the God himself, the counterpart of Godbole's abnegation of personality to achieve a limited version of divine love, Forster describes the unity that is both real and inaccessible:

> Thus was He thrown year after year, and were others thrown— little images of Ganpati, baskets of ten-day corn, tiny tazias after Mohurram—scapegoats, husks, emblems of passage; a passage not easy, not now, not here, not to be apprehended except when it is unattainable: the God to be thrown was an emblem of that. [P. 304]

The paradoxical, ungraspable nature of this vision returns us once more to the idea of conditionality. Like the reiterations of appeal, but with a more restricted focus, Forster's rhythmic uses of the word "perhaps" render the dominance of contin-

10. P. N. Furbank sees Ralph as a young Forster. See P. N. Furbank, *E. M. Forster: A Life*, Vol. 1 (London: Secker & Warburg, 1977), p. 262.

gency. In the deliberate ambiguities of "perhaps," Forster implies a multiple sense of possibility, the simultaneous existence of a complex array of motives or factors, the difficulty of rational comprehension of the universe, and the limitations of man's ability to achieve earthly unity or comprehend a divine one.

Many of the contexts in which "perhaps" occurs are comic and apparently trivial. But the associations invariably have deeper connections. Forster tells us, for example, that Mrs. Moore's famous wasp "perhaps" thought the peg he had occupied was a branch, because "no Indian animal has any sense of an interior" (p. 29). Animals do not differentiate man's order from theirs: to them he is just another creature, and his distinctions are irrelevant to the natural world. "Perhaps" in this context serves the theme of man's separations and exclusions which contrast with the lower animals' instinctive perception of unity, an awareness that in her loving benediction, Mrs. Moore shares. "Perhaps" is again associated with man's exclusions when Forster comments, "All invitations must proceed from heaven perhaps; perhaps it is futile for men to initiate their own unity" (p. 32). Here the conditional mitigates the finality of a statement that would otherwise have the effect of a verdict.

As we have elsewhere seen, truth in India is elusive, conditional, and largely unknowable. The Russell's viper that appeared in the Government College classroom of an unpopular master "perhaps" "had crawled in of itself, but perhaps it had not" (p. 166). At the trial, a comment about Adela's ugliness "fell from nowhere, from the ceiling, perhaps. . . . One of the native policemen took hold of a man who had said nothing, and turned him out roughly" (p. 208). One notes about this passage the ascendancy of truth of mood over truth of fact: ejecting someone from the courtroom satisfied the English need for decisiveness and identification, but the remark that fell from "nowhere" expresses a truth to which this kind of identification is irrelevant. More important is the coalescence, in this brief incident, of "nowhere," "perhaps," and "nothing," thus connecting the essential quality of the caves with the conditional and unknowable nature of truth.

The human capacity to envision a cosmic unity is partial: as noted earlier, this is the meaning of the "perhaps" that qualifies Forster's attribution of pain to stones. Forster's narrative voice is essential to these insights, for the characters can apprehend them far less than he. Thus the narrator is predominantly the source of "perhaps" in the novel. Whereas Fielding and Adela cannot even conceptualize the important questions, the narrator simultaneously passes judgment on their limited consciousnesses and voices the problem.

> Were there worlds beyond which they could never touch, or did all that is possible enter their consciousness? They could not tell. They only realized that their outlook was more or less similar, and found in this a satisfaction. Perhaps life is a mystery, not a muddle; they could not tell. Perhaps the hundred Indias which fuss and squabble so tiresomely are one, and the universe they mirror is one. They had not the apparatus for judging. [P. 251]

The conditional always recalls the limitations of human awareness and capacity. "Before birds, perhaps . . ." (p. 138), the planet must have looked like the approach to the Marabar. The assurance that sounds in Forster's voice throughout the novel expresses his certainty that cosmic answers are not available to man. If "proportion" is to be found anywhere in *A Passage to India*, perhaps it is revealed in the way Forster balances between the powerful negation of the Marabar and the reconciling but transitory assertion of divine unity at Mau. Exemplifying this is a question that, although a whimsical inversion of Mrs. Moore's fragile faith, far transcends whimsy in its implications: "God si Love. Is this the final message of India?" (p. 276).

Forster's reflection on the Hindu inscription implies both its

illustration of the prevailing contingency and the chaotic, topsy-
turvy quality of the Hindu forms. With this, we confront the
question of Forster's attitude to Hinduism and his intentions
regarding the character Godbole.

Godbole is able to comprehend metaphysical complexities
that elude the other characters. His disquisition on good and
evil provides the only direct clarification of the meaning of the
caves. When Fielding, depressed and irritated, is "obliged to
listen to a speech which lacked both basis and conclusion, and
floated through air" (p. 166). Forster affirms Godbole's sagac-
ity and depth: "no eye could see what lay at the bottom of the
Brahman's mind, and yet he had a mind and a heart too, and
all his friends trusted him, without knowing why" (p. 167).
Godbole's reasoned exposition is a refutation of Fielding's ex-
asperated comment that "everything is anything and nothing
something" (p. 169). At Godbole's first entrance, Forster has
associated him with harmony, "as if he had reconciled the
products of East and West, mental as well as physical, and
could never be discomposed" (p. 65). Finally, and most important, it is Godbole who is granted the reconciling vision.

Yet there is much to show that Forster draws back from a
full embrace of Hinduism. His treatment of Godbole is affectionate but detached. The old man changes the subject "in the
same breath, as if to cancel any beauty his words might have
contained" (p. 169). Godbole is as subject as any character to
the indignities that beset human frailty, as Dr. Panna Lal's
diagnosis amply demonstrates. Fielding's observation that for
the Hindu tranquility swallows everything else is borne out in
the details of Godbole's portrayal. He eats in apparent oblivion
to everyone and everything, he misses the crucial train to the
Marabar; he discourses obliquely and with evident triviality in
the face of Aziz's crisis. Forster observes that only a tiny fragment of Professor Godbole attends to worldly matters at all (p.
276), and the comic proof of this pudding is the conversion of
the King George V Emperor School, Godbole's major project

as newly appointed minister of education at Mau, to a granary.

It is true that such affirmation as exists occurs in the context of the Hindu metaphysic. But the gap between vision and achievement exists for all humanity, and the concept of unity is not presented as a solution translatable into action. Moreover, while Forster respects the inclusion of incongruity, merriment, joy, and vulgarity in the Hindu ritual, his development of its chaos and formlessness reveals his fundamental detachment.[11] Forster notes that "this approaching triumph of India was a muddle (as we call it), a frustration of reason and form" (p. 275). He qualifies any notion of climax—"as far as India admits of one" (p. 305), and the festival sums up as a "great blur" of which no one can locate the "emotional centre" (p. 306). This does not vitiate the vision, but it separates Forster's narrative voice from participation in the Hindu aesthetic, even as he insists on the relativism of the Western view—"as we call it." Forster's Western orientation similarly dominates his apprehension of Godbole's song, which he can describe only in the categories of Western music, to which it does not adhere: "The sounds continued and ceased after a few moments as casually as they had begun—apparently halfway through a bar, and upon the subdominant" (p. 72).

Stella Moore, who in her husband's words, is "after something" (p. 308), has discarded the Christianity her mother found wanting and likes Hinduism, but not its forms. In detailing the whimsy, the ineffectuality, and the formless fluidity of both Hindu ritual and the major Hindu character, Forster distances himself from their limitations and withholds endorsement of Hinduism as institution and panacea even as he synthesizes and renders the Hindu vision in its fullest meaning. I cannot agree

---

11. That his portrayal of the Hindu festival is far more sympathetic in *A Passage to India* than in his account in *The Hill of Devi*, I interpret to show not, as Alan Wilde believes, Forster's skill in hiding his real disapproval, but rather the extent to which he supports the spiritual implications of the festival by emphasizing the benignity and joy of the occasion.

with James McConkey that Godbole is "the character-equiv-
alent of the Forsterian voice,"[12] because Forster's voice so transcends Godbole in its comprehensive articulation of a conditional order in the universe and at the same time reduces Godbole, through his particular inadequacies, to the level of the
other characters. Hinduism furnishes Forster with the metaphor of inclusiveness, but no system receives his unqualified
endorsement.

Through the Hindu celebration at Mau, then, Forster makes
explicit the conception of a divine unity that counters the message of the caves. The vision is Janus-faced: in an interview with
Angus Wilson, Forster himself referred to Mrs. Moore's experience as "the vision with its back turned,"[13] and Alan Wilde records Forster as having called the Temple episode Mrs. Moore's
vision "turned inside out."[14] The caves reduce all diversity and
distinction to a single dull sound and collapse the temporal and
spatial categories by which human beings try to order their
perceptions. Characterized by "nothing," the caves transform
the impulses of the phenomenological world in their image:
"everything exists, nothing has value." To this apocalyptic insight Forster offers an opposing vision that both includes and
transcends the nihilistic message of the caves by asserting essentially that "everything exists, everything has value." Thus
the catalogue of diverse elements—birds, railways, foreigners,
stars, stones—for whom "all sorrow is annihilated"; thus also
the necessary inclusion of the untouchable sweepers in the
ceremony of salvation. Thus, finally, the insistence on "completeness, not reconstruction." Neither Mrs. Moore nor the
wasp can be reconstructed, but they can be absorbed into a
vision that signifies a near-universal (balking the stone) ac-

12. James McConkey, *The Novels of E. M. Forster* (Ithaca: Cornell University Press, 1957), p. 11.
13. Angus Wilson, "A Conversation With E. M. Forster," *Encounter*, November 1957, p. 54.
14. Alan Wilde, *Art and Order* (New York: New York University Press,
1964), p. 151.

ceptance of all matter. Similarly, Fielding's well-intentioned attempt to "reconstruct" (p. 293) for Aziz the course of their misunderstanding has no relevance: it requires Ralph Moore's intuitive responsiveness to restore amity and bring the cycle to completion.

The cyclical nature of *A Passage to India* appears in the progressions of Forster's expanding imagery, in the thematic and structural categories of mosque, caves, temple, and the Indian seasons that move from an illusory calm to the destructive hot weather to the regenerating rainy season. In its climaxes and returns the action too illustrates the cyclical movement. Stella and Ralph represent an extension and rebirth of Mrs. Moore; through their appearance, the Marabar is wiped out. The union of Stella and Fielding, and most important, Stella's pregnancy, prefigure a new cycle and suggest the continuity that validates Mrs. Moore's final perception of "the indestructible life of man and his changing faces" (p. 199). In the midst of despair, amid the human chaos that India mirrors so faithfully, Forster has asserted that although God is "the unattainable Friend," he is nevertheless "the never-withdrawn suggestion that haunts our consciousness" (p. 106). The search for unity, finally, has achieved a momentary perception of divine order; evil is absorbed and transcended in a larger vision, the cycle has run its course.

Is *A Passage to India*, then, as Wilfred Stone believes, essentially a revelation of unity, a declaration of independence from earlier repressions, in which Forster displays "spiritual gusto" and immerses himself with "joy" in an orgy of "mud-bespattered hilarity"? Does Forster make less of the cleavages of men "than of the unity encircling them," less of the separations "than of the single context in which they exist"?[15] Some critics would deny what Stone's view assumes, that the novel should be read in terms of its climactic moments, and that one

15. Stone, *The Cave and the Mountain*, p. 303.

mood dominates.[16] But we may read the novel as process and at
the same time identify a pervading intention.

For although Forster suggests the existence of ultimate meaning, his characters grapple with a condition that seems rather
to deny meaning. Seen as a kind of coda to the prehistory that
produced the Marabar, the human span is insignificant. Man's
efforts have resulted merely in a cyclical succession of fruitless
conquests. Such as they were, the glories of man's history are
behind him. Aziz is a sentimental eulogizer, and the triumphs
of Babur and Alamgir have descended into the pettiness of
Anglo-Indian tensions and intra-Indian bickering. The English
are only the last of a series "who also entered the country with
intent to refashion it, but were in the end worked into its
pattern and covered with its dust" (p. 201).

Politics is reduced to "quarrels" that are "the malaise of men
who cannot find their way home" (p. 128). India is inaccessible
to the amenities of a vanished ideal, Edwardian Cambridge,
where "games, work, and pleasant society had interwoven, and
appeared to be sufficient substructure for a national life" (p.
98). Personal relationships cannot bridge the prevailing political atmosphere of "wire-pulling and fear" (p. 98). The dilemma
is paradoxical, for politics "ruin the character and career, yet
nothing can be achieved without them" (pp. 97–98). An end to
imperialism will not engender Indian unity: relieved of the English, the Indians will only reacquire their chronic disunities.
Hamidullah, "on his way to a worrying committee of notables,
nationalist in tendency," knows that "if the English were to
leave India the committee would vanish also" (p. 97). Personal
relationships are similarly transitory. The affirmation of unity
at Mau fades quickly to return us to the frustrations of human
reality. On his final ride with Fielding, Aziz "paused, and the

16. Alan Wilde, for example, reads the novel as process, describing its effect
as dependent not on the climactic moments of caves and temple but rather on
"those scenes, and they constitute the majority, in which it is less easy to find
a dominant mood" (*Art and Order*, p. 157).

scenery, though it smiled, fell like a gravestone on any human hope. . . . The divisions of daily life were returning, the shrine had almost shut" (p. 311).

The vanity of human wishes seems matched by the smallness of the characters, and some critics have complained that Forster's characters are insufficient to his theme. But against the idea of India, vast in scale, complex in its fragmentation, helplessness, and potential unity, the human characters are necessarily small: indeed this is the point. All of them share in the general reduction, to all he presents a detachment laced with irony. The characterizations are nevertheless noteworthy for their diversity and individuality.[17] Forster presents Ronny as arrogant but honest, small-minded but conscientious, human both in his irritation at an unfathomable and inconveniencing parent and in his attempt to see Adela through. The other Anglo-Indians are treated in less depth but with equal justice. Mr. Turton, for all his officialism, does not hate Indians. Forster comes close to approval of his courteous realism in managing the "Bridge Party"; yet the Collector is subject to the raging jingoism that besets English and Indians alike after the caves incident. McBryde, the police superintendent, is treated with sympathy as well as irony. He "was the most reflective and best educated of the Chandrapore officials. He had read and thought a good deal, and, owing to a somewhat unhappy marriage, had evolved a complete philosophy of life" (p. 158). But McBryde is salacious and cynical about Aziz, and Forster hoists him on his own petard by catching him in an illicit affair.

The portraits of the Indians are similarly diverse.[18] Hamidul-

17. The array of minor portraits refutes Frederick Crews's observation that "we become acquainted with a series of insignificant persons whose natures can be summed up in a phrase," *E. M. Forster: The Perils of Humanism* (Princeton: Princeton University Press, 1962), pp. 145–156.

18. Again, Forster's practice disproves Crews's assertion that except for Aziz and Godbole the Indians comprise "rows of characters whose nearly unanimous contempt for the English tends to blur their individuality" (ibid., p. 146).

lah, the Cambridge-educated lawyer, is sentimental about the British and intellectually closer to Fielding than is Aziz. The Nawab Bahadur, a copious mixture of superstition and shrewd-ness, political astuteness and verbose generosity, is a kind of counterpart to the Collector—more sympathetically treated, but aware, as is the English official, of the difficulties both sides must face. Ram Das, the beleaguered Hindu magistrate who presides at the trial, is a man of capacity and understanding. More straightforward and articulate than Aziz, he is a force for unity among Indians themselves. Indeed the only Indian char-acter whose contempt for the English is invariable is the coarse and conniving Mahmoud Ali, whose jealousy and jingoism con-tribute to the estrangement of Aziz and Fielding.

In considering Forster's attitudes toward his important char-acters, we may ask to what degree Fielding represents Forster's voice in the novel.[19] Forster clearly stands behind many of Fielding's perceptions and assessments. Intelligent and intuitive, Fielding is the best of Western rationalists, blessed with the capacity for affection, yet remaining in the Forster tradition of equivocal heroes for whom the world is a plunge beyond the capacities of a humanistic philosophy to mediate. Fielding, moreover, combines the best sensitivities of his forebears with the toughness they so conspicuously lack. Free of Philip's pre-tension and fastidiousness, more hard-bitten and realistic than Rickie, Fielding has managed to function among the trans-planted Sawstonites who are the Anglo-Indians of *A Passage to India* without losing his humanistic ideals, his sense of humor, and his emotional independence.

Yet in his treatment of Fielding, Forster reveals his authorial detachment and the character's limitations. Fielding's motto is "Great is information, and she shall prevail" (p. 181). With all his intelligence and sympathy, the Englishman cannot cope with

19. Alan Wilde, for example, interprets Forster's detachment from the "sub-rational" categories of Hinduism as an intense identification with Fielding (*Art and Order*, p. 149).

events or phenomena that defy rational explanation and reasonable solution. As he looks across from the verandah of the
club to the Marabar hills, they transmit a vision of his incompleteness, as powerful as the one that beset James's Strether in
The Ambassadors:

> . . . the cool benediction of the night descended, the stars spar-
> kled, and the whole universe was a hill. Lovely, exquisite mo-
> ment—but passing the Englishman with averted face and on
> swift wings. He experienced nothing himself; it was as if some-
> one had told him there was such a moment, and he was obliged
> to believe. And he felt dubious and discontented suddenly, and
> wondered whether he was really and truly successful as a human
> being. After forty years' experience, he had learned to manage
> his life and make the best of it on advanced European lines, had
> developed his personality, explored his limitations, controlled
> his passions—and he had done it all without becoming either
> pedantic or worldly. A creditable achievement, but as the mo-
> ment passed he felt he ought to have been working at something
> else the whole time—he didn't know at what, never would know,
> never could know, and that was why he felt sad. [P. 181]

Fielding, so superior to Adela Quested in his intuitive capacities, is reduced to her footing when confronted with the irrational. Forster's final judgment, that they are "dwarfs talking,
shaking hands" (p. 252), represents the chilling reduction of a
character whose capacities, infinitely greater than those of his
earlier versions, have become irrelevant to the contemporary
condition. Forster's most important humanistic hero, Fielding
embodies the "proportion" that represented moral success in
Howards End. But his wisdom, maturity, good will, and affection avail little. They do not allow him fulfillment in personal
relations; more significantly, they do not enable him even to
perceive the metaphysical question that animates the novel.

Forster's position as the unique interpreter of metaphysical
truths is not, of course, new. His moral and aesthetic distance
from the objects of his creation, however, reaches an unprece-
dented height in *A Passage to India,* and this distance is signif-

icantly paralleled by the situation of the character closest to
Forster's insight. The search for ultimate truth that began with
Philip Herriton's pilgrimage across Italy toward salvation has
led in *A Passage to India* to a vision whose agent, Godbole, is
notably detached from worldly matters. That Godbole's antics
are the object of his creator's comic irony reveals him as cast in
the same framework of limitation as the other characters. Withdrawal does not solve the political and social problems that the
efforts to create personal relationships have so conspicuously
failed to assuage. Yet although the moment is temporary,
Godbole participates in an experience of reconciliation whose
meaning lies in its analogy to the transcendent unity of divine
love. But more significant than the ephemerality of Godbole's
vision is the condition of its attainment. The possibility of insight can exist only through abnegation of self, through denial
of will, through withdrawal from personal engagement. The
attempts at human connection which the action sought unsuccessfully to sustain have yielded in the end to the tranquil
indifference of a character who has "never been known to tell
anyone anything" (p. 295). Detachment is thus seen as necessary to the inclusive vision that provides the only suggestion of
God's presence, the only redemption from the certain frustrations of human effort. Between the first novel and the last,
Forster has moved from the celebration to the abandonment of
personality. Whereas in the earlier novels he resisted asceticism
and withdrawal, the spiritual exploration of *A Passage to
India* ends uncomfortably with a vision that precludes achievement in the world of action, a unity whose condition is the
withdrawal from human concerns.

The implications of this radical change in position inform
the language of *A Passage to India*. Forster's prose retains the
comic irony, the deft reversals, the catalogues, the balanced
phrases, the logical discriminations, the juxtapositions of apparent incongruities that characterized his technique in the earlier novels. His narrative presence is equally pervasive. Nor is it

less didactic: it is only less personal. The impersonality that characterizes Forster's authorial presence in his final novel manifests itself in two major ways. The first appears in the combination of his narrative voice with the technique of purposeful repetitions of key words, images, and ideas—Forster's use of "rhythm." The second is to be found in the qualities of Forster's voice itself, as it simultaneously projects and embodies his bleak vision of man.

Voice and theme coalesce in the evocation of setting, as Forster presides directly over the Indian environment that engenders all the relevant terms of symbolic reference. The language of narration provides the images whose symbolic meaning evolves throughout the novel: the speaker's voice and the images it controls are integrated into a single context. At the same time, the purposeful repetitions create a new and impersonal sense of process and structure, in which such words as "caves," "arch," "echo," and "appeal" transcend their immediate contexts to acquire with each reappearance an increased breadth of suggestion and symbolic resonance.

Rhythm also appears in the novel in the simpler sense of beat or meter, and here too Forster replaces an earlier narrative directness with a different kind of emphasis. Repetitions of twos and threes play continuously around the major themes. Such rhythms may derive directly from the narrator, as when, describing the caves, Forster twice remarks on the "nothing, nothing" that characterizes them. They appear in the narrator's personification of setting—examples of this are the "pomper, pomper, pomper" of the train that accompanies the travelers to the Marabar, and the "ponk ponk" of tropical birds. They pass between narrator and characters, as the observation about the need for "kindness, more kindness, and even after that more kindness" moves from Aziz to Fielding to Forster's own voice. And they emanate directly from characters, as Aziz's furious "Madam! Madam! Madam!" when he thinks Mrs. Moore has desecrated his mosque by wearing shoes, and Mrs. Turton's estimate of men as "weak, weak, weak." In all their variations, however, the double and triple rhythms project an instinctual energy that counterpoints and augments the subtler and more complex repetitions.

But Forster's own voice in *A Passage to India* provides the most salient expression of his change of vision, as, constantly manipulating the relationship between environment and the limited human animal, he develops a world of ennui, indifference, and limitation. The remote perspective that dwarfs all the characters and regards them as part of an anonymous and helpless humanity dramatically illustrates Forster's own detachment from the agonies or triumphs of human personality. Concomitantly his narrative voice withdraws from the display of personality. Gone are the geniality, the chattiness, the essayistic interventions, the confidential air that implied a personal relationship with the reader. *A Passage to India* contains but a single incident of direct address—and it is directed with chilling irony to the terrors of Mrs. Moore's experience: "Visions are supposed to entail profundity, but—wait till you get one, dear reader! The abyss also may be petty, the serpent of eternity made of maggots" (p. 198). Earlier Forster implied the reader's capacity for insight and generalization; he now identifies the reader with the limitations of his characters.

The somber and impersonal voice of *A Passage to India* speaks of uncertainty in secure accents. Trilling's view that Forster's voice in his final novel is faltering and less prominent is belied both by the extent of the narrative interventions and by the declarative quality of the narrator's language.[20] Forster insists on the reality of alienation with unequivocal verbs. His relentless repetition of detail creates the chaotic diversity of the Indian universe. His concrete diction defines an indifferent natural environment of sounds, smells, filth, dust, kites, and corpses that intensifies the revelation of human helplessness.

20. Lionel Trilling, *E. M. Forster* (Norfolk, Conn.: New Directions, 1964), p. 145.

Forster's narrative language, his detached tone and remote perspective, dominate the novel, and the view they project testifies to the artist's degree of withdrawal from the world he has created. The human scale approaches the vanishing point, as Mrs. Moore and Adela play cards, indifferent to the rest of humanity:

> . . . the day generally . . . acquired as it receded a definite outline, as India itself might, could it be viewed from the moon. Presently the players went to bed, but not before other people had woken up elsewhere, people whose emotions they could not share, and whose existence they ignored. [Pp. 90–91]

Man's spiritual and biological vulnerabilities merge in what is perhaps Forster's most extreme statement of human limitation. Stupified by the heat, the "Chandrapore combatants" soon yield to sleep: "Those in the Civil Station kept watch a little, fearing an attack, but presently they too entered the world of dreams—that world in which a third of each man's life is spent, and which is thought by some pessimists to be a premonition of eternity" (p. 226). Awake, man engages in trivial and fruitless bickerings. Unconsciousness consumes a significant part of his existence: even alive, he is close to the nothingness of death. Most important, man's impotence implies God's absence. In attributing his observation to "some pessimists," Forster intensifies his impersonality while maintaining the bleakness of his view.

As the illustrations above suggest, Forster's withdrawal is integral to his vision of man's situation. But his detachment has further implications. As in the case of Godbole, Forster's withdrawal is the condition for his insight. The remote voice of the final novel is the primary means to revelation. Forster as narrator implies the connectedness of matter: it is he who interprets the moment of Krishna's birth and the significance of "passage." Like his first hero, Philip, "nobody but himself would ever see round it now. And to see round it he was standing at

an immense distance" (*Where Angels Fear to Tread*, p. 147).
Forster has demonstrated in *A Passage to India* what a little
way good will, intuition, and human effort will go. He has
also, if briefly, transcended the implications of his story to
speak of completion. In a prophetic voice and from an immense distance, he has suggested the unity of matter in a vision
of divine love.

But the prophetic voice that separates itself from limited
humanity is incompatible with the circumscribing devotion to
human efforts. That the perception of divine unity is not translatable into social or personal fulfillment, the chronicle of historical exhaustion and human impotence makes clear. The scope
of Forster's vision depends ultimately on his detachment from
human claims or solutions. And for this there is a price. Amid
the near-perfection of its ordered language, the narrative voice
of *A Passage to India* has acquired the human exhaustion it
so eloquently describes. In its detachment from character and
reader alike, in its remoteness from the near if not complete
futility of human action, Forster's voice projects a certain dead-
ness of tone. Gone are the chatty disquisitions of *Where Angels
Fear to Tread,* the passionate inconsistencies of *The Longest
Journey.* In their place is an evenness, a deliberation by which
Forster embodies a rich and coherent structure whose meaning,
like that of music, is integral with its process and reverberates
beyond its final sounding. But with the loss of hope and enthusiasm, with the unrelenting portrayal of limitation, with,
above all, the extremity of withdrawal, Forster's voice moves
toward confrontation with the implications of his vision. As
his perspective recedes to infinity, so, as events have verified,
Forster the novelist reaches impasse.

7 ～

Conclusion:
The Price of Unity

FOR Philip Herriton, still in his twenties, all the wonderful things are over. The curious implications of this conclusion, which initiates both Philip's adulthood and Forster's novelistic career, attain their full significance in *A Passage to India*. For in that novel, humankind seems at last to have reached not maturity but exhaustion. Furthermore, the detachment to which Philip retreated is now presented as substitute for the failures of human relationships that the earlier novels canvass. However incomplete the achievements of Philip and Rickie, their good intentions paved the way to salvation. But good intentions go a very little way in *A Passage to India,* and any achievement is largely obliterated in the aftermath of the Marabar. The anti-ascetic ideal, the humanistic belief in self-realization through personal relationships, has yielded to a vision whose form and content alike suggest the irrelevance of these values to the only insight that provides redemption from chaos—the conception of an ordered and impersonal unity.

Yet although a final withdrawal lurks beneath the formulations of Forster's first novel, the narrator who moves Philip

toward engagement with the world differs greatly from the
remote speaker of the final novel. Although *Where Angels Fear
to Tread* ends on a note of limitation, Forster's voice and the
action he dramatizes are marked by energy, optimism, and
playfulness. His description of the opera at Monteriano rings
with mischievous joy:

> . . . the chorus of Scotch retainers burst into cry. The audience
> accompanied with tappings and drummings, swaying in the mel-
> ody like corn in the wind. Harriet, though she did not care for
> music, knew how to listen to it. She uttered an acid "Shish!" . . .
>
> The people were quiet, not because it is wrong to talk during
> a chorus, but because it is natural to be civil to a visitor. For a
> little time she kept the whole house in order, and could smile at
> her brother complacently.
>
> Her success annoyed him. He had grasped the principle of
> opera in Italy—it aims not at illusion but at entertainment—and
> he did not want this great evening party to turn into a prayer-
> meeting. But soon the boxes began to fill, and Harriet's power
> was over. Families greeted each other across the auditorium.
> People in the pit hailed their brothers and sons in the chorus,
> and told them how well they were singing. When Lucia ap-
> peared by the fountain there was loud applause, and cries of
> "Welcome to Monteriano." [P. 94]

This scene derives much of its effect from Forster's pleasure in
contrasting the staid Harriet with the spontaneous and child-
like Italian crowd. Moreover, his focus is personal. The purpose and outcome of the episode is Philip's moral benefit, and
Forster sympathetically identifies Philip with his own perceptions in explaining that the young man "had grasped the principle of opera in Italy" (p. 94).

The humorous moments of *A Passage to India* invariably
occur within contexts of human ugliness or limitation. Dr.
Panna Lal comically pacifying a mob is averting real tragedy.
Servants spy or neglect to come; in this way they illustrate the
prevailing distrust and parody the greater neglect of the God
who avoids the appeals of all creation. Humorous discussion of

Godbole's ailments only emphasizes the schisms between Moslem and Hindu. Dr. Panna Lal's ineptitude with his horse, assurance to the English of their racial superiority, offers Aziz the occasion to antagonize the Hindu. Their ensuing enmity illustrates political, social, and religious cleavages.

Two selections from *A Passage to India* dramatically illustrate the distance Forster has traveled between the first and final embodiments of his vision, the distance from hope to pessimism, sympathy to indifference, energy to ennui. The Collector's "Bridge Party," an attempted meeting of East and West, illustrates the sense of human failure that pervades the novel:

> The shorter and the taller ladies both adjusted their saris, and smiled. There was a curious uncertainty about their gestures, as if they sought for a new formula which neither East nor West could provide. . . . Miss Quested now had her desired opportunity; friendly Indians were before her, and she tried to make them talk, but she failed, she strove in vain against the echoing walls of their civility. Whatever she said produced a murmur of deprecation, varying into a murmur of concern when she dropped her pocket-handkerchief. She tried doing nothing, to see what that produced, and they too did nothing. Mrs. Moore was equally unsuccessful. Mrs. Turton waited for them with a detached expression; she had known what nonsense it all was from the first. [Pp. 36–37]

Forster's language renders motifs central to the novel, embodied with apparent casualness in the use of "echo" and "nothing." A mirror image evoked when Adela, doing "nothing" produces "nothing" in the Indians, anticipates the echo in the Marabar caves. Forster's diction and the details of the encounter intensify the sense of unease and conditionality; his verbs—"smiled," "sought," "provide," "tried," "strove," help portray the unsuccessful but continuing search for unity that the scene illustrates. But where the narrator of *Where Angels Fear to Tread* stood approvingly close to his character's growing insight, the speaker of *A Passage to India* anatomizes East and West alike from the remote perspective that elsewhere in the same episode defines kites, vulture, and the sky above the characters as components in an endless series. Against such a setting, the human actors are revealed as tiny, their efforts as futile.

The loss of hope implied in this early episode is chillingly embodied in the brief but unequivocal description of Aziz's party as they retreat from the Marabar: "in the twilight, all resembled corpses, and the train itself seemed dead though it moved—a coffin from the scientific North which troubled the scenery four times a day" (p. 151). From a belief in personal relations and the importance of individual fulfillment that weathered the increasingly somber formulations of four novels, Forster has come nearly to the end of human hope, at least as such hope may historically be expressed. Although the momentary vision of a transcendent love annihilates the previously dominant evil and completes a cycle, evil will reappear. Forster does not suggest that, armed with the Hindu vision, man will be more capable of vanquishing it in the future than he was in the past. Withdrawal, nevertheless, provides the only avenue to vision, and Forster's narrative voice embodies this insight that represents the paradoxical culmination of his metaphysical quest.

The possibility of this conclusion was implicit from the beginning in Philip's young world-weariness, and in Forster's use of a voice that, however engaging, remained consistently separate from all his characters. Action and voice in *Where Angels Fear to Tread* and *The Longest Journey* reflect the disjunctions in Forster's position: preaching fulfillment through personal relations, he removes his central characters from the possibility of participation. Illustrated in Philip's withdrawal, shown in the discrepancy between the narrator's pronouncements and Rickie's fated hopelessness, seen ultimately in Rickie's removal from a world in which he cannot function, the strain that besets Forster's humanistic philosophy reaches its climax in *Howards End,* where a prevision of existential chaos and the action's Pyrrhic victory for the intelligentsia lead directly to the coherent pessimism of *A Passage to India*.

Forster's vision in *A Passage to India* thus has precedents in the earlier novels, where it lurked unheralded beneath the exhortations to comradeship and connection. Nevertheless, the vision of the final novel is unique. A concept of nature as both source and conservator of the fundamental values that make humanism possible suffuses the prewar novels. But *A Passage to India* presents a new cosmos. Vanished are Italian landscapes and English countryside. Instead, Forster has given us India, monstrous, extraordinary, chaotic, a context in which humanity can never be easy, a symbol, rather, of man's helplessness and alienation. No longer the center of his universe, man is an exile, divided from his fellows and separated from the sense of ultimate meaning that the Wiltshire downs so comfortably embodied. Thus reduced, he is a petitioner, seeking to define and to discover his God, appealing for some evidence of divine presence amid the conflict and chaos of an alien world.

Environment, time, and space all dwarf humanity. Fielding, the most enlightened version of Forster's characteristic hero, is himself merely a dwarf. Whereas in the earlier novels Forster generalized the attitudes of his characters to the rest of humanity, in *A Passage to India* he generalizes humanity first as the mudlike inhabitants of Chandrapore and fits the individual characters into a preexisting frame of limitation. The narrative voice that projects such a view is far removed from the earlier narrator who sought to move favored characters toward his own perspective of insight and observation, who actively engaged the reader through techniques of intervention and inclusion in his own comprehensive view. The voice of *A Passage to India* has accepted the implications of its position. Although the earlier Forster strikes us as sometimes uncertain, the impersonal voice of the final novel is always perfectly assured. The remoteness of this voice illustrates Forster's separation from human concerns. But the detachment is a necessary means to revelation, and Forster's act of dissociation is rendered not only through his perspective and tone, but by the enactment of his themes in the phenomenological universe of his novel. For the first time, Forster integrates voice and symbol into an artistic order, a reverberating musical structure, that reveals a unity more fleetingly glimpsed in the world of the novel itself.

Why then is *A Passage to India* Forster's final novel? The answer to this question, as hindsight provides it, seems to lie in the inseparability of Forster's narrative voice from the substance of his vision.[1] The action demonstrates, the voice develops, variations on the theme of man's limitation: unity cannot be realized through earthly effort. Concomitantly, the voice that simultaneously pronounces God's unity and man's incapacity has detached itself from man; it speaks from a perspective so remote that it sometimes seems recognizably human only in its replication of the indifference it attributes to humanity. This withdrawal was prefigured from the start, but the geniality of *Where Angels Fear to Tread,* the passionate concern of *The Longest Journey,* the ambitious though strained formulas of *Howards End* all express hope, all assume the worth of continued effort. From his remote perspective in *A Passage to India,* Forster concedes the value only of survival. The possibility of a man-centered universe has disappeared. In its place is the religious vision that Forster sought earlier to embody in a humanistic framework. But as we have seen, the inclusive vision has its price. Godbole's perception of wasp and lady depends on his abnegation of personality; his transcendent moment mimics the more inclusive synthesis of the narrative voice.

---

1. This is not to deny the significance of psychological factors, as Furbank describes them in the biography. See P. N. Furbank, *E. M. Forster: A Life,* Vol. 2 (London: Secker & Warburg, 1978), pp. 131–133. Yet as the culmination of Forster's inspiration and art, *A Passage to India* seems also to embody a logic that makes Forster's cessation of novel-writing both comprehensible and appropriate.

Observing Godbole's achievement, Forster incorporates it into that larger unity that required his own withdrawal, a movement that becomes more final as the insight and its embodiment achieve near-completion. Where the price of vision is withdrawal, where the most inclusive vision requires the greatest retreat, a voice that moves to the vanishing point engenders its own annihilation. It is perhaps not surprising that Forster was unable to speak again, that he was able to assert and to embody the existence of unity once only.

After *A Passage to India* Forster the writer himself falls back on survival—on the humanistic efforts he portrayed ultimately as feeble and ineffective. The voice that in the final novel so transcended the formulations and insight of all the characters becomes, simply, Fielding, an often wittier and more knowledgeable schoolmaster, but Fielding nonetheless. Nowhere is this more evident than in Forster's essay "What I Believe," where he adumbrates his humanistic creed, right down to the famous injunction that it is better to betray one's country than one's friend.[2]

A Passage to India, then, provides the final revelation of Forster's artistic presence and the ultimate formulation of his metaphysical position. His narrative voice speaks with the metaphorical imagination, the ironic wit and generalizing propensity of the voice of earlier novels. But the radical change in Forster's view of man, and his acceptance of humanism's insufficiency to cope with a world of apocalypse have produced equally dramatic changes in the voice that narrates and controls the final novel. A new and complex unity pervades the association of voice and symbol; new also are the tone, perspective, and the diction through which Forster renders a universe to which man's needs are irrelevant and which itself expresses the chaos and irrationality of contemporary life.

2. E. M. Forster, "What I Believe," *Two Cheers for Democracy,* Abinger Edition, 11, ed. Oliver Stallybrass (London: Edward Arnold, 1972), p. 66.

Forster's retreat, finally, is the logical outcome of the vision that informs his every word. Detachment is the condition of a transitory perception of divine unity that redeems man from worthlessness but scarcely mitigates his fate on earth. The vision is qualified, the hope small: in its final withdrawal, Forster's voice echoes into silence.

Index

245

Forster's Narrative Vision

Designed by G. T. Whipple, Jr.
Composed by Eastern Graphics in
10-1/2 point Sabon (Linotron 202), 2-1/2 points leaded,
with display lines in Sabon.
Printed offset by Thomson-Shore, Inc.
on Warren's Number 66 Text, 50 pound basis.
Bound by John H. Dekker & Sons
in Holliston book cloth
and stamped in Kurz-Hastings foil.

Library of Congress Cataloging in Publication Data
Rosecrance, Barbara.
Forster's narrative vision.

    Includes bibliographical references and index.
    1. Forster, E. M. (Edward Morgan), 1879–1970—
Criticism and interpretation.   I. Title.
PR6011.O58Z836   1982   823'.912   82-71598
ISBN 0-8014-1502-0